WOMEN'S RITES VERSUS
WOMEN'S RIGHTS

Women's Rites Versus Women's Rights:

A Study of Circumcision Among the Ketu Yoruba of South Western Nigeria

BY

EMMANUEL BABATUNDE

Africa World Press, Inc.

P.O. Box 1892
Trenton, NJ 08607

P.O. Box 48
Asmara, ERITREA

Africa World Press, Inc.

P.O. Box 1892
Trenton, NJ 08607

P.O. Box 48
Asmara, ERITREA

Cover Design: Linda Nickens
Book Design: Wanjiku Ngugi

Chapter 7 was first printed on the Editorial Commentary page of *The Philadelphia Inquirer* Saturday, October 26, 1996

Library of Congress Cataloging-in-Publication Data

Babatunde, Emmanuel D.
    Women's rites vs women's rights: a study of circumcision among the Ketu Yoruba of South Western Nigeria / by Emmanuel D. Babatunde.
        p.   cm.
    Includes bibliographical references (p.   ) and index.
    ISBN 0-86543-625-8. -- ISBN 0-86543-626-6 (pbk .)
    Female circumcision--Nigeria. 2. Women, Yoruba--Social conditions. 3. Women, Yoruba--Rites and ceremonies. 4. Sex role--Nigeria. 5. Sex differences--Nigeria. I. Title.
    GN484.B2 1997
    392. 1' 4' 09669--dc21   97-32516
                                                               CIP

CONTENTS

DEDICATION

It is in keeping with the theme of this work that I make a special mention of my late mother, Juliana Abẹjẹ Babatunde, to whose undying memory this work has been dedicated. She was an epitome of kindness, illustriousness and altruism. She lives on in all her children and her grand children, most particularly in my twin daughter, Iyabọ, her splitting image who now carries all her names into the future. The pain of death has been overcome by the joy of birth and rebirth. I dedicate this poem also to her memory.

ON THE LOSS OF MOTHER

You were the epitome of motherliness
A Powerful shock absorber, an unrelenting mother hen
Vulnerable, outnumbered, without a chance
Yet indefatigable in a last ditch fight to save her brood

Oh! You mother of mothers
Content to live vicariously through your brood,
Their joy was your joy, their sadness yours too
Praying as they lay dying, in the hope that they will live,

Judged by the number of your surviving children
Three out of seven, with seven miscarriages to add,
A laughing stock they made out of you
Their wicked jokes could not hide their crocodile tears

Lone monogamy in a compound of polygynous marriages
The rule of your religion they credited to your potent "sorcery"
Otherwise how could such a wealthy man
Stay married to one whose children cannot even stay alive.

Every jealous "co-wife" laughed you to scorn,
Their sadistic mirth increasing with your every new stress

Attributing your pains to the taboo of maintaining monogamy
Among a proudly polygynous royalty

Mother, the stories you told I remember clearly,
Terrible gossips meant to keep you perpetually sad
Adding stress to stress that you might your destiny detest
And run to mental to make their prophecy fulfilled

The seventh miscarriage was particularly devastating
Coming only days after the brilliant Jacob died
Upon completing the school-leaving examinations
In flying colors that resounded from village to village

That miscarriage pushed your body to the limits
Your soul temporarily freed from its agonizing prison
Hovered over watching the frantic efforts below
Intended to bring you back to life.

Savoring the awesome peace of release
You made as if to turn away
Intending to go as far from that mask as you could,
Only to find your deceased father blocking your way
Commanding you to get back, that plenty was still to be done

Grimacing at the thought of a return to that caste
Your objection you shouted painfully from the subterranean recess
And in shouting you woke back to the world of the living
The presumptuous men below praised the potency of their medicine

Even in your pathos, as you recovered your tried to act right,
Serving everyone in the extended family compound
Friend and foe, adult and child alike
Your famed delicious Christmas rice and chicken

Tongue untied with the delicacy
The world went forth from the wench
That the only way your husband would have another child
Was to marry another wife

Dedication

Mother, you kept everything in your heart of gold
Prayed hard that the God of your new religion
Would vindicate you with just one more child that would live
To prove them wrong that called your body deadbeat.

Then came the nurse with the dispensary to the town
In desperation you sought her company whom other women avoided,
You became a rebel to the cultural taboos that forbade
The eating of eggs and meat and anything helpful to pregnancy

Then your pregnancy stayed past the accustomed time
Five months, six, seven, and eight months you counted
Fearing it would come down like the other seven before it
Until carried to term it was!
This product of positive deviance

The child became a symbol of the new God's triumph
They called him a child of prayer
They named him Emmanuel
God is with his people they said.

ACKNOWLEDGEMENTS

The late Edwin Ardener supervised this work in its thesis form for Master of Letters degree at Oxford. I thank his cherished memory. Shirley Ardener O. B. E., his widow and an accomplished anthropologist, one of the founders of the dynamic Oxford Women Studies Group, based at Queen Elizabeth Hall, Oxford, has been a constant inspiration and encouragement for publishing this work. I am grateful to her. Dr. Wendy James, at the Institute of Anthropology, Oxford University, has also been of great help. The late Lienhardt brothers, Godfrey and Peter, were more than teachers; they were friends of unsurpassed kindness, thoughtfulness, candor, insight and humility. Godfrey's house was known as the "African Commonwealth." The late Fr. Paul Edwards (S.J.), a scholar and gentleman, advised me on style. Of their memory one can only quote St. Chrysostom, "Those whom we love and loose are no longer where they used to be but wherever we are. We carry in our hearts, the sweet memories of their life."

I am grateful to Fr. Paul Yarnold (S.J.), Campion Hall, Oxford and Dr. B. E. Harrel-Bond, Queen Elizabeth Hall, Oxford in providing me with insights from their own works, which helped me to analyze my data. In thoroughly revising the work for publication at Lincoln University, I am grateful to Dr. Niara Sudarkasa for the lively discussions and for persuading me to adopt this more relevant title. Mr. Edward Wilmot Olatunde Blyden IV, a young man of uncommon talent and patience, assisted me with setting the index and dealing with the tedium of blending Yoruba language characters in two completely different font software programs. I am grateful.

I am most indebted to my wife, Dr. Kelebogile Ouma Virginia Setiloane-Babatunde, a great mother, a fantastic home-maker, and a resourceful scholar. I am equally indebted to our children: Arámide, Ọmọlolú, Iyábọ̀, Àkànbí and OnaLenna Fọláṣade, the newest addition to the family.

LIST OF ABBREVIATIONS

Am. Anthr.	*American Anthropologist*
Am. Ethno.	*American Ethnologist*
AJOG	*American Journal of Obstetrics and Gynecology*
ASA	Association of Social Anthropologists
CUP	Cambridge University Press
CDSA	Cambridge Papers in Social Anthropology
EAMJ	*East African Medical Journal*
IAI	International African Institute
JHNS	*Journal of the Historical Society of Nigeria*
LUP	Lagos University Press
MAN/JRAI	*Journal of the Royal Anthropological Institute*
MUP	Manchester University Press
Mss.	Manuscript
NGJ	*Nigerian Geographic Journal*
NISER	Nigerian Institute of Social and Economic Research
NJESS	*Nigerian Journal of Education and Social Studies*
HRAF	Human Relations Area File
n.d.	No Date
n.s.	New Series
OUP	Oxford University Press
OUP/IAI	Oxford University Press for the Internal African Institute
UNESCO	United Nations Educational, Scientific and Cultural Organization
UIP	University of Ibadan Press

The Ketu in Relation to the Other Yoruba Subgroups

PREFACE

Definition of the Problem

The Kétu perform fertility rites for girls in preparation for marriage. Aside from the desire to enhance fertility, these rites also mark the passage of Kétu females from youthful asexuality to adult sexuality. These ceremonies have a symbolic structure, expressed in the three classical stages of *separation, transition,* and *inclusion* (van Gennep 1909), but the rites can be understood only in relation to the larger system of which they form a part, that is, Yoruba culture. This study through the examination of ritual, will show the importance of females within Kétu society.

The existing literature on Yoruba women may be divided into two categories. The first category consists of recent writings that glorify women's autonomy and prominence in the economic sphere (Sudarkasa 1973, 1977, 1978, 1982, 1987 1996; Little 1970 Hoch-Smith 1978). These imply or argue that, effective economic prominence makes women independent. The second category (Ward 1938); Longo 1964), in contrast, stresses the suppression of women, particularly in the political sphere. The aim of this study is to show that the status of women cannot be relegated to simple, clear-cut terms of "independence" or of "subordination". It will be suggested here that the sexes have prominence in specific areas of social activity. Thus, males may be prominent in the political sphere, while females enjoy prominence in the economic sphere. The crux of the matter is not the dominance, rather the specific areas where each of the sexes enjoys prominence. The individual area of prominence of either sex is seen not in isolation but in relation to the whole system of spheres that compose the total area of male-female relations in the society.

Research on the status of women in those societies whose dominant structures are said to be "male-oriented" necessitates analysis in order to answer questions such as "How do females express their views?" Through which cultural channels do females achieve such expressions? What do such expressions say about the male-female relationship If it is found that females have more prominence in certain areas than the males concede to them, does any cultural institution provide a paradigm by which one can understand those "transformation rules" (Ardener 1978; S. Ardener 1978, xiv) that bind the views of the females to those of the males without serious friction?

In the patrilineal Kétu society, the male perspective is prominent regarding the affairs of the community. The female perspective often remains virtually ignored. It has been argued that although female views may appear to be ignored in ordinary affairs, they become more prominent in symbolism. It is suggested in this work that ritual does reveal areas of female prominence. It is further suggested that men are, in part, conscious of the strength of females in society and, therefore, try to maintain the balance by emphasizing areas of male prominence. Thus, the function of the Kétu girls' fertility rites as a product of the male-oriented structure is to socialize the girls in these structures, i.e., of male prominence.

Of the models that exist in anthropological literature, I eventually chose Audrey's Richards' 1956 study of the *chisungu*, Bemba girls' fertility rites, easily the most exhaustive study of fertility rites yet made. Richards' model, best suited as a basis for the interpretation of Kétu ritual, helps to explicate the importance of fertility rites within that society, highlighting the tensions inherent in the society while encouraging concern for the didactic aspects of the rites. Most of Richards' suggestions regarding Bemba ritual find equivalences and confirmation in Kétu ritual.

I have not, however, been content with presenting the Kétu fertility rites in terms of any one analysis. Following the suggestion of Richards herself, I have looked at the rites from several of points of view. When and where necessary, I have utilized categories of other models, for instance, the idea of "the wild" (Ardener 1972, 151).

I have also stressed that Kétu fertility rites have unique characteristics. Unlike rites of passage, which appear to be analyzed in isolation, that is, individually, Kétu rites form a series, beginning with rites of marriage and continuing with the subsequent rites of birth and the naming of the first child. Furthermore, each component of the series of rites is, in itself, a micro-rite of passage, having a period of separation, a period of non classification, and, finally, a period of inclusion. In isolation, however, the components do not effect the major transition that is achieved by the series as a whole. It is the gradual progression through the series that makes the status change possible.

INTRODUCTION

A THEORETICAL BACKGROUND:
FEMALE GENITAL SURGERY AND ALICE WALKER AND THE ANTHROPOLOGY OF FEMALE CIRCUMCISION.

> In all this we do not even debate the point as to whether an educated and trained member of a community is entitled to observe it with profit and competence. We do not place taboos on Psycho-analysis, because the psycho-analyst himself may be of the same race and culture as his patient, and at times even in the same neurotic condition. We do not send our Behaviourist to Central Australia because, being white, he might be unable to study white children. The English economist is allowed to work on the commerce and banking of the City of London, and the French jurists have given us excellent analysis of the Code of Napoleon (1953; vii-viii).
>
> —Bronislaw Malinowski's
> Introduction to Jomo Kenyatta's *Facing Mount Kenya*

Female Genital Surgery

Female circumcision belongs to those forms of cultural practices characterized as traditional female genital surgery(Howard 1984; Gunning 1991-92). The issue of female genital surgery has had wide-ranging ramifications and galvanized a dynamic albeit a some-what emotionally charged debate on various aspects of human interaction in contemporary society. It has generated discourses on gender relations, public health, and cultural reconstruction of human identity. It has also sparked squabbles of cultural imperialism, as well as accusations of cultural relativism. Interesting discourses on the notion of "public" and "private" spheres have arisen from the consideration of the method of eradicating female genital surgeries (Charlesworth et al 1991; Bunch 1910; Romany 1993; Rosenthal 1994). Even a critical body of legal literature has been generated by the disquisitions on female genital surgery, questioning the universally representative nature of the foundations of human rights laws as presently conceived (Boulware-Miller 1985; Smith 1992; Dallmeyer 1993; Toubia 1993; Cook 1994; Lewis 1995).

Studies on female genital surgery have also led to the examination of the bases of perceived imbalance between the sexes in the utilization of opportunities for self-enhancing and power-sharing activities in the society. It is suggested that because the social institutional structures are male oriented, men have assumed the right, as one natural to them, of re-creating human being in and through cultural practices. The intention in these labeling and re-creating exercises is to perpetuate the male-oriented hegemony interwoven into the fabric of the principles of the society.

Put in the terminology of Noam Chomsky's Transformational Generative Grammar Structure (TGGS), all segments of society—men, women, adolescents, children—have views unique to them that they express at the deep structural level in the society. But since men constitute the vital majority, only their views are verbalized at the surface structure as representing the views of the society. The views of the other constituent groups of the society, groups often referred to as minorities, remain unheard, even though their views are crucial to a truly representative embodiment of views in their society. The conceptual plane of verbalization at the surface structure has been overrun by views generated by dominance. Dominance has, in the attempt to perpetuate its own interest, rearranged things in the surface structure so that any views generated on that conceptual plane verbalizes views in consonance with its own interest. Primary to that rearrangement is the deliberate creation of interstices, little holes that connect to the surface structure, to give the impression that all views generated at the deep structural level, including minority views have equal access for verbalization. Yet the strategy is to construct the interstices in such a way that, as minority views pass through them, they are changed in the process, expressing themselves in the language that suits the male hegemony.

Other male-oriented structures of contemporary societies to be gleaned from religion, law, politics, education, economics, socialization practices, and even practice theory, which generates the knowledge base upon which male-oriented hegemony is based, are being re-examined. The intention of the re-examination is to pursue a methodical deconstruction of these male-oriented structures in order to rebuild a more complementary gender-sensitive structure made from the contributions of the female and of the male human agents as equal participants in the business of social reconstruction (Ortner 1996; Moore 1994).

The Traditionalists and the Abolitionists

Two distinct reactions have dominated the polemics surrounding issues of female genital surgery, viz:- the traditionalists and the abolitionists. The traditionalists see female genital surgery and the ritual acts surrounding it as crucial to the maintenance of traditional culture. They further argue that any attempt to abolish it will undermine the total fabric of traditional culture. The abolitionists assert that it is a practice that dehumanizes the female and that it should be abolished since the human rights of the female supercedes the cultural impositions placed on her in the female rites. The abolitionists work assiduously at various levels to put an end to female genital surgery, preferring to call it female genital mutilation. Through this nomenclature, they intend to focus attention, not only on the pain the surgery inflicts, but also on the notion that it is an unnecessary and cruel deprivation.

At the institutional level relating to law, considerable effort has been given to the expansion of relevant legal concepts as well as to the reinterpretation of human rights in the attempt to present female surgery, not as an issue to be confined to the private sphere, but one that belongs to the public sphere (Abdullahi 1994). Once this transition is established, it would become the responsibility of the state to abolish the practice. Efforts directed to this end maintain that human rights supercede cultural rites that try to recreate women to satisfy men's preferences. Since cultural rites such as female genital surgery dehumanize females, the argument alleges, such rites encroach on women's natural ability to achieve complete self-enhancement and full personal realization. They constitute an abuse of women's human rights (Rosenthal 1992, 1993) which should supercede efforts to remake women through cultural rites. Therefore, it becomes a matter of human rights to abolish rites that prevent women from full physical and sexual fulfillment of themselves.

This school of thought is propelled in the main by the feminist agenda which tends to employ two tactics. First, it lumps together all forms of female genital surgery under its most severe form and creates a language of discourse complete with its taxonomy intended to inveigle what has passed for normalcy. A typical example emanating from this tendency is the identification of a category of violence referred to as "gendered violence," which male-oriented socialization process imposes on females. Gendered violence is defined as:

> physical, verbal and visual brutality that is inflicted disproportionately on members of one sex. Gendered violence includes gender intimidation, sexual assault, violence between intimates, sexual harassment, genital mutilation, and selective murder of women. (Wood 1996,310)

The second disposition of the abolitionist perspective, consequent upon deliberately lumping together of all female genital surgeries, is a more subtle strategy of identifying sub-Saharan Africa as the place that practices the most extreme form of this surgical procedure—infibulation. Besides distorting the fact, this tendency is indicative of a disturbing trend that is easily noticeable in the print and audio-visual arms of the Western media in relation to sub-Saharan Africa.

As the world moves towards globalization through the aid of improved technologies that make internationalization of capital and labor crucial foundations of interaction, continents poise to participate in the rewards of the global village. Efforts that identify the goriest practices with sub-Saharan Africa conjure up the same derisive language employed to characterize Africa as the "dark continent," so named at the Berlin Conference of 1884/1885 to justify colonial occupation of Africa.

This strategy is not new. It is a calculated methodical effort aimed at inducing, in the African, both mental paralysis and overwhelming self-doubt. It has been launched from different angles, particularly through selective media blitz of the macabre, through the use of the derisive language from religious propaganda, and through an hegemonic use of education built on an epistemological assumption that Africa has nothing to offer except barbarism. African religion whose symbolism provided the hermeneutic codes for generating meaning, was rejected as a religion. As Mudimbe noted:

> The missionary language of derision is basically a cultural position, the expression of an ethnocentric present outlook. The aspects of refutation and demonstration rationalize the initial ethnocentric moment and are aimed explicitly towards an intellectual reduction that would complement the rules of orthodoxy and conformity (1988,52)

African political structures, with their clear-cut checks and balances against tyranny, were rejected. African traditional political arrangement accepted, *de jure* and *de facto* that power was vested in the community, and that leadership ought to pursue majority interest arrived at through compromise and sensitivity to community concerns if it were to continue to be relevant. These traditional political structures were rejected as obsolete and useless. They were replaced by alien vampire clientage systems built on the notion of the person as an individual responsible only to himself, perpetually at war with others in the same community to whom he owes no allegiance except that imposed by the fear of punishment.

Through such derision, the opinion was sold that Africa had nothing to offer and had everything to gain from being colonized. The statement credited to H.E. Egerton, professor of colonial history at Oxford in 1922, that precolonial Africa was "blank, uninteresting, brutal barbarism" (Davidson 1992,66) epitomizes this position. That disposition was still so alive in 1963 that even the Regius Professor of History at Oxford described African history as "no more than barbarous tribal gyrations" (Trevor-Roper, 1963). This instance of *argumentum ad magistatem*, argument by the majesty of the speaker,—one of fallacies of Aristotelean logic—is reminiscent of an age-old practice in the Catholic church couched in the maxim, *Roma locuta est, causa finita est* "Rome has spoken, the cause is finished"; If the luminaries from Oxford have spoken, then it must to be true.

It would be a serious mistake to assume that the view that Africa in general, and sub-Saharan Africa in particular has nothing to offer belongs to the past. It is astounding that as this century draws to a close, the images projected by the West are images of Africa in decay. The West makes no effort to show the strengths and the lasting contributions of Africa to world civilization. What is particularly disturbing is the sanitized manner in which they present this image of decay, that is, making effort to conceal the fact that these images are a function of their endeavors to re-create and re-structure Africa in the image and likeness of the West.

It is instructive to note that *The New York Times Magazine*, one of the very few authoritative sources on any topic for a good number of the reading American public, carried an article titled, *Our Africa Problem* (Sunday March 2nd 1997). The writer, besides shuttling through the capitals of some beleaguered African countries traveled from the Kenyan frontier town of Lokichokio to the Sudanese village of Chukudum, a distance of only seventy miles. In one of the most promising examples of parachute journalism, he generalized, *inter alia*; "But tropical Africa—hot, wet, and poor, and home to an unmatched diversity of animals, plants and microbes - has been an especially fertile petri dish for pathogens"(1997,35). To this writer, "Africa, after all, is the fourth world, an incomprehensible dystopia of random murder, tribal depravity and political corruption" (1997,36). He suggested that since altruism was no longer a tenable reason for engagement and foreign aid assistance (when has it ever served as such a foundation?), America must see it as a matter of self-interest to ensure against the incursion of new incurable diseases from Africa by ensuring political stability. Political stability, he argued, would bring biological stability.

Yet the fact is that the African rain forest supplies at least fifty percent of the earth's oxygen, and that Africa is home to a plentiful supply of botanical medicinal herbs to which Western medicine is only beginning to give grudging recognition. In addition, Africa is home to the seventeen most sought after minerals resources, for example, gold, diamond, copper, cobalt, uranium, and vast quantities of petroleum. The presence of these mineral resources turned sub Saharan Africa into the battle ground for much of the cold war period. The experience of Africans is that the Western proponents of democracy are only too eager to push aside democratic principles when there is considerable economic gain to be made in the Third World.

As long as the effort to abolish female genital surgery is predicated on the identification of gore and barbarism with sub-Saharan Africa, the impression will endure that such effort is yet another example of the extent to which those with little understanding of African culture, will go to wage relentless cultural warfare against the continent. Antagonisms create a siege mentality that will only translate into an increase rather than a decrease in the practice as a way of demonstrating the autonomy of the practitioners. The second part of this chapter treats Alice Walker's novel *Possessing the Secret of Joy* (1992) as representing this strategy; to abolish female genital surgeries by focusing on the horrific.

Some Western activists have styled circumcision as an unnecessary surgery that ought to be abolished. Yet, in European and American societies, special images of beauty have become deified as the norm to be achieved. Numerous million dollar industries, e.g., the weight loss and cosmetic surgery industries, have arisen to exploit this culturally created obsession for the perfect figure. This has resulted in a myriad of silicone-based body additions and subtractions in varying forms of unnecessary surgery.

To return to the critical review of the perspectives on circumcision, easily the most articulate exponent of the traditionalist viewpoint is still by Jomo Kenyatta's 1953 classic *Facing Mount Kenya*. It is an essentialist argument. It, too, suffers from the lumping terms together; Kenyatta uses circumcision interchangeably with clitoridectomy (1953,130, 132-134). The work is an apologetics for the continuation of the rites that are seen as central to the very essence of Gikuyu culture. As he noted:

> The real argument lies not in the defense of the surgical operation or its details, but in the understanding of a very important fact in the tribal psychology of the Gikuyu - namely, that this operation is still regarded as the very essence of an institution which has enormous educational, social, moral, and religious implications, quite apart from the operation itself. For the present it is impossible for a member of the tribe to imagine an initiation without clitoridectomy. Therefore the abolition of the surgical element in this custom means to the Gikuyu the abolition of the whole institution. (1953,133).

As if this view were not sufficient to drive home the point, Kenyatta goes on to stress the significance of the practice as a ritual in the same category of similar practices accepted as rituals in the Judaeo-Christian tradition (1953,133).

Given the historical context in which he was writing, although one may not agree with him, it is easy to understand why Jomo Kenyatta pursued an essentialist approach. His book was published eight years after the end of the Second World War when anticolonial sentiment was at a fever pitch. He was destined to take a leading role in mobilizing cultural values in the anticolonial struggle through the Mau Mau indigenous resistance movement. He was to become the first president of independent Kenya. The name "Kenya," an elision of *Kiri-Nyaga*, "the abode of the gods" (1953,137); provided symbolic support for the eventual success of the struggle. Since the gods were in charge, so long as the living kept to the traditions of their ancestors, victory over the foreigners was ensured.

But the essentialist position does not constitute an explanation for the cultural logic of why things came to be in the first case. Its logic, if it can be framed adequately, is: *our ancestors have always done it, and it helps us to connect disparate aspects of our culture. That is why we must continue to do it.* But many pertinent questions are left unanswered: Why did the ancestors do it in the first case when they were alive? What needs or fears were these practices trying to assuage or satisfy? If the "why?" can be explained and understood in terms of the three principal component categories of Gikuyu culture—ideas, institutions, and material technology—instead of a simple statement of antecedent event, then a deeper understanding of the reasons for their occurrence will be achieved. The intention of this study as an exercise in social engineering is to arrive at new more effective solutions to treat the cause of the fears and the needs for which group logic had initially prescribed the female genital surgery.

In other words, the indigenous anthropologists, as social scientists, cannot be excluded from studying aspects of their own culture. They bring an enriched inner and intuitive insight from within, from the emic perspective. But if they are to write anthropology and not an apology *pro vita sua* of their culture, they must be ready to look at things both from within and from without. Indigenous anthropologists are not excused from seeking a scientific explanation of what they observe. Scientific explanations move beyond the Millsian notion of explaining a thing by its antecedents or causes in preference to the Popperian notion which draws on critical or conventional dualism by claiming that explanation is effected in terms of two crucial factors. The first factor has to do with the general rules that produce an event or act. The second factor pertains to the specific initial conditions of needs and fears that a culture is trying to satisfy or cope with in and through its cultural practices and institutions.

One might infer from the evidence of such basic institutional factors as low mechanized farming, low health care delivery and the dire need for labor intensive force to eke out a living in the demanding African environment as plausible reasons that make fertility such a crucial preoccupation for the survival in most African cultures. In this context, rituals that enhance fertility may be seen as central to the survival of the group. The implication is that when such rituals are not performed, the whole culture will be undermined. This is not an explanation of the reason why the practice of circumcision to enhance fertility started. Rather it is an apology that circumcision should continue. Indigenous anthropologists should be able, by virtue of their training, to detach themselves intellectually for qualitative interpretative analysis if they are not to plead guilty to the accusation that attachment to one's culture constitutes a barrier for qualitative anthropological work. Kenyatta's otherwise outstanding ethnographic work seems again and again to reveal this weakness; that explanation relies solely in establishing connection between elements or in citing antecedent causes. As Kenyatta, again, noted:

> The real anthropological study, therefore, is to show that clitoridectomy, like Jewish circumcision, is a mere bodily mutilation which, however, is regarded as the *conditio sine qua* non of the whole teaching of tribal law, religion, and morality. (1953,133)

The usefulness of arriving at an understanding at the two levels of critical dualism is that it allows us to generalize as well as to compare. Once the general rules are ascertained and slotted against the specific initial conditions of a culture, a clearer understanding can be achieved. Pertinent questions, useful in revealing these rules and the context of the specific initial conditions of Gikuyu culture, include the following: Is circumcision connected with fertility? Is fertility crucial to survival in the subsistent economy? What has the unmechanized nature of the productive system to do with the connection between circumcision and fertility if there is any? What is needed for productivity given the presence of land? What is the surest source of continuous human labor? What militates against this need? Answers to these questions take the analysis to the next level of satisfying old cultural needs by new and improved means in the contemporary scheme of things. Since cultures are dynamic, there may be newer and better ways of dealing with the fears and needs that generated the practice of circumcision in the first case.

The fundamental point is that the same questions can be applied to the Yoruba of Western Nigeria, and they will provide the same answers. When fertility is linked with circumcision, because the unmechanized system of farming, fishing, or cattle rearing demands intensive human labor, the most steady sources of labor are those of one's family. But poor health care manifested in high infant mortality, and high maternal morbidity combine to militate against the overriding need for surviving children to maximize economic resources. So culture sets child rearing as its *summum bonum*—highest good—by making the number of surviving children as the ultimate measurement of self-worth. The human desire to seek its own survival, under very difficult human and environmental conditions, is, I suggest, the more fundamental cause of the practice of circumcision. Once human survival is assured, the emphasis will shift to the desire to achieve success by acquiring skills of the new status ascribing professions. The controversy of the traditionalists and the abolitionists begs the question of why circumcision continues. As Sherry B. Ortner has succintly noted:

> Writing in terms of old binaries—structure/event, structure/agency, habitus/practice —is, I think, a dead end. The challenge is to picture indissoluble formations of structurally embedded agency and intention-filled structures, to recognize the ways in which the subject is part of larger social and cultural webs, and in which social and cultural "systems" are replicated upon human desires and projects. (Ortner 1996,12)

This singular concern for human survival in order to achieve economic well-being has been taken to its extreme form in a cultural ceremony practiced among the Mba-Ise Igbo of Eastern Nigeria; *Ewu uku* which literally translates "goat for the waist," that is, the ceremonial goat is killed to celebrate and recognize the labors and pains endured by the waist of a woman. A woman celebrated in this ceremony has given birth to ten surviving children.

As the rational choice school of thought would surmise, the ritual is a rationale for the preservation of the traditional occupational system that goes invariably to support the male-oriented hegemony. Men do not give birth to children. They depend on their women to perform that duty. Yet men need many hands to cultivate larger farms that will produce the abundance of yams on which they build their prestige and status in the society. Women go through the demanding biological changes of pregnancy and the traumatic experience of labor. It is convenient for men to give token recognition for the mother of ten surviving children whose life is reduced to successive phases. Within that society, all other women, as part of their socialization, set her up as the model to emulate. Thus, men's interest in having more hands in their farm is perpetuated.

Circumcision was a ritual symbolic prestation to ensure fertility. In Marcel Mauss' language, prestation was the gift that is given that compels the recipient, under pain of metaphysical sanction called *hau*, to give something better in return. It was called counterprestation, which, in turn, made reciprocity obligatory. It was a gift given, *do ut des*, in order to receive another in return. The connection between circumcision and fertility was dictated by the poor health-care conditions. It was characterized by high infant mortality and maternal morbidity. Cultural logic preferred polygyny and multiple children to ensure that an appreciable number of children would survive. It also recommended circumcision to increase the blessings of fertility. When, health care delivery improves by deliberate efforts in social engineering, infant mortality and maternal morbidity will improve. As the survival rate improves during infancy and adolescence, the main concern of the society will shift from survival to a concern for achievement demonstrated by the desire for one's children to succeed, e.g., becoming physician, lawyer, teacher and now (with the frequency of military coups detat) military officers. This phenomenon will lead to severing the link between circumcision and fertility. I suggest that it is the duty of the anthropologist to reveal these deep structural connections between the disparate aspects of traditional life. It is further suggested that in order to abolish circumcision, its link to fertility ought to be broken through improved health care delivery. In this way, anthropology will prove quite useful to those whose duty it is to formulate public policy on such sensitive issues as female genital surgery.

To avoid doubt, I argue in this work for the need to understand the cultural logic behind the genesis and continuation of circumcision. That will not be achieved by politicizing the issue of female genital surgery. It will be achieved through qualitative cultural analysis that is neither derisive nor apologetic. Through this understanding, solutions can be derived to deal with the initial fears and needs that generated this practice in the first case. I argue that the effort to end circumcision will pay dividend when the method moves away from superficial attacks and defense antics. To that extent this work falls into the category of Hope Lewis' monumental work, "Between *Irua* and 'Female Genital Mutilation': Feminist Human Rights Discourse and the Cultural Divide, *Harvard Human Rights Journal,* vol.8, 1995." It shows that interpretation of circumcision in terms of domination or cultural imperialism merely scratches the surface of this rather complex practice.

Terminology

Considerable confusion and controversy surround the usage of terms that relate to female genital surgeries. The confusion arises from the fact that many writers, including those who have persuasively written for or against female genital surgeries, use terms like circumcision and clitoridectomy interchangeably (Kenyatta 1953, 130, 132-134; Cloudsley 1984,110; Wood 1996,325). The controversy comes from the politics of the embattled discourse between the abolitionists and the traditionalists. Even the term "female genital surgery" (credited to Isabelle Gunning 1991-1992), which has been used thus far does not meet with the approval of the abolitionists. They believe that this designation gives the impression that the genital surgeries are done using same system as in the West, complete with anesthetic and antiseptic know-how. They insist that the use of the word "surgery" distances the reader from the painful trauma involved in the traditional process of physical alteration. To this group, "genital mutilation" is preferred.

The traditionalists, of course, object to the use of the term "genital mutilation," which they say prejudges the issue by introducing the notion of a deliberate and premeditated intent to do harm. They suggest that such an understanding creates the impression that those who do female genital surgeries are either barbarians or sadists. They claim that such impressions tend to stop the discourse at the superficial level of condemnation. Given the amount of controversy over designation alone, it is justifiable to assert that, "Just as there is no single, all-encompassing 'solution' to the feminist controversy over FGS [female genital surgeries], there is no one term that is appropriate in all contexts" (Lewis, 1995,7-8). It should suffice to define, in brief, the different types of female genital surgery in accordance with the terms accepted by the World Health Organization. Circumcision involves the removal of the clitoral prepuce. It is the mildest and rarest form of female genital surgeries. It is also known in the Muslim world as *sunna* which stands for "traditional." *Excision* is said to involve the amputation of the labia minora. It is often used synonymously with clitoridectomy.

Infibulation is the most severe form of female genital surgeries. It involves the amputation of the clitoris, the whole of the labia minora, the whole of the middle part of the labia majora; and the stitching together of the two sides of the vulva with catgut or thorns. A tiny piece of wood is inserted to keep an opening for urine and menstruation purposes. It involves the binding together of the female's legs from ankle to knee until the wound has healed. This extreme type of female genital surgery is also known as *pharaonic* circumcision.

Ethnographer of Female Genital Surgery by Accident

December of 1962 marked the beginning of the three year cycle of the rites of passage for the group of females whose time of marriage was near in the Olola ward. Circumcision is one of the important stages in these rites of passage. The Olola ward is one of the wards of the ancient Kétu town of Imękǫ in the present-day Yewa Local Government area of Ògùn State of Nigeria. It is one of the custodian wards entrusted with preserving aspects of Yoruba tradition as practiced in this particular section of Yorubaland. It is, therefore, considered a conservative ward. The name Olola means "those who own the art of giving ethnic marks." The Olola ward is known for extravagance in preparing its female initiands as a display of wealth, in this context, tends to improve the standing of the ward members in the community. The behavior of Olola's initiands sets the standard of good behavior for the other wards.

Preparation for this ritual took half the year. The extended families of the initiands and the extended families of the wife takers(husbands to be) work hard to provide victuals for the six-week seclusion period. Hunters accumulated smoked meat. Farmer's wives made copious quantities and varieties of local foodstuffs that were taken to the ritual site located at the Idi-Oro compound.

As the rites of passage proceeded the consensus of opinion was that no preparation in the past came close to those of ikola-abe, the circumcision rites of that year. There was a reason behind the lavish proportions of the 1962 ceremony. Akanbi Babatunde had just assumed the enviable role as head of the family with the prestige that came in representing the ward. He was also known as "Ògùnsinyin," the local rendition for the Christian name August-ine. To the anguished consternation of the other family members, Ògùnsinyin had converted to Catholicism rising to the position of lay preacher in that religion. Although age was a crucial qualification, there was a lot of uneasiness in the family and the town circle as to whether he should be allowed to serve as the elder of the family. The feeling was that he could not preserve that from which he had now distanced himself. But the pragmatism of the Yoruba set in. Not only was Ogusinyin willing to assume the responsibility with a vigor, but he somehow managed to leave the impression that his fervor for Catholicism was equally undiminished. Family politics fueled by sibling rivalry made some silent opponents watch keenly for any drastic flaw that might impugn his integrity as the sponsor of the rites.

Ògùnsinyin nevertheless, worked hard to ensure that everything would be perfect, and it seemed that he had achieved perfection. The parade dance through the town displaying the beauty of the initiands and the wealth that accompanied them to the seclusion hut was impressive. The mentors of the initiands were resplendent in their special ceremonial dress. The extended family was in full support. The town's people were ecstatic. Proceedings, including the circumcisions, went quite well until the evening before the graduation parade through the town, when suddenly it was discovered that one initiand had absconded from the seclusion hut and eloped, not with her intended husband, but with a lover the day before. It was also discovered, upon opening the **bembe** the locally made tin containers, where the expensive presents and cloths intended for the marriage were kept, that big stones were packed to mislead an inquisitive mentor into believing that everything was intact. Upon further enquiry, it was discovered to the consternation of the larger family, that some of the initiands had colluded with the wayward girl against the best interests of the family.

This was unheard of. It disheartened the family that had worked so hard and so trustingly. Internal family politics put the blame on Ògùnsinyin whose conversion to modernity had made an inroad into this haven of cultural stability. In the whirlwind of the controversy surrounding this event, the family masquerade, Asoroko, a symbol of ancestral family triumph over enemies during wars in ancient times, came out unannounced in the night to decry this offense and show that extreme actions must be met with extreme reactions. Local intelligence sources went to work with haste to capture the offending initiand by all possible means.

It was at that juncture that Ògùnsinyin, the harbinger of modernism, reminded the family that they ought to exercise caution so that the situation would not go from bad to worse. He pointed out that life now was regulated by the rules of government. If people took matters into their hands, they would go to prison (a heinous social stigma at that time in every part of Nigeria). This would be tragic. He suggested that the event would lead to a court case, and that court cases demanded documentation to support a grievance. The family members accepted his suggestion to use the family lorry to follow leads early the next morning.

But there was a cultural taboo at issue. It is taboo for young adult males to enter the seclusion site. The only man allowed to enter is the ritual marker himself. Even then he must enter on female terms, wearing women's clothes and his hair braided in the Yoruba women's fashion. But even the ritual marker could not help since he was not literate. Only minors, twelve years old or younger were allowed at the site. But all educated males who could read and write well were in their twenties or older, all except Gbadebọ , the youngest son of Ògùnsinyin and he would be twelve years old at the beginning of the new year, about four Yoruba weeks (sixteen days) away. So by fortuitous accident Gbadebọ became the contact person between the initiands in their seclusion and the outside world of the ancient Kétu town traumatized by the initiands unspeakable offense. He had to keep documents of the statements from the other initiands for the anticipated court case. Thus Gbadebọ became the community's intermediary in its preparation for the long arm of the European court.

All the attention subsequently paid to Gbadebọ was beyond his understanding. After all, he had no option but to obey when Baba commanded. He did his duty to the extended family and forgot all about it. Gbadebọ went on to Ibadan for his high school studies at the Catholic Minor Seminary, Ibadan. Then he proceeded to do his first degree in philosophy and theology at the SS. Peter and Paul's Major Seminary, Bodija, Ibadan, affiliated with Urban University in Rome, after which, he did a diploma in religious studies at the University of Ibadan. Later, he was given a scholarship to study social anthropology at the Institute of Anthropology at Oxford as a member of Campion Hall, the Jesuit Private Hall of

Oxford University. After a first year spent in the excrutiating program of diploma in social anthropology at Oxford in 1978, the events
surrounding the elopement of the initiand from the author's ancient
Kétu town of Imẹko in 1962 suddenly made sense.

Alice Walker and the Anthropology of Female Circumcision

Alice Walker's novel *Possessing the Secret of Joy* was a monumental masterstroke of timing, content relevance, and suitability. Published close to the first anniversary of the Anita Hill/Clarence Tho-
mas debacle, an event that put a definitive stamp on the 1992 elections as the year of women's accession to political power in America,
the timing could not have been better. So, too, was the relevance of
the content. The central issue was to keep the struggle —or, more
appropriately, the battle —for women's rights from losing steam.
The strategy was to shock American society, in the frontline of the
war between the sexes, into resentful awareness by selecting a cultural practice that epitomized the brutalization of women. The bone
of contention for some, was that the work itself was one of fiction,
one that distorted the anthropological realities of the subject in order to push through a hidden agenda. It is important that the wider
anthropological context be addressed for the purpose of clarifica-
tion.

Walker's story is built around the practice of circumcision demonstrating its horrific consequences on the protagonist—the epitome
of the exploited, overly abused female—a character with whom most
contemporary women could identify. Ritual circumcision,
clitoridectomy and infibulation is practiced in parts of the Horn of
Africa and Arabia. In Walker's novel, the protagonist, Tashi, otherwise known as Evelyn, is, the sacrificial lamb who vicariously
carries the pain inflicted by man's inhumanity to women in the name
of culture for nothing other than the need for control and for domination. Tashi marries Adam, the African-American pastor, and
moves to America with him. She becomes mentally unstable because of the pains she has suffered, but suppressed, as a result of
losing her sister, Dura, a hemophiliac who died after undergoing the
excision. Returning to Africa, Tashi killed M'Lissa, the elderly
woman who performed the excision on her sister and on countless

other women. Before her execution, Tashi comes to the conclusion that resisting historical brutalization of women amounts to "possessing the secret of joy."

Africa is the land of torture and mutilation. America is the center of healing. The intermediaries, as usual, are the missionaries. This time, however, the missionaries are African-Americans. America is also the land of well-motivated female freedom fighters who must take the battle of liberation to other lands on behalf of all abused women. By choosing to focus on circumcision rather than the more severe infibulation prevalent in some areas of Islamic influence such as in regions around the horn of African and Arabia, sub-Saharan Africa is targeted, identifying it, as usual, as the source of the unsavory while transforming the motivation of this selective attention to one of chivalry, protecting the weakest of the weak. Such is the new image that Africa commands in the present world order, and it comes with a language of derision, a language associated with weakness and falability.

It is this language of derision, this condemnation of "barbarity" that comes through clearly when the exercise (regarded as so "sacred," as many anthropologists discovered during their fieldwork, that one could not discuss it) becomes so disparagingly trivialized in Ms. Walker's hands. Hence, the gory detail intended to shock when she writes:

> Abruptly, inside, there was silence: And then I saw M'Lissa shuffle out, dragging her lame leg, and at first I didn't realize she was carrying anything, or it was so insignificant and unclean that she carried it not in her fingers but between her toes. Chicken -a hen, not a cock - was scratching futilely in the dirt between the hut and the tree where the other girls, their own ordeal over, lay. M'Lissa lifted her foot and flung this small object in the direction of the hen, and she, as if waiting for this moment rushed toward M'Lissa upturned foot, ground, and in one quick movement of beak and neck, gobbled it down. (1992,73)

Quite apart from the transformation of hen from an herbivorous to a carnivorous animal, the supposed nonchalance with which the excised part is treated is sickeningly false. The level of barbarity that it conjures is only equal to the offensive language that the slave

18

raiders used to describe Africa, that is, to justify slavery. The practice of genital mutilation will not stop through condemnations of barbarity. It will not stop through patronizing postures intended to export the high sexual tension prevalent in some industrialized areas to traditional areas of the world. Conquest and control are not the prime motivations undergirding interpersonal relations in traditional societies. Rather, complementarity and co-existence are the crucial principles promoting group survival. Culture, traditional or industrialized, must change by accommodating new experiences. When it does not, it slowly dies out.

Alice Walker is not the first to write compellingly on the subject of circumcision, and she was swift to recognize this fact. She detailed her gratitude to, among others, Esther Ògùnmodede, Nawal El Sadawi, Frank Hosken, Lila Said, Awa Thiam, Gloria Steinem, Fatima Abdul Mahmoud (1992,285). Neither was this piece of literature intended to be a sympathetic presentation along the line of Ngugi wa Thiongo's *The River Between*. A practice of such barbarity according to Walker's thesis, does not deserve an iota of sympathy. Her work is a piece of social engineering that exploits an abhorrent cultural practice to force the discussion of issues that Alice Walker sees as crucial to the total emancipation of women. In line with this intent, *Possessing the Secret of Joy* advances new controversial norms.

The brilliance of Walker's novel resides in veiling the promotion of these new cut-edge norms in the cloak of righteous indignation against circumcision, a practice generally seen to be unacceptable, obsolete, exploitative, and downrightly dehumanizing. Ms. Walker sensationalized the horrific to draw attention to the deplorable, while surreptitiously advancing the controversial which she sees as crucial to the dethronement of men from the pedestal that male-oriented structures have placed them. That timely defeat of men should lead to the establishment of that prototypical society in which women are freed of the nuisance of men in general and black men in particular. She selected this strategy solely because of her consummate knowledge of American psychology. It is generous, quick to come to the deliverance of those it considers downtrodden, short in temper, and easily bored. The excitement *Possessing the Secrets of Joy* generated was even more short-lived in the American psyche in 1992 because of its preoccupation with the ritual of national political elections. It is precisely to keep this discourse on-going that it becomes crucial to dig into the more latent but equally portentous hidden agenda of the book. Three areas of preoccupation are significant; cultural practices that (i) disempower women, (ii) the condition of black men in America, and (iii) human sexuality.

Aspects of human culture are products of human creativity in the struggle for survival in competition with one another and against their peculiar environment. A major preoccupation in the process of culture formation is the maintenance of order predicated on social and political arrangements. These arrangements occur primarily to meet basic societal needs. Such needs include the fulfillment of the urge for procreation, the production, distribution and consumption of goods and services, the cultural stipulations guiding behavior, the urge to explain baffling aspects of the human experience, and notions of socializing the young into adult roles with commensurate responsibilities.

These cultural processes take time and different characterizations. Often, aspects of dominance are built into it and presented as representative of the interests of the various segments that make up a society. In some societies, the female is dominant. In most others, the male is dominant. In others still, descent from both sexes is crucial to having access to resources that will ensure success. Whether male or female, the tendency is to create ideological grounds for the superiority of the dominant sex by presenting the nondominant sex as somewhat inferior. Dominance ensures that cultural traits that disempower the marginalized be built into the process of socialization. When these traits are internalized, they serve the interest of dominance.

Every society has what it regards as the *summum bonum*, the highest good. To some, the ability to bring—forcefully if necessary—people of other lands under their control for the purposes of exploitation is the highest good. For others, begetting children and effecting the continuity of the descent line is the highest good. For the latter, the socialization process ensures that, females who may not be dominant in that society internalize the importance of reproduction, tying each birth to success and self esteem in the society. When the socialization process is successful, both men and women identify with the basic message of the social expectations. Call this "false consciousness" or "brutal manipulation," the fact is that quite a number of women identify with this tendency and see their self-worth as tied up to performing the duties that culture ear-marks for them. This is a crucial point.

It is important to note that any cultural practice, and circumcision is an example, that impairs the natural ability of any sex to realize its potential fully—whether intellectual, physical, or emotional—ought to be abolished. In trying to ensure abolition where circumcision is practiced, it is equally crucial that the condition of women not be exacerbated because of precipitous methods of approach based on false notions. It is not correct to imply that in most areas, the primary concern of the practice is for purposes of control and power. As this work from data gathered among the Kétu Yoruba and as anthropologists who have worked in the field will testify, views regarding continuation of the practice seriously differ from those of men, some of whom tend to see things in power dimensions.

It is a fact that women are the backbone of religion in most societies, even in those religions that treat women as second class. To quite a few women in different parts of the world, children are not pawns in the game of power, mere instruments of resource accumulation, numbers in the army of self-interested power-hungry "generals" euphemistically called heroes. Children are soulful persons whom women bring into the world in an intimate way that men can never fathom even though, out of feeling of deep insecurity, men make laws giving themselves rights of ownership of the children over and above the rights of women. It is not surprising that women with such feelings see procreation as a special duty that gives their lives meaning, joy, or sorrow. They fret about the possibility of not begetting children. They agonize over the health and worldly prospects of their children, hoping their children will have happier and more successful lives than themselves. They give a tiny part of themselves to the source of fertility in return for, as counter prestation, more fertility. Procreation is as crucial to them as individual satisfaction is to a contemporary American feminist. They live for and in their children as some others only want to live for and in themselves. It is a terrible injustice not to consider this aspect.

Is this so difficult to understand? Perhaps so for some who live in the postmodern and postindustrial Western world. Most women in nonindustrialized societies live in conditions where health care is very poor, where infant mortality and maternal morbidity is very high, and yet the yardstick of success is the number of living, successful children. In these societies, matters relating to fertility take on aspect of religion. Perhaps, this is why Tashi, in Africa, submitted herself for the operation and countered the suggestion that she not do so with the words, "Who are you and your people never to accept us as we are? Never to imitate any of our ways? It is always we who have to change." (1992,23)

The practice of circumcision for this purpose will not diminish until its link to fertility is severed. How can this be done? Today as infant mortality and maternal morbidity diminish, there is less desperation to resort to symbolic gestures for fertility enhancement. But when infant mortality is still high in cultures where the highest good is procreation, any attempt to seek interdiction will be resisted. When such attempts are couched in the language of derision, traditional people begin to feel persecuted, which encourages men to make more rigid demands on the women. This is why care should be taken so as not to exacerbate matters in the desire to find solutions.

In most of Alice Walker's novels, the image and character of men in general, and of black men in particular, are not wholesome. The television series that came out of *The Color Purple* endeavor and *Brewster Place*, were no exception. There was the usual grudging concession to a good man. The rest were pathetic; an irresponsible, unreliable consort, a mean-spirited and ruinously grabbing only son, and a philandering itinerant pastor. Even alternative sexual preference was justified because two young black men had raped one of the women in the relationship. Walker pushes this theme further in *Possessing the Secret of Joy*. The book opens with the myth of Narcicissus turned on its head in the story of Baba and his two wives. The message it assumes in Walker's literarily supple hands is that women should ignore men. The prescription, if the line of the myth is to be adhered to, is that women should, like Narcicissus, drown in selfadmiration (1992;5). Then, typical of men, the brutality of male hunters creates the incidence of divide and rule between Tashi's pregnant mother and the Leopard mother whose cubs and mate were killed (1992,20). In the preceding page the obviously white male doctor complained that the reason Negro women do not receive good diagnosis is that "they can never bring themselves to blame their mothers."

More specifically, the men in *Possessing the Secret of Joy* live up to the reputation associated with men in Walker's novels. Tashi's husband Adam, is a philandering pastor who lies glibly to cover his illicit affair with his French consort Lisette. The product of this liaison is Pierre, who comes to the rescue of his half-sibling, Benny, born handicapped as a result of complications from Tashi's circumcision. The only man completely clean is Mzee (The Old Man), whose professional services and field movie of newly circumcised young girls drags from Tashi's subconscious (to employ Freudian language) long-repressed feelings of pain about her sister's death, which was the commencement of her own lack of sexual pleasure. One wonders why Walker selected Mzee to be the only clean man. Is it because he is white or because he constantly proclaimed that "Europe is the mother of all evil" (1992, 83)?

A disturbing aspect of this presentation of the image of black men is that it perpetuates the historical stereotypes that institutional structures have long established about black men in America. It encourages the adversarial pattern of relationship between black men and black women that the divide and rule structures of slavery and overt and covert variants of racism have entrenched.

Of course, there is copious evidence that the black male is experiencing untold difficulties. Black-on-black violence has increased with the rise in drug addiction, one in every four black male in the United States is either in jail or in some correctional facility, and fathering children without assuming responsibility for them is making single parenthood untenable in a traumatized economy. But focusing on this without looking at the institutionalized bases of black exclusion is tantamount to blaming the victim. For the sake of self-interest, black women must vigorously pursue policies that will enhance the chances of black men to succeed. If there are to be stable middle class black families, they will emerge when situations allow black men to take full advantage of the opportunities of self-enhancement. In a pluralist society, where race is a crucial variable, where the number of professional black women far outreach available professional black men, marital instability is the inevitable fallout. It is high time that Walker directs her special talents to present positive images of black men.

In the final analysis, Alice Walker's book is as much a review of genital surgery as it is a commentary on alternate sexual preferences and the need for women to be completely free of men. Barring this, those men who are accepted will have to come in the image and likeness of Pierre, the Harvard-trained anthropologist. Pierre, is happily bisexual, naturally so, he claims, because "he is the offspring of two sexes and two races" (1972,170), and if "no one is surprised that he is biracial why should they be surprised that he is bisexual?" (1992,170). Pierre's girlfriend, an unnamed Berkeley student, on the other hand, is pansexual. She had been brought up by earth-worshipping parents to believe that men were not crucial to the achievement of sexual pleasure. "She could achieve orgasm doing almost anything. She said that at home there were favorite trees she loved that she rubbed against. She could orgasm against warm, smooth boulders... she could come against the earth itself if it rose a bit to meet her." (1992,176) She prefers to achieve orgasm by riding her horse bareback. Pierre was the only man she ever went with. She left him for an elephant. The ideal point is that women should do everything to be free of men. *When all avenues for freedom from men fail, they should resort—like Lara and Torabe who committed suicide (1992,5,136)— to seeking the ultimate freedom from men.*

When the relationship between the sexes becomes so terrible that women prefer death to life, the civilization to which they belong is in crisis. It is here that Africa, in its naturalness, can teach the new world a few things.

CHAPTER ONE

THE KÉTU

The Kétu in the Larger Yoruba Group

The Kétu are a subgroup of the larger Yoruba people which, together with the Hausa, the Fulani and the Igbo, forms one of the major socio-linguistic groups [1] in Nigeria. The other subgroups of the Yoruba in Nigeria are the Awori, the Ijesha, the Oyo, the Ife, the Egba, the Egbado[2] the Ijebu, the Ondo, the Ekiti, the Yagba, and the Igbomina. The population of the Yoruba in Nigeria is between six and twelve million[3] (further population figures referring to the Ke;tu will be treated later). Because of binding cultural factors such as a generally intelligible language, common tradition of origin, and basically similar political structures, all these subgroups have been described as belonging to a cultural category of their own, known since at least early nineteenth century as the Yoruba(Koelle 1845, 5).

All Yoruba people have an emotional attachment to the story that Ile-Ife, the cradle of Yoruba civilization, is their common ancestral home(Idowu 1962; Asiwaju1976,9)[4] With the exception of the the Igbomina and the Yagba, all the subgroups formed the administrative area of the defunct Western Region of Nigeria. This area has been subdivided in the last twenty years into four administrative states: Ògùn, Oshun, Oyo, and Ondo. The relationship between the traditional subgroups and the new states is as follows:

Subgroup	State
The Kétu of the former Egbado Division[5] of Egba province, now Yewa Local Government	Ògùn
The Egbado and Awori of the Egbado Division of Egba province	Ògùn
The Ijebu of the former Ijebu Division of Ijebu province	Ògùn
The Ijebu of the Epe and Ikorodu of the former Ijebu-Remo Division of Ijebu province	Lagos
The Oyo, the Ife, and the Ijesha of the former Oyo, Ife, and and Ilesha Divisions of Oyo province The Ondo and the Ekiti of the Ondo, Ekiti, Okitipupa, and Owo Divisions of Ondo province Ondo	Ọ̀yọ̀
The Ibadan, the Oyo, of the Ibadan and Oyo Divisions of Ondo province	Oyo
The Iwo, the Aiyedaade, the Ijesa and the Igbajo	Oshun
The Yagba and the Igbomina of the Kabba and Ilorin Divisions of Ilorin province	Kwara

Besides Nigeria, the country with the largest concentration of Yoruba, subgroups of Yoruba descent exist in other areas of the world as a result of various historical factors such as the protracted Oyo-Dahomey wars of the last quarter of the seventeenth century; the inter-subgroup hostilities that originated with the political vacuum created by the demise of Oyo military power (Ajayi and Smith 1964); the Atlantic slave trade, which gave the neighboring coast the misnomer of the Slave Coast; and the 1889 boundary settlement[6]. As a result of these factors, there are a considerable number of the Yoruba in Dahomey (now the Republic of Benin), in Sierra Leone, In Cuba, In Surinam, in Trinidad[7] and in Brazil.

The Yoruba in these different places have acquired different appellations. Those in French Dahomey are known as *Nago* (Dalzel 1793,20). Those in Cuba are known as the *Lucumi,* derived from the Yoruba greeting *oluku mi*, my friend. The Yoruba in Sierra Leone are referred to as Aku possibly from the common prefix to most Yoruba greetings—*E ku* .

To return to the Yoruba in Nigeria, a broad cultural unity combines with local variety in detail; in areas like kinship and political organization, where one might expect close similarity, there is sometimes a surprising degree of variation. While in myths of origin, there is similarity; in kinship, patriliny is not common to all the Yoruba, some subgroups having a cognatic descent system (Lloyd 1966,484). As to ritual, among the Ife (Bascom 1969,61) and the Kétu, circumcision is performed on girls at approximately age twenty as part of the immediate preparation for marriage, but other Yoruba subgroups tend to perform it for their females much earlier at approximately age fourteen. The diversities noted warn the researcher among the Yoruba to resist any temptation to generalize, except in certain very obvious areas of concurrence. One ought to realize that:

> The factors of local and historical variety must always qualify the remarks of those who seek to generalize about the ecology, settlement patterns, kinship system, political organizations and social stratification of the Yoruba....(Peel 1968, 19)

The Kétu in History

The town of Kétu, from which the subgroup derives its name, was the capital of an ancient kingdom. Its traditions have been unusually well-preserved as a result of existence of the customary office of royal bard, *Baba Eléégun*, whose duty at coronation ceremonies was to recite without mistake, on the pain of death by hanging, the names and parentage of all preceding kings (Parrinder 1956,23; Smith 1969,68).

In the pattern of settlement of the established Yoruba kingdoms, Kétu town in the eighteenth century was under the king, *Ala*, "the owner of ." He asserted his authority over a number of smaller towns that were under the jurisdiction of chiefs or heads, *Baale*, whom he approved. chiefdoms such as Meko and Egua acknowledged the supremacy of the AlaKétu.

Kétu was not the original name for the people of this kingdom. Tradition asserts that the original group migrated from Ife under *Sopasan*, a grandson of *Oduduwa*. (See the Appendix for further information on the story of Kétu migration from Ife). This group settled first on a hill called *Oke-Oyan*, and later at a site called *Aro* (Parrinder 1956, 11; Smith 1968, 68). It was not until the reign of the seventh king, Ẹdẹ, that descendants of the members of the original group arrived at the site of what would be known as *Kétu*, where for some centuries they lived in undisturbed peace (Smith 1969:70).[8]

In the last quarter of the eighteenth century, however, the Kétu kingdom found itself in an unusually precarious position, being sandwiched between the hawkish kingdoms of Oyo and Dahomey (which was transforming itself from a collection of bickering, independent city states into a centralized kingdom whose units were bound together by its recurrent wars with neighboring ethnic groups). Kétu, in this precarious location, endeavored to protect itself by building fortifications. These included the circular wall, outer ditches planted with thorns and a "sentry gate"— *Idena*—with inner and outer covered gateways and a central courtyard. Kétu lore, testifying to the immensity of the project, holds that it was completed with the aid of two giants (Parrinder 1956,26; Smith 1969,69). The fortifications have been described as the most impressive example of Yoruba military architecture in existence (Parrinder 1956,27; Smith 1969,69).

Kétu tradition claims that the *Idena* gate was erected on the spot where a hunchbacked weaver was immolated. This ritual sacrifice was a form of symbolic riddle. Its efficacy rested on the homoeopathic principle of magic—the effect of like on like—"Who can straighten a hunchback's hump? Who can break our town?" *(Ke itu ike? Ke ifọ ilu?)* The etymology of the name Kétu. Kétu is thus an elision of the first two words of the riddle. The implication is that since it is impossible to straighten an hunchback's hump it would be impossible to "break up" the town. The Frazerian concept of homoeopathic magic serves as the link between the major and the minor premises of the rite and its symbolic riddle. From the completion of the fortifications and the signing of the Anglo-French partitioning agreement of 1889, Kétu never enjoyed long periods of peace.

After the beginning of the eighteenth century, Oyo kingdom had extended its military hegemony to most parts of Yorubaland

28

and even beyond (Peel 1968a, 19; Smith 1969, 71). By 1730, it had representatives in Abomey, the capital of the slowly emerging Dahomey kingdom. Kétu eventually became subordinate to Oyo, which had previously annexed the two Kétu towns, *Ifoyin* and *Ikolaje*. As an expression of its subordination, its king was required to travel in the company of rulers of the annexed towns to pay an annual tribute of thatching grass to the *Alafin* of Oyo.

The extensive military power of Oyo has often led some observers and researchers among the Yoruba to the error of thinking that the whole of Yorubaland was formerly one vast kingdom under the leadership of the *Alafin*. Such observers described incorrectly, the subgroup boundaries as new developments expressing the state of anomie. E.D. Morrel's observation is representative of this attitude. After his tour of Nigeria at the beginning of the twentieth century, he recommended that the colonial government should embark upon:

> ... the general reconstruction of the machinery of traditional government over the whole province, and the welding together under the headship of the Alafin of Oyo, "the king and Lord of Yorubaland" as he is described in the British Treaty, working with a council representative of all Yorubaland, of the separate districts which internal anarchy and external aggression between them have caused to fall away from the central authority. (1911,87)

In the *History of the Yorubas* (1921) Johnson tended to support the myth of a formerly united Yorubaland under the awesome direction of the Alaafin. C. R. Niven, writing in 1937, stated that "with Abiodun came to an end the unity of the Yorubas. He was the last Alaafin of an undivided country ..."(1937,70-71).

During the last quarter of the eighteenth century, the military power of Oyo weakened. This led to the ascendancy of Dahomey kingdom, which made incursions into its neighboring Yoruba kingdoms a matter of frequency. Dahomey invaded Kétu in 1789 (Smith 1969,71). In the nineteenth century, during the reign of Ghezo, the incursions became more persistent. Kétu was at the mercy of Dahomey throughout most of the century. The British in 1853, proffered the Kétu some hope of deliverance from the Dahomey menace.

The Egba defeat by the Ikorodu in 1853, with the alleged assistance of Glover, the administrator of Lagos, led the Egba to close their boundaries in retaliation (Newbury 1961). This closure was calculated to disrupt the improved trade conditions. It had been hoped that trade in such agricultural commodities as palm oil and cotton would, given a peaceful political atmosphere, replace trade in slaves. The industries in the European metropolitan centers, products of the industrial revolution, needed raw materials most of which could not be grown in the European climate. The profit from these new products formed the new basis of wealth. The industrial machinery, over time, made slave labor expensive and precarious. Both relatively peaceful and secure environment were needed if raw materials were to feed industry in an uninterrupted fashion. The hope of creating these conditions was being gradually realized when the Egba closed their boundaries. To avoid a situation where trade was not possible, the British, who were by this time in control in Lagos, thought that two alternatives were open to them. The first was territorial expansion by force; the second, to open alternative routes either through Ondo or Kétu. The first line of action, at that time, was out of the question because tact and caution characterized the attitude of both the British and the French in their relation with the rulers of West Africa. Their aim was to court the friendship of groups of people in preparation for the establishment of political control. Any use of force by one European power would have driven the attacked group straight into the arms of the other.

The second proposition, namely, the opening of alternative routes, looked more appealing. It was, however, virtually impossible to open a route through Ondo without enlisting the cooperation of the Ijebu, who had unequivocally stated their unwillingness to co-operate in such matters. Kétu was the only choice. There were two points in its favor:

> If Porto-Novo could be informally "protected" and a new route through Egbado country opened, not only would the trade of Lagos be safeguarded, but also the Egba could be blockaded without difficulty and eventually persuaded to keep open the doubtful road from Ikorodu to Ibadan. (Newbury 1961:90)

The plan did not materialize. In retrospect, it is unfortunate that it did not, because it would have given an economic boost to Kétu which was relatively poor. Kétu's economically strategic position would have led the British to defend it against Dahomey kingdom. Besides, the importance of Kétu would have been established, affording it better treatment than it had received under the French. From the moment the plan fell through, Kétu sank back into its impoverished condition, and Dahomean attacks continued until Kétu was destroyed in 1888.

In the winter of 1884-85, Chancellor Bismarck of Germany convened a meeting of the European powers interested in demarcating areas of interest in Africa (Aydelotte 1937; Crowe 1942, Asiwaju 1984). This meeting, the Berlin Conference, resulted in the partitioning of Africa among the Europeans. Towards the implementation of the agreements reached at the conference, the Anglo-French demarcation treaty was signed on August 10, 1889, partitioning West Africa between the British and the French spheres of influence. In effect, the event dealt a political and, perhaps, a psychological blow to the indigenes of the capital of Kétu kingdom. The boundary lines excised Kétu town itself not only from its most important satellites but also from the main Yoruba group, which was now under the British. Thus, Kétu became a leader without a considerable following, a head without its parts. Kétu town was integrated into French Dahomey, where it gradually waned in importance from a distinct *protectorate* (1894, a year after the Dahomey were defeated by the French) to *canton* (1910) and then to a simple *poste*. The psychological blow came when, at the partition, the French Kétu *indigenes* became known as Dahomeans, adopting the name of their leading nineteenth century enemy and persecutor (Parrinder 1956,1; Asiwaju 1976,61). Newbury succinctly recorded the confusion caused by the boundary arbitrary lines:

> the extent to which the Yoruba had been divided was not appreciated at Lagos till this re-delimitation of the boundary. With the exception of Ilorin, Nigeria had lost the whole kingdom of Save from Kokot in the north to Okpara in the south, bounded by the Weme and Okpara rivers. The kingdom of Kétu had been divided in half, extending to Agombo and Ilemon. The eastern sector, without the capital of Kétu itself from Japata to Igbo-Iro formed the district

of Mekko on the British side. The small chiefdoms of
Isale, Ifonyin, Ikolaje, each with an Oba formerly under
the Alafin of Oyo, were also split up. Isale, according to
the British boundary Commissioner, Partridge, was a particularly 'hardcase', for while the very reluctant Oba and
people live in the village which is just inside Dahomi,
nearly all their land including the large farm of Mojama,
is in British territory (Newbury 1961,170).

The fate of the Kétu in Dahomey was less comfortable than that of
their kinsmen in Nigeria because of the differing policies of the
European powers towards their colonies. These policies were based
upon the different principles encapsulated in the ideologies of "indirect rule" and "Assimilation." The British partitioned the Kétu into
native authorities, aimed at making use of the traditional political
systems after the paradigm of indirect rule that Lord Lugard had
initiated in Northern Nigeria (Perham 1937,160-79; Peel 1968,39).
This system of government was said to be indirect because it was
carried on through the indigenous political authorities and not directly through Europeans or European-appointed administrators
(Beattie 1964,251). Consequently, traditional political institution
was strengthened to provide adequate means of "native control."
To clarify the source of native authority, the power of kings was
increased while that of the chiefs (that served, in the traditional
political arrangement as a system of checks and balances to the
power of the kings) was suppressed. The tension this imbalance
created was ameliorated by an understanding of traditional systems
achieved through increased anthropological research—embodied in
the series of Intelligence reports—led to a modification of the system in line with traditional methods (Peel 1968,39).

The French showed that they, on the other hand, were unsym-
pathetic to traditional African political institutions. As Asiwaju
noted, "French rule in the Yoruba districts of Dahomey deliberately
and irreparably damaged the prestige and the dignity attached to the
position and the office of the Oba"(1976,105). The principle of
assimilation, a product of the cultural "altruism" of French Revolution, set out to "civilize" the Kétu by absorbing them into French
culture. To become civilized they had to become French. In 1930,
Brevic, the governor-general of French West Africa stated his aim
unequivocally:

The recruitment of the cadres of natives more and more content more and more assured, and by a vigorous and progressive selection more and more advanced. It is diffusion of the French language, by the contact established more intimately and more completely with French life and activities; it is the constitution of a native elite to the greatest possible extent, in whom the passionate striving towards a culture completely and jealously French could be strengthened (Quoted by Han 1949,22)

In line with this aim, Kétu traditional authority structures were a liability rather than an asset, and the French proceeded methodically to undermine and destroy them. They suppressed the institution of kingship and interfered with the procedures of succession (Asiwaju 1970;, 1974). They made appointments to traditional offices without consideration for the feelings of the people or the social structure. In 1910, for example, Ida Alaba, a Kétu woman of royal parentage, was appointed head or *chef de canton* of the intensely patrilineal Kétu (Parrinder 1956; Asiwaju 1976,271). Subjected to such a trying fate under the French, it was not surprising that some Kétu families moved across the boundary, away from Dahomey to the Nigerian side (Asiwaju 1976, 272).

Kétu Location and Population

The Kétu in Nigeria are situated in the southwestern corner of the country. This territory lies between the Yewa and *Ọya* rivers. The latter flows in a southeasterly direction to join the Ògùn River, a few miles north of Abeôokuta. Kétu territory has an estimated area of 534 square miles. It is bounded approximately by latitudes 7° and 7°30 north and longitudes 2°45 and 3° east. It is a low-lying area, generally, with the only alteration found around Imẹkọ with its boulder-strewn hills that rise to height of 1000 feet above sea level.

It is as difficult to give the exact population figure of Kétu as it is to attempt to ascertain that of Nigeria.[9] In recording the figures of the 1921 census for the Ilaro division of Abeôokuta Province, nothing was recorded for Imẹkọ and Egua, the two leading Kétu towns in Nigeria (Forde 1951:43-4). The census for both 1952 census recorded 12,503; Idọfa - 1,100; Ilara - 1,651; Iwoye - 980;

and Egua (grouped with the Northern-Ọhọri-Kétu)-1,043. The 1962 and 1973 census' were invalidated. The projected figures for administrative purposes of the Egbado-North Local Government area with headquarters at Aiyetoro (1979) was 66,100 for the Kétu. Its distribution is as follows: Imẹko- 40,000; Egua-10,000; Iwoye-6,000; Ilara-3,600; Ijaka-3,500; Idofa-3,000.

Several reasons may account for the meteoric rise in the Kétu population between 1952 and 1979. The 1953 census was alleged to be underestimated partly because the calculations depended on taxation roles. Since tax evasion was quite popular, it was unreliable to use tax records to ascertain census figures. Census-taking was often carried out by group estimates rather than individual count, since the Yoruba had taboos against the census (Eighmy 1968). Yoruba custom prohibits the counting of one's children. Children are the highest good for the Yoruba, who believe such counting is a vain show of wealth, attracting the evil eye. Since independence on 1 October 1960, the awareness that large populated areas qualify for government-provided amenities such as piped water, electricity, cottage hospitals, and institutions of higher learning (amenities associated with development) forced the Yoruba (and other groups) to suppress their fears of a taboo that could no longer hold in the face of the new value systems that gave preference to enthusiastic cooperation with the censustakers. The result of this change in attitude was a willingness to exaggerate figures.

Environment and Human Activity

The Kétu area, like most of Yorubaland, has two major seasons: the rainy season and the dry season. The rains are largely caused by the moisture-laden monsoon winds blowing over the Atlantic. When these winds subside in October, its front is driven southward by the northeasterly winds blowing across the arid Sahara desert, bringing with them a desiccation that affects all varieties of life.

Farming is the major occupation of the Kétu. The rainy season (April-October), given over to planting and weeding, calls for intensive labor on the farms. Since Kétu agricultural methods are unmechanized, farming groups implement rudimentary tools such as hoes and cutlasses for clearing, cleaning, hoeing, mound making, planting, and weeding. Group labor ensures not only the cultivation of sufficiently large portions but also the prompt weeding choke crops during the wet season. As Ojo noted, "three months of uninterrupted growth of weeds on a yam plot from, say April to June, is all that is required for the farm to revert to bush and the crops to be suffocated" (1966,59).[10]

Yam was the most highly prized farm product before the introduction of cash crops transformed farming from a preoccupation with subsistence needs to concentration on market economy. William Bascom, who did fieldwork in Kétu area of Imękǫ, recorded thirty varieties of yams. Other varieties of farm products include cassava, *paki* (Manihot utilissima), cocoyam, *koko* (Colocasis esculenta), oil palm, *epo-ǫpę* (Elaeis guineennis), maize, *agbado* (Zea mays), cow pea, *ęwa* (vigna unguiculata). Other food crops such as paw-paw, *ibępę* (carica papaya), banana *ǫgędę* (musa sapientum), mango, *mǫngoro* (magnifera Indica) and mushrooms, *olu* (pennisetum purpurem) are not cultivated. Okro, *ila* (hibiscus esculentus), garden egg, *ikàn* (solonum melongena) and different varieties of pepper are also grown. As Captain H. Clapperton who went through the Kétu area on his way to the ancient city of Oyo (Eyeo or Kaltunga) noted:

> The country, well cultivated and beautiful risinginto the hill and dale, from the tops of the hills are had distant views, the road leading through plantations of millet, yams, avalanches and Indian corn (1829,10).

"Corn porridge"(*ękǫ mimu*), is a beverage made from corn. It is to the Kétu what tea is to the English or coffee to the Americans. As Bascom noted, "it is the typical breakfast drink, and for many individuals it constitutes the only meal taken in the mornings" (1951,128).

With the introduction of such crops as cocoa and cotton, the cultivation of domestic crops became secondary. Rank and status used to be built on the surplus food products, perhaps a reasonable way of disposing of surpluses in the absence of means of storage and preservation. With the introduction of money economy and cash crops, food-crop surpluses no longer conferred status, is now measured in terms of the amount of liquid cash one could command and display.

The dry season (November-March) is given over wholly to harvesting and hunting. It is also the season for intensive ritual activities. The dry grasses are set on fire, and there is a great deal of hunting. The abundance of hunting game and the farm produce harvest provide for the feasting. Since there is little to do on the farm, the gregarious and urban instincts of the Yoruba, which Simpson so well noted (1937,6), are given scope and expressed in ritual dances such as the *egungun* festival (a dance celebrating the return of the ancestors) the *gèlèdè* (a transvestite fertility dance),where men dressed as females perform in order to placate women said to be witches, inducing them to employ their mystical powers for the service of the society.

Yoruba Language and Kétu Dialect

The Yoruba language is said to be a "dialect continuum," comprised of geographically contiguous and linguistically related languages (Bamgbose 1966,1). It belongs to the Kwa family of the Niger-Congo branch of the great Congo-Kordofanian language group (Greenberg 1963,1). The languages of the Kwa family extend along the coast of Guinea from Liberia to the Cross River of Nigeria and in land for some two hundred miles (Armstrong 1964:10). Although languages of the Kwa family are said to number more than sixty (Armstrong 1964:10), the best known are Kru, Baule, Twi, Ga, Ewe, Fon, Yoruba, Edo, Igbo, Idoma, Ijo, and Efik. In basic vocabulary all the Kwa languages have a considerable number of words that are similar both in form and meaning, as the cross-referenced arrangement below will illustrate.

Similar Words of Kwa Family Languages

	to steal	to count	white	market	mouth
Yoruba	ji	ka	funfun	oja	enu
Twi	wia	kan	fufu	egwa	ano
Gun	wi, yi				
Igbo	ohyi,	ahya			
Nupe	yi		ufufu	nusu	

Igbira	yi		oruru	irenu	
Idoma	wi	k'	oja		okonu
Igala			aja		alu
Bini			fwofwa	unu	
Ishekiri		ka	fife		aru

(Based on the word list provided by Armstrong 1964).

The Yoruba language has a three-term system of tones for the syllable (Abraham 1958:x-xi); the high, the middle, and the low. I use the Yoruba words—*fọ*, *agbọn*, and *o bẹ*—as illustrations. When spoken in the high tone fọ connotes "break," *agbọn* means a "bee" and *o bẹ́* means "he jumped." When the middle tone is employed, agboôn means "coconut" and *o bẹ* means "he is too forward," *fọ* means "to wash". When they are spoken in the low tone *foô*, *àgbọn* and *o bẹ̀* connote "to speak", "jaw" and "he begs for pardon" respectively. In other words, the surface structures of these Yoruba words, like many Yoruba sentences, are ambiguous because they are transformations of three different deep structures.

Farrow highlighted the subtlety of Yoruba when he noted:

> the Yoruba language is one of particular subtlety. Its most important feature is musical intonation and a frequent method of deceit is to utter the words of one sentence and put upon them the tones of another conveying a totally different meaning, which only a person with an expert knowledge of the language can detect. (1926,2)

The relevance of this subtle use of language to enrich the symbolism of ritual will reveal itself when the ritual symbols of the Ke;tu girls' fertility rites are interpreted. The Ke;tu dialect differs in form from the *koine* a formal language that is used for contact, writing, and teaching purposes. Thus, as an illustration, we have the following:

English	Yoruba	Kétu
What is that?	*Kini yen?*	*Keno?*
Where are you going?	*Nibo lo nlo?*	*Ibisi i lo?*
Head	*ori*	*eri, eeho*What is
your name?	*Kini oruko re?*	*Ke leeko e?*

There is underlying agreement with the basic stem of the group vocabularies that a Ke;tu can understands spoken Koine, although one brought up using Koine may find it difficulty to comprehend in its entirety the message of a rapid Kétu speaker.

The Kétu Concept of Time[11]

The Kétu idea of time may be classified in two ways; absolute time and contingent time. Absolute time records the eternal rising and setting of the sun and the passing of every minute in the day. The day is the smallest unit in Kétu time. In reference to absolute time, Kétu parents exhort their children to be diligent because "time waits for no one"(*àkókò kò duro dẹnikan*). The Kétu do not have a way of reckoning absolute time, although they often say, Time passes as a mirage (*Igba nlọ bi orére*). The only aspect of absolute time that the Kétu account for is contingent time.

Contingent time is real time to the Kétu. It is made up of events and reckoned in two ways; the ecological system and the structural system.[12] The Kétu ecological time system is reckoned by the annual cyclical rhythm of the seasons. The seasons control human activities and regulate the occurrence of social events. The rainy season, which provides ideal conditions for farming, does not leave much room for feasting. The energetic activity of mound making (to plant seeds) combine with the unremitting growth of weeds. In addition, the sporadic downpour of heavy tropical rains discourages the large number of public performances that Kétu feasts entail. Thus, during this season, the concept of time is very narrow, limited to the daily drudgery of farming, which is disrupted at four-day intervals by market day .

The Kétu day begins at dawn and ends at dusk. Dawn is heralded by the crowing of the cocks while the roosting of the hens and cocks informs the Kétu that the day is ending. When the sun is in the vertical position (noon) the Kétu say they are about to begin the second half of the day. Since reliance is put on the crowing of the cocks for the beginning of the new day's activities, it is important that cocks crow only at the appropriate time. Thus, the Kétu have a rule that if a cock crows at the wrong time, that is, perhaps in the evening, the men take it out of the village to be killed, cooked, and eaten.

The Kétu week is comprised of four days.[13] The first day of the week is 'the day of wealth and enterprise' (*ojo aje*), normally the market day. The second day is the "day of secrecy" (*ojo awo*), a sacred day to *Ifa*, the refraction of the omniscience of the Supreme Being. The third day is "the day of Ògùn" (Ògùn is the refraction of *Olodumare's* wrath), a day sacred to all hunters and markgivers. With the introduction of vehicles, it also became sacred to all drivers. The last day is *Obatala's* day (*Obatala* is another name for the archdivinity *Orisha-nla*).[14] Seven Kétu weeks make a month, which is measured as the period between the appearance of a face of the moon and the next.

The Kétu structural system of time reckoning is not determined by the annual movement of the heavenly bodies. It is a reflection of the sets of relationships between social groups. It is subjective in that it deals with events that particular social groups consider unique. It also makes use of the specific distance between age sets and kinship and lineage orders. Thus, the four-generational depths of the kinship system differentiate relations (that is, grandfather, father, son, and grandson), forming not only a time-depth to the kinship group but also points of reference in a line of ascent by which relationships are determined. A Kétu man may reckon time by saying, "during the time of our grandfather" (*nigba awoôn baba nla; wa*). The limitations in both the ecological and structural systems of time-reckoning is that they do not make a standard judgement of time possible as values of time-change relative to season and group.

The Kétu maintain that all time and its reckoning depends on the will of the Supreme Being and his cohort of divinities. If the Supreme Being does not guarantee through his refractions the normal rhythm of the seasons, if he fails to make the earth and all who live on earth fertile, then the Yoruba sense of time in both the ecological and structural perspectives is arrested. The events that compose time, either in the remembered genealogical points or in the cyclical rhythm of the ecological process, do not occur. In the Kétu sense, there is virtually a chronological vacuum because worthwhile time is time reckoned through events.

The connection between the Kétu idea of time and Kétu belief system echoes Emile Durkheim's assertion that the basic categories of the human mind such as time, space, and other structures through which the individual experience becomes assimilated and ordered derive from religious beliefs. He observed that when simple religious beliefs are:

> systematically analyzed, the principal categories are naturally found. They are born in religion and of religion; they are a product of religious thought (Durkheim 1915,9)

Durkheim's theory of the role of religion in society is useful in understanding Kétu religion and Kétu notions to time.

NOTES

1. The word "tribe" has been avoided here in preference for "group" not only because its definition, like that of "ethnicity," is difficult (mercer 1961; Fried 1968) , but also because the criteria for specifying a tribe has become controversial. Bohannan (1966: 121) has placed the blame for what is called the "myth of tribal exclusiveness" on the colonial governments that, in an attempt to ease political administration, had to create a tribal map of Africa with clearly defined boundaries. In reality, the "tribes" ran together and intermixed, and between them there existed a s high degree of interdigitation. See Harrell-Bond *et al.,* 1978' 12-20 for more dis cussion on this topic.

2. Although the Kétu in Nigeria are referred to as "Egbado-Kétu" in documents, "Kétu" is the appropriate term. They were referred to Egbado-Kétu with the constitution of the federated council of the Egbado and the Kétu, becoming the Egbado-Kétu district of Ilaro division of Egba province. More recently, the Ke;tu belong to Yewa Local Government of the Ògùn North administrative area of Ògùn State.

3. The 1952 Census, which was alleged to be an understatement, put the Yoruba as 6,359,717 while the equally controversial 1962 Census gave the figure as 11.2 millions.

4. Some historians question the traditional position given to Ife as the ancestral home of the Yoruba.(See Abayomi 1978)

5. A division was comprised of four or more districts; a district is comprised of a number of villages and towns. A province was

comprised of two or more divisions. (Duze 1963,521)

6. For details, see, for example Ajayi and Smith, 1964, Asiwaju, 1984).

7. See the seminal book by Maureen Warner-Lewis *Trinidad Yoruba; From Mother Tongue to Memory* published in 1996 by The University of Alabama Press

8. This is an instance where myth and history seem to merge in explaining the past of a non-literate people.

9. The 1952 census gave the figure 31,152,027 as the total for Nigeria, *Nigerian Census, Ministry of Statistics, 1953*. The 1962 census, highly controversial, gave the total figure as 53, 200,000 without indicating its distribution among the groups of people in Nigeria. The equally controversial 1973 census, which was later invalidated, estimated 86, 000,000. The United Nations population projections estimate 80, 000,000.

10. For the elaborate system of cooperative farming the Yoruba have developed to meet with the geographical hardships such as *aaro*, *owe*, and family lineage farming see Ojo 1963, 31- 38; Morton Williams 1953, 23.

11. See Krapf-Askari (1966, 3-18) for a scholarly work on the time classifications of a Yoruba subgroup.

12. The concept of time as ecological and structural is borrowed from Evans-Pritchard's analysis of Nuer time. But for the variations in ecology between the Nuer and the Kétu, the basic contents of that analysis fits, to some extent, the Kétu conception of time (Evans-Pritchard 1940).

13. Ellis recorded a five-day week for the Yoruba (1892,145), most probably because the Yoruba refer to the last market day which is the first day of their week as "five days ago"(*ija run*).

14. See chapter two of E. D. Babatunde (1992) on Yoruba metaphysics for further reading on Yoruba and Bini divinities.

REVIEW OF SOME MODELS FOR THE ANALYSIS OF INITIATION RITUALS

> What I have in mind can be exemplified by reference to initiation ceremonies. In terms of van Gennep's model they are the means of marking and organizing the transition from childhood to socially recognized adulthood. Restated in terms of the model I am proposing they are the means of divesting a person of his status as a child in the domestic domain and of investing him with the status of actual or potential citizen in the politico-jural domain. Ordeals and mutilations are more than the new status. The right to exercise adult sexuality, that is sexuality in marriage for procreative purposes, as opposed to childish sexuality, is one of the distinctive prerogatives and responsibilities of citizenship. One purpose of initiation rites, and for that matter, the main purpose of female initiation, is to confer this right and to do this in such a way that the commitments implied in its acquisition are accepted as a necessary moral and jural concomitant of citizenship(Fortes 1962:87).

This quotation gives rise to some basic questions such: What is van Gennep's model? What does it say about the significance of transition rites? Does the quality of van Gennep's analysis do justice to the variety of initiation roles in ethnic societies? What is the difference, if any, between van Gennep's celebrated features of ritual transition and Fortes' idea of "divesting a person of his status as a child in the domestic domain and investing him with the status of actual or potential citizen in the politico-jural domain"? Finally, why should ordeals and mutilations be 'the conspicuous ways of emphasizing entry into the new status'? These questions and others posed by the examination of other models will be given some attention here.

Frazer's works have little to do with the ritual of initiation. However, they recognized the importance initiation in the life of traditional ethnic people. Frazer asserted that initiation ceremonies are "the central mysteries of primitive society" (1922, 278). His preoccupation with tracing the origins of religion under which initiation ritual is subsumed and his assumption that religion is the fruit of defective mental processes arising from wrong associations seem to have prevented him from conducting a more penetrating study of the social implications of initiation rites in tribal societies. Arnold van Gennep was the first to study the importance of rituals of initiation in the society.

In his work *Les Rites de Passage* (1909), [1] van Gennep provided an elaborate enquiry into the nature and mechanism of the rituals of transition in tribal societies, in Christian societies and in societies of antiquity. These rituals were used to institute a change in social positions. He pointed out that there is a similarity in the features of such rituals, as are those celebrating the movement of individuals and groups on the land, the movement of persons between social groups, those occurring at important points in the life-cycle like pregnancy, childbirth, betrothal, marriage and funerals. He claimed that these noticeable similarities were not only peculiar to the aforementioned instances but also to rituals occurring at the change of seasons, phases of the moon, at planting and harvesting periods, and even at ordination and installation rituals. These ritual occasions had a three-fold feature in common: (i) *separation* from the existing state, (ii) a period of *transition* when the object of the ceremony is unclassified (in Mary Douglas' term, 'anomalous'); and (iii) the final state of integration.

Social life consisted of a series of movements between the sacred and the profane worlds, since the groups between which the movements were made and the societies themselves were established on a strong magico-religious basis. To emphasize this dichotomy, van Gennep noted:

> In such societies every change in a person's life involves actions and reactions between the sacred and the profane —actions and reactions to be regulated and guarded so that society as a whole will suffer no discomfort. (1960,3)

Developing this idea further, van Gennep observes that, since many of these transitional rituals aimed at the same goal, they took a similar pattern, dramatized in a form where the initiand dies, leaves the present existence, remains temporarily unclassified, and, finally, resurrects into a new existence. The different social situations to which the rituals arise emphasize aspect of the tripartite ritual feature germane to it. Thus, at death, the rite of *separation* is paramount; at marriage, that of *integration* is emphasized; the rite of *transition* or *liminality* predominates at the initiation to cult societies and status groups.

Female circumcision, in the context of Kétu fertility rites, is considered to be related to procreation since it is marriage oriented. Kétu marriage aims at procreation, especially of sons who will continue the patriline. This view is contrary to that of van Gennep, who insisted that he did not "see any relation between circumcision and procreation"(1960,73). He gave two reasons, none of which seem to apply to the Kétu. First van Gennep notes the wide variability in the age initiands, whereas the Kétu always perform circumcision about the twentieth year as a preamble to marriage and procreation, because the Kétu are not ignorant of the physiological basis of procreation. The relevance of van Gennep's second point, that the reduction of sexual excitability as showing the unrelatedness of circumcision to procreation, is difficult to comprehend. One would have thought that since in those societies where the utmost aim of marriage is procreation, not solely loving companionship, every attempt would be made to streamline this aim by cutting away what may distract attention from that aim. Seen in this light, circumcision becomes necessary to show that the sexual act is a means to an end. It is a means to achieving the highest good of those societies

—children—and not an end in itself. The removal of an erogenous center only makes this point clear.[2]

Initiation rites van Gennep concluded conferred social puberty by incorporating initiands into adult society. He claimed:

> These are rites of separation from the asexual world, and
> they are followed by rites of incorporation into the world
> of sexuality and, in all societies and all social groups, into
> a group confined to persons of one sex or the other
> (1960,67)

Meyer Fortes, who did his anthropological work among the Tallensi and the Ashanti of Ghana, emphasizing that it is responsible adult sexuality that characterizes the new status of the graduand of such initiating rituals noted:

> The right to exercise adult sexuality, that is, marriage for
> procreative purposes, as opposed to childish sexuality, is
> one of the distinctive prerogatives and responsibilities of
> citizenship. (1962,87)

In circumcision and its attendant surgeries, van Gennep saw two symbolic meanings. First in his view, the permanence of the individual's incorporation into the group required, among other things, the performance of the surgery. Second, he thought that mutilation involved operations of inconvenient dispensable parts of the body, such as tooth extraction and nail-cutting. Seen in this light, clitoridectomy becomes an attempt to remove an appendage which blurs the male/female distinctions or promotes female resemblance of the male. He asserted that such

> mutilations are a means of permanent differentiations such
> as the wearing of a special dress or mask or body painting
> (1960,74)

Van Gennep's assumption of the prevalence in tribal societies of the rigid dichotomy between the sacred and profane (an assumption that formed the basis of his model) has continued to perturb modern ethnographers. Evans-Pritchard has criticized this assumption stating that fieldwork data do not confirm its veracity. In tribal societies, he claimed, there is a constant shift between the two concepts, since it is situations that confirm sacrality to an object in common use for "profane purposes."

Van Gennep proposed that birth, puberty, marriage, death as well as other crises in man's journey through life prompt ritual ceremonies that differ only in detail from one culture to another but are, in essence, universal. He seemed, following the manner of scholars of the *Année Sociologique* circle to which he belonged, to have reposed a great deal of trust in the validity of this thesis by showing its prevalence over a wide area of the world. This appeal to the universal was a characteristic Durkheimian preoccupation. Robert Hertz in *Death and the Right Hand,* first published in 1909, had shown, in like manner, that different funerary practices such as embalming (to preserve the flesh while transforming the corpse into a skeleton) and cremation (to transform the body rapidly by destroying it) are similar in that both express the liminal status of the dead person. Mauss' classic work, *The Gift* also rested on a method of demonstration. As Gluckman says:

> The argument becomes overwhelmingly convincing by rep-
> etition and recapitulation; it remains at the same point for
> we are shown the same stages of passage, variously em-
> phasized, in different types of society. (1962,11)

Thus, van Gennep's analysis, like those of his colleagues, stopped where it should have begun. Max Gluckman wondered why van Gennep failed to continue his examination of the sources of tribal ritualization. Claude Levi-Strauss made a similar observation about Mauss. He claimed that the latter's concern mainly with accumulating examples of exchange and its coercive "power" prevented him from making the theoretical break that led to the structuralist understanding of exchange; that also applies to van Gennep. They are both "like Moses leading his people to a promised land of which he would never contemplate the splendor" (1966,37). This drawback notwithstanding, van Gennep's contributions form one of the main foundations upon which later researchers have built.

Junod (1913) applied van Gennep's model to Tsonga society. He showed among other things, that for the Tsonga, living involved progressions in time and space and a set of activity changes and status alterations for the individual. Each stage of alteration, progress, and transition was marked by a ritual and its attendant taboos.

Gluckman (1962) Evans-Pritchard (1960) argued that the answer to initiation rituals does not lie in the dichotomy of the sacred and the profane, which van Gennep claimed to be the basis of social life in tribal societies. He also disagreed with Durkheim's explanation that the large-scale ritualization in these societies was a result of the low level of division of labor. Rather, he argued, many play several roles in the same social environment and with the same people, thus giving rise to the possibility of confusion. The attachment of ritual to each role was to clarify their boundaries so as to minimize such possibilities. Meyer Fortes (1962) expressed a similar opinion. He regarded society as a network of offices and a complex of linkages between status and roles. Ritual established and maintained theses complexes.

Further insights are to be found in Audrey Richards' work on the Bemba girls' initiation ceremony (1956); in Victor Turner's works on the Ndembu (1962, 1967); and Edwin Ardener's work on the Bakweri (1972). Their models have furthered the understanding of female rites of passage. These models will be reviewed in so far as they help in the analysis of the Kétu girls' fertility rites. Before reviewing the salient points of these models, however, some background information on symbolism will prove useful to the subsequent analysis of Kétu ritual symbols. Mircea. Eliade's work *Birth and Rebirth* and B. Bettelheim's *Symbolic Wounds* are useful in this regard because they typify, respectively, the approach of the religion historian and that of the psychoanalyst, to initiation rites in general, and female initiation in particular.

Eliade's view of initiation provides data for comparison. His basic assumption seems to be that the significance of initiation lies in the religious context of regeneration and the ascent of the initiand to a different mode at the spiritual. This is perhaps not surprising for a scholar who has given much of his time to the study of religions and to the task of confirming the assumed influence of the sacred and the profane in the universal culture (1958). One may be somewhat skeptical about the goals of the initiation of boys and girls. He holds that the boys gain access to a transcendental state in which they share in divine attributes by acquiring the power of re-

48

creation. Initiation for girls, on the other hand, merely reminds them of what is "natural" for them, i.e, the beauty of motherhood. This interpretation which attributes the achievement of transcendental(i.e, superior) quality to the male while apportioning nothing other than the mundane to the female, amounts perhaps to a sexist perspective generated by Eliade's male-oriented perspective. Such an interpretation is contradicted by an objective analysis from a religious dimension. Eliade suggests that initiation reminds the female of the beauty of motherhood, while it elevates the male to a transcendental state. In religious studies and theology, two major attributes of the divine are transcendence and creatorship(Idowu 1962; Awolalu, 1976; Babatunde 1992). Motherhood is a participation in divine creatorship, yet it does not qualify the female, according to Eliade's view, for transcendence. The female carries the foetus for nine months, delivers it, and has naturally, primary responsibility for its nurturance. These unique functions are a natural extension of the creatorship of the divine. The male initiand, on the other hand, who is being prepared to join with the female to begin the subsequent procreative process that will continue in and through her, achieves trancendence by that momentary union. This rather subjective interpretation is a demonstration of the extent to which the male hegemony filters through the prism of the scholar.

Eliade attributes two religious meanings to circumcision practiced within the ritual of initiation: (a) the acquisition of bisexuality and (b) the religious value of blood. In some cultures, the divinities were regarded as being bisexual in nature. Divine bisexuality had to do with the concept of divine totality, which implies the coexistence of all attributes, and so the coalescence of the sexes in God. The aim of circumcision, then, was to participate in the divine attributes by acquiring bisexuality, for the "subincised member represented both the female and the male organs essentially in the process of fructification"(Eliade 1958,16). Eliade also asserts that the religious purpose of presenting novices as asexual or bisexual was that the novice had a better chance of attaining to a particular mode of being (for example, becoming a man or a woman,) if he first became a totality. Circumcision aims at blood letting a symbol of strength and virility. Eliade sees the primary purpose of subincision as providing fresh blood—the symbol of creativity.

There are some *prima facie* objections to these assertions. How does circumcision provide an initiand (a boy) with a bisexual nature, when in actual fact it removes the outer coating that makes the masculine genitals resemble that of a female? If circumcision achieves this in boys, does it do the same to girls when it removes that part of the female reproductive organs having the greatest resemblance to that of the male? Furthermore, contrary to Eliade, it can equally be argued that circumcision puts a decisive end to that phase that Eliade has in mind—the bisexual phase. Thus, for van Gennep, it marks a definitive difference between the sexes.

Eliade also sees the girls' initiation rites as qualitatively inferior to those of boys. The boys initiation rites introduce them to a world "not immediate"; to the superior sacral world. On the other hand, the initiation of girls was just a revelation to the girl-initiands of the sacred meaning of a phenomenon that is apparently natural —the visible sign of their sexual maturity. He wrote:

> Girls' initiation is determined by a mystery natural to the female sex, the appearance of menstruation, with all that this phenomenon implies for primitives: e.g. periodical purification, fecundity, curative and magical powers. The girl is to become conscious of a transformation that comes about in a natural way and to assume the mode of being that results from it, the mode of being of the adult woman. (1958,47)

He does not explain why a girl needs a ritual to make her conscious of what comes naturally to her. Besides, one would have thought that the revelation of the sacred and a share in the divine attributes, the goals of initiation, involve among other things, the ability to procreate. If so, girls who are, at initiation, made aware of their creative ability participate in the creative power of the Creator. With this participation, therefore, initiation of girls attains the same end, and does so with a more basic claim than that of boys.

The Psychoanalytic Approach to Initiation

Sigmund Freud popularized circumcision as the point of departure for the psychoanalytic study of initiation. In establishing the analysis of initiation rites conjecturally as originating from the Oedipus complex, he wrote:

> We have conjectured, that, in the early days of the human family, castration really was performed on the growing boy by the jealous and cruel father, and that circumcision, which is so frequently an element in puberty rites, is an easily recognizable trace of it. (1933,120-121)

In a later work, this assumption was elevated from conjecture to certainty, as he wrote with an air of authority:

> Circumcision *is* the symbolic substitute of castration, a punishment which the primeval father dealt his sons, long ago out of the fulness of his power, and whosoever accepted this symbol showed by so doing that he was ready to submit to the father's will, although it was at the cost of a painful sacrifice. (1952,129).

Thus, the psychoanalytical study of initiation was founded upon the treatment of circumcision. The analysis of the incidence of circumcision itself was established on this rather unproven conjecture. Circumcision was seen in this imaginary dialectical perspective of the revenge of an autocratic and vengeful father on his son. Female circumcision could hardly be explained in these terms, as the Oedipus complex was confined to sex (father and son) since the mother was neither autocratic nor vengeful. One feels that a primaeval, cruel father should be in existence if psychoanalytical work on initiation is to be done. If he is not, it is part of the work of the psychoanalyst to discover him.

Bruno Bettelheim thought that the Oedipus complex theory would not explain adequately the phenomenon of circumcision. He argued that its origin lies precisely in "insecurity about and dissatisfaciton of both boys and girls with their own sex, and envy of the other"(1955,21)[3]. In Bettelheim's approach, there is a noticeable shift from father-son conflict to that of the individual versus society. Circumcision ceases to be a problem of castration anxiety and assumes the posture of the individual's resistance against social integration. Initiation, then, seems to him to be "efforts to integrate, rather than discharge asocial instinctual tendencies".(1955, 22) To prove his point, Bettelheim made another disturbing conjecture, that the mental activities of schizophrenic children in some cultures are similar to the mental processes that motivate the ritual actions of mentally fit adults in tribal societies. He states categorically that:

> The more we speculate on the children's motivations, the more impressive became the similarity between what they wished to do and certain features of puberty rites as practised by preliterate tribes. (1955,55)

He maintained that one of the major purposes of boys' circumcision was to assert that men , too, are capable of doing what women do —give birth. The purpose of subincision was to give men the apparatus and the functions equal to women. He interpreted the secrecy surrounding male initiation as a conscious attempt by men to disguise the failure of the rite to achieve this end. He quoted another author, van Waters, to advance the view that male initiation rites originated from the desire to create an analogous operation for women.

This argument goes round in a circle. Asserting that male circumcision originated from the desire to acquire female characteristics of menstruation and the simulation of giving birth; female initiation originated to emulate men's initiation, Bettelheim wrote:

> In concluding this discussion it seems safe only to say that anthropological observations lend themselves to the interpretation that initiation rites were designed to compensate for what might have been considered male physiological deficiency in procreation, perhaps reinforced by woman because of penis envy or resentment of menstruation than to the more familiar anthropological and psychoanalytic interpretations (1955,205).

Objections to Bettleheim's approach to the study of initiation rites present themselves. There was a time in the history of research when generalizations were based on conjecture; participant observation in fieldwork experiences has cleared the ground, making a place for more cautious suggestions. This significant academic breakthrough seems to have been ignored by some psychoanalysts. Besides, the tendency to relate and equate the mental processes of schizophrenic children in industrialized societies with those of mentally balanced adults in nonindustrialized societies reeks so much of the early works of Lucien Levy-Bruhl and other intellectualist scholars as to be unbelievable in ongoing research.

Bettelheim's use of anthropological material to force recognition of psychoanalytic observations lends weight to one obvious anthropological truism—that the researchers find in what they observe what they expect to find; the order they find is the order they have imposed (Leach 1967,xix).

Audrey Richards' Model

Audrey Richards' study of *Chisungu*, the Bemba girls initiation rites, provides a useful model for the study of girls' initiation rites. The Bemba of present-day Zambia, among whom she worked, are a matrilineal agricultural people with uxorilocal marital residence. They do not possess durable property in which status can be expressed; ranking and social prestige being confirmed in terms of how much one can command of the service of others. One way of building status was through affinal relationships and the ability of the matrilineage to entice young men of other lineages into marriage and to remain in these lineages. The Bemba perform the chisungu rite for their girls before marriage. Much of the agricultural work among the Bemba devolves on the women since the men prefer to "cultivate by the sword," an enterprise that, in terms of social evaluation, seemed to hold more reward than the tedium of farming. The slaves as well as the booty captured during the wars are expended to build up prestige.

In the precolonial era, chisungu rites lasted for six months. The pressures of modern living have caused a dramatic curtailment. The chisungu, for the two girls that Richards witnessed, lasted for thirty days. At the onset of the first menstruation, any would-be initiand goes through the *ukusolwela* ceremony, which consists of the act of pulling out doctored seeds from ritual fire and eating them. This brief rite purifies her. At a suitable time, she is made to dance the chisungu under a mistress of ceremonies, *Nacimbusa*, who must be an elderly woman who has proved herself to be a successful midwife. With the aid of her assistants, *Banacimbusa*, she organizes the rites. On the first day the initiands receive blessings, go into the forest where they are hidden, perform the jumping feat, and then triumphantly return to the village. On the day after the conclusion of their endurance test of catching insects with their mouths, food is offered to the initiands. Then follows the ritual of lighting the fire; the ritual of eating the porridge, which is itself concluded with the invocation of the blessing of the ancestral spirits. The ritual of drinking beer takes place on the seventeenth day. The ritual of killing of chickens, which is a test of the girls' maturity, follows. The ritual of cleansing of the girls, the final rite of bathing and an index of ritual purification, precedes the ceremony of congratulations. The days in between these major activities are spent in making *mbusa*—emblems, as well as modeling objects like lions and snakes, and painting wall designs.

In her interpretative analysis, Richards distinguished between the "expressed" and the "deduced" purposes of chisungu. The expressed purpose constitutes what the actors believe they are achieving by the rites. The deduced purpose is either derived from indirect evidence that helps one to arrive at the beliefs and objectives about the rites or "by an analysis of other ceremonies performed by the same community in which an identical or similar act occurs" (1956,115). This, in other words, combines what Victor Turner would later call the "operational" and the "positional" levels of meaning.[4] The expressed purpose is of two kinds—primary, what the actors of the rites claim their objective to be, and secondary, the acknowledged motive it entails, for example, the ceremony as a source of amusement.

The primary purpose of the chisungu included these two; (a) to "grow"—magically—the initiands into fertile and nubile young women and (b) to effect this and remove the anomaly and danger that surrounds the girls by "securing the transition from a calm but unproductive girlhood to a potentially dangerous but fertile womanhood" (1956,125). Other such purposes included the teaching or reaffirmation of the tribal dogma and the maintenance of traditional values, for the chisungu, like most other initiating rites, serves as the vehicle for linking generations in the transmission of tradition. Concerning the task of detecting the pragmatic effects, Richards would want a clear line of demarcation made between the intention, conscious or unconscious, of the actors and the effect they produce on the state of mind of the individual.

The end result of Richards' patient analysis is the revelation of different levels of information that the rites of passage convey. On the one hand, chisungu is an index to the social structure understood as a series of social roles which are associated with membership in the different social groups of which the society is composed; on the other hand, it reveals Bemba religious beliefs and fears. On the one hand, it is a medium for gaining access to the secret knowledge of women; on the other hand, it provides an opportunity for instruction. And again, on the one hand, it concerns an event that is of universal importance since it deals with tensions connected with puberty; on the other hand, it has peculiarity of its own as it concerns Bemba attempts to resolve the tensions and paradoxes arising out of the rule of descent and marriage residence.

Some of the deep-seated tensions in Bemba society arise from a situation where exogamous matrilineages have to attract men from other lineages to marry their females and mate to create children over whom the husbands have no right of possession. The insistence on uxorilocal residence strengthens the position of the wife further, while it heightens the frustration of the husband on a twofold level: first, the fact that marriage means for him moving away from the secure environment of his own kinship group, and second, the stronger feeling of defeat, i.e., not being the owner of the children. As a paliative for his trying position, as insurance against marital breakups, and as encouragement to remain as faithful as possible to one's own spouse, Bemba tradition has ritualized the otherwise shaky marital union and has evolved a complex set of taboos and beliefs about sexual relations. By insisting on unflinching respect for the husband and on honesty in marriage as the qualifications for gaining access to the ancestors, tradition has soothed the nerves of the husband as well as restricted his freedom to disavow his marriage.

Two paradoxes emerge out of the traditional compromise. The first, is the constantly shifting image of the man between that of the domineering husband and the submissive son-in-law. The second is that between the well-ensconced wife and the submissive partner. Richards rightly observed that these contradictions find

> expression and perhaps resolution in the Chisungu which
> might be regarded as an extreme expression of the dilemma

of a matrilineal society in which men are dominant but
the line goes through the woman. (1956,51)

This somewhat extensive treatment of Richards' work is to show,
among other things, that Yoruba girls' fertility rites, which com-
mence at circumcision and end at the naming of the first child, com-
prise a series in a continuum of symbolic activities that ritualize the
dilemma between male dominance and male dependence on the female[5].

Edwin Ardener's Model

In his work, in the edited publication of *The Interpretation of Ritual*,
Ardener made an important contribution to the study of symbolism
by drawing attention to the analytical shortcomings that result from
the attempt to base analysis of matters about the "muted" group on
the evaluations provided by the "dominant" group in the same society. He maintained that the study of symbolism unravels certain
evaluations of women that expressly present female views about
themselves. He used the Bakweri of West Cameroons as a case in
point and showed how the views of Bakweri men differed so essentially from those of the women on rite of passage central to Bakweri
culture. Since a similar difference in the views of men and women
exist with regard to Kétu female circumcision rites, and since
Ardener's analytical insight has proved useful in this study, I shall
give a summary of his treatment of *liengu* rites.

The Bakweri have a myth that attempts to explain the male
concocted artificial boundaries of nature and culture. It postulates
that once upon a time, the bickering of four quarrelsome brothers
escalated to such an extent that they reached a unanimous decision
to part company forever. To discover which brother would go to
which of three places—the village, the forest, and the water—they
set themselves the task of detecting who amongst them would light
a fire that would remain burning until evening. The cunning Moto
succeeded and won the right to live in the village as man ("man" as
a generic term for both sexes). Ewaki and Eto went off to live in the
forest, one as an ape, the other as a mouse. The fourth brother,
Mojili, went to live in the river as a water spirit. The symbolic
dichotomy of the Bakweri, therefore, pits Moto, the brother resid-

ing in the town, against those living outside the town, rendering binary sets:

culture - nature; man - animals; village - forest; matter- spirit.

The paradox in the Bakweri symbolic taxonomy is that the Bakweri men bind themselves and their women in the camp of culture against the camp of nature, populated by anything outside the village. This classification put Mojili, who "turns"Bakweri girls into water-maidens (a transitory state that men abhor and classify as dangerous) in the camp of nature. However, it is this same liengu rite tha Bakweri women regard as the condition for the "transmission of girls" to adulthood. During the liengu rites, the girls are admitted to a corpus of secret knowledge and language peculiar to women. The initiands are also given ritual instructions that ridicule male symbols. They treat rats, *veto*, (which belong to the men's "wild" or wildness) as their husbands, and they engage in other inverted acts interpreted as dealing with a "total symbolic reversal whose effect is the 'feminization' of the male symbol" (S. Ardener 1977,51). The discrepancy occurs when men interpret the *liengu* rites that transforms Bakweri girls into women as dangerous to their women-folk. Such differences in interpretation occur in the attitude of Kétu men to Yoruba circumcision rites, and this difference will be highlighted.

Victor Turner's Model

In a series of works (1962, 1967), Turner has developed a model that was styled the cryptological approach (Sperber 1975,16). He maintained that one has to employ three levels of interpretation if one is to find a fuller meaning of symbolism. He called the three levels, the exegetical, the operational and the positional. The exegetical level contains the actors' statement about what they are doing, i.e., what they interpret their ritual acts to be. (This corresponds to Richards' expressed purpose.) The second level, the operational, is the preserve of the ethnographer, and it pertains to the deductions arising from his/her observations of what the actors say and do. To achieve meaning at this level, the ethnographer will rely both on his theoretical training and on his considerable knowledge of the social structure that has given rise to the ritual. The third level, the positional, arises from cross-checking the meaning of the symbol in different rituals in the same complex or by "an analysis of other ceremonies performed by the same community in which an identical or similar art occurs".(Richards 1956,115)

Although I will employ some of the ideas from Ardener's and Turner's models, where necessary, to to elicit more meaning, I will rely on Richards' model. I have chosen Richards' model because its manner of interpretation immediately relates the ritual to its pivotal place in society. Besides, with clarity, it throws light on the tensions inherent in the society arising from the delicate interplay of the rules of descent and those of residence at marriage. It also highlights the modifications and alignments necessitated by the ascription of status and rank associated with maturity or, more precisely, the attainment of adulthood in the society. It suggests the possibility of looking at the fertility ritual as a didactic mechanism, a suggestion that has been taken up and confirmed with reference to the Kétu series of fertility rites. Also, it is Richards' model that accommodates the treatment of those unconscious tensions and conflicts, the identification of which is so vital to gaining an understanding of the dynamism of the Kétu series of rites.

The more one reflects on fertility rite data the more one sees clearly the tensions and paradoxes originating from within the culture. These tensions relate to the new pressures that cannot be resolved or accommodated by obsolete methods of formalizing access to economic resources and hence to rank and status; paradoxes of male dominance and male dependence on the female; the tension inherent in the patrilineal ideology that insists on tracing, through the father, the descent of children born and delivered by the mother, who alone can say whether the *pater* is the same as the *genitor* in a society where old mores are beginning to relax. The paradoxes are expressed in myths and ritualized in Yoruba girls' fertility rites, which end when the patrilineal group has received proof of the profitability of the venture—the birth of the first child.

NOTES

1. Arnold van Gennep, *Les Rites de Passage*, Paris (1909). All references to this work are taken from the English translation by M. Vizedom and G. L. Caffee, Arnold van Gennep, *The Rites of Passage* London: Routledge and Kegan Paul, 1960.

2. Actually, the different reason that the Kétu men and women give for circumcision will be seen below, where I will use it to support Edwin Ardener's view that if the researcher intends to have balanced data about matters related to "muted" groups (for example, women in Kétu society) he/she has to try to get at what these groups say about themselves, not just what the dominant group says about them.

3. Psychoanalysis seems to conduct its analysis by creating hypothetical confrontations, at times even having to reach int. Arnold van Gennep, *Les Rites de Passage*, Paris (1909). All references to this work are taken from the English translation by M. Vizedom and G. L. Caffee, Arnold van Gennep, *The Rites of Passage* London: Routledge and Kegan Paul, 1960.

4. Without the slightest intention to depreciate, the contributions of Victor Turner to the study of ritual, the more deeply I read Audrey Richards' work on the chisungu, the more strengthened my conviction becomes that, but for the terminologies, Richards has touched on some of what Turner would say later.

5. Compare Appendix: the section on Yoruba myths of origin and their interpretation

CHAPTER THREE

OUTLINE OF THE KÉTU LINEAGE SYSTEM

Kétu Kinship System

Kétu Kinship Terminology

The Kétu patrilineage is the widest group of agnates tracing their descent through the male in each preceding generation to a common ancestor. In settlement terms, the lineage is divided into segments. The *segment* is the basic Kétu settlement unit, and it is constituted primarily by a corporate group of agnates living together in the *ìdílé*. Also living in idile, are "wives of the house" (*aya ile:*) along with their children (*ọmọ ilé*). A third group is made up of "strangers" or "those who live with the members of the *ìdílé:*" (*alabagbe, àlejò*). After some time, these strangers are usually absorbed into the kingroup. They must acknowledge and accept the tutelage of the "divinities and the ancestors of the lineage" (*òrìshà ìdílé*). They must comport themselves according to the lineage norms, obeying in particular, one stated in the Yoruba proverb "The enemy of my friend is my enemy, the friend of my friend is my friend"(*Ọ̀tá ọ̀rẹ̀mi, ọtami ni. Ọ̀rẹ ọ̀rẹ̀ mi, ọ̀rẹ̀mi ni*). A stranger who fulfils these conditions is assimilated into the idile. Thereafter, he can enjoy every privilege the lineage can offer, with the exception of succession to office.[1] The frequent occurrence of these assimilative phenomena recalls Evans-Prichard's remarks about the Nuer:

> The adoption and the assimilation of cognatic to agnatic ties are two ways in which community relations are transmitted into kinship relations; in which living together forces residential relations into a kinship pattern. (1940, 228)

From the male point of view, which the patrilineal ideology tends to stress, affinal relatives are members of the wife's patrilineage (called àna) without specification as to age or sex, because the Kétu believe: "Just as there is no small bee, so also, there cannot be a little affine or in-law"(Kòsí kékeré agbọn, bẹni kòsí kékeré àna)[2]. The affine or in-law has given you your greatest treasure (your wife), and so you must always show your appreciation to him.

Each in-law upholds the integrity of his own lineage into which a son-in-law has married. A wife is like a ward from her lineage. A Yoruba proverb of the modern era brings out one aspect of the caution and deference expected when one is interacting with affinal relatives: "He who speaks English in his in-laws' house must provide a suitable interpretation" (Ẹni tí óbá sọ òyinbó nílé àna, dandan ni kótúmọ rẹ)[3]

The family of a man, his wives and their children, are collectively referred to, not by any particular kinship term, but by a spatial term having to do with their position in the homestead or compound of the extended family (group of married agnates living together in a big, long, and circular house within the idile. This territorial space is called ojú ilé the ("section of the house") or, in Kétu dialect, ọdèdẹ̀. Most authorities (Forde 1951; Lloyd 1955, 1962, 1965; Schwab 1955 and Krapf-Askari 1969) use the double term "my own house" (ilé tèmi) to describe the unit I call ọdèdẹ̀. The effect of the loose and classificatory nature of Yoruba kinship terms is to strengthen lineage unity. The use of any specific possessive terms as "my own house" (ilé tèmi), "my own wife" (ìyàwó mi) is seen as tending to create exclusive groups within the lineage that may threaten the unity of the lineage. Such possessive terms tend to emphasize individual rather than collective interests. Thus, where specific kinship terms occur, in social relations and dealings, they are ignored in preference to more classificatory terms that are in line with the spirit of Kétu kinship behavior.

Kétu Kinship - Terminology[4]

The key to the genealogical formulae employed here is:

F = father; M = mother; B = brother Z = sister;
S = son; H = husband; W = wife; e = elder; y = younger;
F + M = P (parents); B + Z = G (sibling); S + D = C (children); H + W = E (spouses)

1. *Baba àgbà, Babalákú*	-	FF, MF, FFB, FMB, MMB, MFB
2. Iyá àgbà, Iyálákú	-	MM, FM, MMZ, FFZ, MFZ, FMZ
3. Baba	-	F FB^e, MB, FFBS, FFZS, FMBS MFZS, MMBS, MMZS
4. Iyá	-	M, MZ, FZ, MFBD, MMZD, MMBD, FFBD, FFZD, FMZD, FMBD, Hw^e
5. *Qomólójú*^{5}	-	CS, CD
6. *Qkọ*	-	H
7. *Iyàwó, Aya*	-	W
8. *Àna*	-	ZH, DH, MMZDH, MZH, FZDH, FFBDH, FFZDH
9. *Iyèkan*	-	Ego's MB, MZ, MBS, MBD
10. *Qmọ ĭyá*	-	Full sibling and their descendants
11. *Qbàkan*	-	Half sibling
12. *Àbúrò*	-	Any member of Ego's generation that is junior to Ego
13. *Ẹgbon*	-	Any member of the lineage who belongs to the generation of Ego's elder brother or elder sister.
14. *Qmọ*	-	C can refer to Ego's own child; children of Ego's collateral kin. The sex of the child can be specified by the addition of *oôkunrin*, (male) or *obìnrin* (female).

These ordinary kinship terms of reference offer some insight into basic Kétu attitudes towards kinship ties. The table itself shows certain characteristics: (a) stress on generational difference except where modified by age; (b) the indication of seniority among kinsmen.

Some problems of Kétu terminology parallel some that Ardener has mentioned with reference to the Mba-Ise Igbo (1954, 1959). The Iba-Ise Igbo have a segmentary lineage system, where the units are labeled by using terminology derived from the basic extended family unit. The system of land-use in Mba-Ise vests heritable ownership of the land in men; day-to-day management devolves on their wives. In a polygamous household, the land is divided for use among the wives, who thereby determine to some extent the amount of land to be inherited by their sons. At the death of the head of the family unit, the land is not divided equally among all the sons. The eldest son (*ophara*) receives a special portion in recognition of his special financial and ritual responsibility. The remaining land is divided into the mothers' spheres of interest. Within his group of full siblings (*omo nne*) the ophara receives another share of land for his personal use.

The social distinctions within the family between groups of siblings who stand in relation to each other as half siblings or children of the same father (*omo nna*) are built on this system of land sharing. The distinction is emphasized in the sharing of game, food, in cooking arrangements, and in other forms such as the physical layout of the extended family with its separate kitchen for each wife. The omo nne term extends to embrace the children and the children's children of the omo nne of the first generation. Yet at each generation, new groups of the *omo nne/omo nna* are formed as the original existing group of omo nne engage in polygynous marriage. This aspect makes the use of the term omo nne so fluid as to be meaningful only in the context in which it is used.

There are some significant differences between the Mba-Ise and the Kétu. First, Kétu women, like most Yoruba women, do not engage in farming (Fadipe 1970, 147),[6] therefore their husband's land is not divided for use amongst them. In addition, the rights of their children are not affected by their mother's junior or senior marital status. Second, there is no such arrangement of separate housing and cooking facilities for the wives in a polygynous Kétu family, so that the ọmọ-ìyáọbàkan social distinctions, the equivalent of the Mba-Ise omo nne/omo nna have no foundation in the housing arrangement. Third, children of the same ọ̀dẹ̀dẹ̀ are made to eat together while those of the same sex are made to sleep in a group as part of the drive to unity.

Kétu Lineage

Kétu patrilineages[7] are exogamous, and they are called ìdílé. Residence at marriage is normally virilocal. The ìdílé is the largest group of agnatically related persons who trace their descent in the male line through usually not more than four generations to a common known or fictive ancestor called "the fountain head"(*orisun*). The ìdílé divides internally into segments. A tendency towards segmentation and fission is counteracted by two factors that work for the solidarity of the lineage. The first is the corporateness of the lineage, which transforms members into an active interest group of people who are ready to protect their rights. The second factor is the short depth of genealogy, which never seems to reach beyond four generations from the ancestor to the living members (Lloyd 1965,251). This creates an intense sentiment of close kinship, both vertically and horizontally. Vertically, the living members feel a sense of closeness through the male line to the apical ancestor, who, in their genealogical reckoning, is not far removed from them. Horizontally, foreshortening the genealogy also shortens the distance between the living relatives, since the closer one is to the first generation, the closer the kinship tie between members. The sentiment of closeness affects the daily relations of the living members with one another. For the Kétu, accurately tracing one's genealogy is neither important nor even desirable.[8] An accurate tracing may in fact reveal greater kinship distances between living members, while a shortening of the chart for social purposes reduces such a distance. When the chart is shortened, the lesser segments are thrust up the rungs of the genealogical ladder, perhaps as far up as the region of the major lineages. As a result, the members feel that they are more closely related to the common ancestor, whose protection forms the basis of the sanctions validating the authority of the heads of the individual segments. Viewed in this light, Meyer Fortes' point regarding the social function of the category "ancestor" is applicable to the Kétu Yoruba;

> The ancestor cult is the calculus of the lineage system, the mechanism by means of which the progressive internal differentiation of the lineage is ordered and is fitted into the existing structure. It is also the principal ideological bulwark of the lineage organization. (Fortes 1945,33)

Relationship within the lineage is regulated by emphasizing cooperation between the segments to ensure the functioning of the whole. One often hears the proverb reiterated: "It is when the right hand washes the left and the left hand washes the right that both hands get clean"(*Ọ̀tún wẹ òsìn, òsìn wẹ ọtún ni ọwọ fi nmọ*). Another proverb that the Kétu use to emphasize this desired end is "Give me, I give you, croaks the toad at the depth of the river"(*Bù ú mi ki mbù un ọ ni ọpọlọ nké lálẹ odò*). The moral of lineage cooperation and solidarity runs through these and other proverbs.

Other peculiar features that express the solidarity of the lineage include the possession of common facial marks called *ilà*, praise songs *oríkì* that narrate the heroic deeds and important events of the lineage. Other basic features common to members include the observance of certain taboos *èèwọ*, the worship of some specific divinity *òrìshà*. All these features serve to emphasize the importance of unity among members if the lineage is to survive. As Fortes states:

> A lineage is a temporal system. Continuity in time is its fundamental quality. Its constitution and dimension at a given time represents a phase of a process which, as the natives see it, has been going on in exactly the same way from the beginning of their social order and is continuing to the future. The contemporary face of a lineage is more than a product of its past; it embodies all the significant changes that have occurred in it through the past, and it is at the same time, the embryo of its future organization. (1945,32-3)

Kinship Relations

Deference to old age and the recognition of seniority are two important aspects of Kétu etiquette that also reflect on Kétu kinship behavior. One often hears the mistress of ceremonies of the fertility
rites reiterate the proverb "No matter how rich a child is in beautiful clothes he cannot have more used clothes than his parent" (*Kòsí
bi ọmọde ṣe le ni aṣọ to tí yio ni àkísà tó obi rẹ*).[9] Elders must be
given respect because of their age and their experience therein. Kétu
tradition stresses that because parents are their children's first teachers, and the father, especially, should not make light of this task,
since any faulty traits noticed in the child is blamed on the parents.
The father's strong tendency not to spare the rod and spoil the child
s born out in another proverb: "The child behaves foolishly and
instead of reprimanding it, we pray that it may not dieÑwhat kills
more quickly than foolishness?" (*Ọmọ kògbọn ani ki ómáku, kini
npa ọmọ bi àïgbọn*). Hence, the father/child relationship is very
cool and formal.

This image of the father as a strict disciplinarian is comple-
mented by that of the mother, who is a refuge, a kind of "human
shock-absorber." She is, in the Kétu image of parenthood, the "gentle
side." The father represents the right hand of firm discipline, which
intimidates the child. The mother represents that of gentleness, which
brings the child around and consoles the child. The proverb, "When
we use the right hand to flog the child, we use the left hand to draw
him back to ourselves" (*Ti abá fi ọwọ ọtún na ọmọ afi òsìn faa
mọra*) makes the point clearly. The mother provides the
reconciliatory medium, and, hence again, the Yoruba child makes
no mistake as to which parent is higher in his affection. It is a
common Yoruba saying: "The mother is gold, the father is glass!"
(*Iyá ni wúrà baba ni dìgì*).

The symbolism of this saying brings out the valuation of the
parents. The affection of the father is fragile and hard to come by;
glass was both foreign and scarce to Yorubaland. It is short-lived.
Mother-love is as durable and as fine as gold. She is the mainstay
in the child's life. While the father's affection—like a piece of glass
—can break into splinters, irretrievably lost because of the child's
misbehavior, in which case the father can disown him, the mother
will never disown the child. With reference to the unending love of

the mother, the Yoruba say: "No matter how terrible the mouth is, the owner will always lick it" (*Ti ẹnu kòba sunwòn ẹlẹnu ápọnla*). While the mother is most likely to be blamed for every fault in the child, she does not receive the credit for the child's good qualities. The Yoruba say: "When the child is good, it belongs to the father; if it is bad, it is the mother's" (*Ti ọmọ ba dára ti baba rẹ, ti oba bàjẹ́, ti ïya rẹ*).

The relation of the child to its grandparents is affectionate, almost to the point of over-pampering. Traditionally Kétu grandparents bring up some of their grandchildren. The paradox of a disciplinarian tradition, like that of the Kétu, is that while it insists on the discipline in the children, it allows them to enter into the care of their grandparents even though experience has confirmed that grandparents do not haved much corrective influence on their grandchildren. Yoruba people often say: "The child of the elderly one is as spoilt as the left hand"[10] (*Ọmọ arúgbó bajẹ bi ọwọ òsìn*). Yet they will not hesitate to allow their children to be brought up by the grandmother.[11]

The father's sister and the mother's brother regard the children of their brothers and sisters as their own. The mother's brother, even though the rule of patriliny has established his sister's children in another patriclan, treats them with great affection, as they symbolize the fertility and the creative power of his own lineage. The brother always makes his sister's children welcome and cases abound of children who have broken off or have been expelled from their patrilineage going off and setting up their abode with the *Iyèkan*, their maternal patrikin.

Since seniority is one way of regulating social relations (Bascom 1942), relative age affects a lineage member's behavior. While he is expected to treat those members of his generation who are older than himself with respect, he treats any member of his parent's generation, who is his junior, as his inferior, the emphasis being place on seniority rather than generational difference.

A man maintains some distance and caution with his affinal relatives. The degree of distance varies with the group of affinal relatives in question. He is expected to treat those who belong to the generation of his wife's father with great respect and at times with avoidance. He enjoys an asymmetrical "joking relationship" with his wife's brothers who are of the same generation with himself (Radcliffe-Brown 1965,90). This seems to be balanced by the same sort of joking relation existing between his own brothers and his wife. His wife, too, is expected to respect and avoid her husband's parents. This is most rigidly enforced as the situation in the extended family means that the husband's parents are often thrown together with the wife. Avoidance and respect reduces the tension between the mother-in-law and the wife.

Among the Kétu there is no practice of bride-service[12], which was a common feature of the institution of marriage of some east African sociolinguistic groups like the Bemba of Zambia (Richards 1956) and the Kimbu of Western Tanzania (Shorter 1972). For this reason and since residence at marriage is patrilocal, the instances of contact of the husband with his affinal relatives are reduced to the minimum. Meetings occur in the course of certain traditional duties of a son-in-law to his affinal relatives that include the provision of group labor such as thatching the roof of the house or clearing a sizeable piece of land in readinesss for the planting season at the onset of the first rains. The son-in-law also has an obligation to seek redress in cases of assault against an in-law.

Kinship and Residence

Kétu lineage members live in large compounds called *agbo-ilé*[13] which have a genealogical depth that extends to about three or four generations. As Krapf-Askari, who termed it ilé tiwa (as did Forde and Lloyd), observed, it consists of

> a head (*bale tiwa*), his wives, his younger brothers and sons and their wives and children his unmarried sisters and daughters, and sometimes, the sons of his father's younger brothers with their wives. (1969,72)

There are three categories of people living in the agbo-ile. First, there are the *ǫmǫ-ilé*, the hard core of the lineage, the agnatic members associated with ownership of the territory on which the residence is sited. This group is often jokingly referred to as the "sons of the soil," an appellation that has a strong political overtone distinguishing the natives of a town against its "foreign elements." The second group is comprised of the wives (*ĭyàwó*) of the agnatic members. The third group is comprised of the strangers (*alábagbé*). A smaller unit of the residential group is the *ọdẹdẹ*. The basic Kétu kinship unit, therefore, does not correspond to the nuclear or elementary family of father, mother, and children.[14] This is the natural outcome of a polygamous marriage system.

The *agbo-ilè*, or extended family, is not an undifferentiated mass of people related by birth, marriage, or residential link. Within the extended family there is an hierarchical structure that runs down from the *baálé*, the head, to the newly born child. The conditions for asserting or determining seniority depend on the nature of one's affiliation to the lineage. Among the children, seniority depends on birth; among the wives, it is determined by the time of marriage into the group. For the strangers (*àlejò*) who, for some reason, have not been assimilated either by the process of translating "residential relations into kingship pattern" (Evans-Pritchard 1940,228), or of transforming "ties of contiguity to those of common descent"(Ardener 1959,129) the position is often ambiguous. In line with Yoruba etiquette, children are encouraged to respect elderly people, including the strangers who, however, are given to realize that discipline is left to the elders.

The *ọdẹdẹ,* the smallest unit of the extended family, is composed of the husband (*ọkọ*), the wives (*ïyàwó*) and the children (*ọmọ*). Within this unit, there is a realignment of children in terms of a common primogenitrix. The children of the same mother are called *ọmọ-ïyá*. It is thus the equivalent of the Mba-Ise Igbo category for full siblings (*omo nne*). Children of the same father but different mothers are called "one father" (*ọbàkan*). Collectively, the groups of omo-iya in a household are called *orígun*. In most cases, they form an economic unit. While omo-iya-obakan social distinctions are recognizable, after keen observation within the ọdẹdẹ, the conscious working of Yoruba kinship ideology is to ignore, neutralize, or even deny the existence of these boundaries. Hence, unlike the Mba-Ise Igbo, Kétu wives do not have separate living quarters detached from those of others; hence the wives cook for all the odede members. The wives eat together just as the children do.

At about the age of five, children of the same sex are encouraged to eat together, sleep in the same area of the ọdẹdẹ and, naturally, play together. While distinctions among the Mba-Ise Igbo omo nne/omo nna are encouraged by such things as sleeping arrangements, eating arrangements, the division of game and, ultimately, the pattern of land inheritance, among the Kétu (omo-iya/obakan), distinctions have none of these underpinnings. Yet, among the Kétu, attempts to break down the barriers of the distinction do not seem to have yielded the desired goal, especially in the areas of inheritance and succession. Before studying this more closely, it would be profitable to examine the extensive field of reference of the omo-iya/obakan terms.

The term omo-iya is confusing. Applied in the strict literal sense, it means "children of the same mother". But this does not necessarily make them full siblings. Among most of the Yoruba, and especially the Kétu, widow inheritance is a common practice. The children from such unions are not considered to be born to the memory of the deceased. Unlike the Nuer and the old Jewish customs (Jones 1966), they are not the deceased's children. They are the children of their genitors. The children of such a woman, both those born before widow-inheritance and those begotten by the widow, are classified among the omo-iya. Yet they are not full siblings since they belong to different fathers. Krapf-Askari wisely avoided this confusing field of reference of the omo-iya term by restricting "it as the Yoruba do not, to a woman's children by the same husband" (1969,64). Children who are born after divorce (which is said to be rare in the past) are also classified along with those begotten in marriage as omo-iya. Yet this latter group of omo-iya will, normally, belong to two distinct lineages as it is forbidden for a lineage member to take as wife any woman who has been divorced by a kinsman.

When the term omo-iya is restricted to full siblings the Yoruba terminological problem is not over. It only shifts focus to another area—that of the extensive field of reference. The members of the original group of the omo-iya in the odede group are naturally closer together. The term omo-iya is extended to include their own children, that is, members of the second generation. Yet, at this generation as well as the next, the practice of polygyny implies that new groups of omo-iya and obakan are formed. Therefore, while the original omo-iya (those of the first generation) call themselves and their children omo-iya, their children will only use the term omo-iya to refer to their own full siblings as against the rest of their father's children by other wives. For these they will use the term obakan. In the same way, obakan gets more and more relativistic with each succeeding generation. This contracting and expanding field of reference of omo-iya and obakan means that "any attempt to assign them to groups of definite size, and especially to arrange them in any hierarchy of magnitude is doomed to failure" (Ardener 1959,117). The relativity of their field of reference implies that it is the context in which they are used that gives precision to them (Green 1947).

Inheritance and Succession

With Kétu inheritance, the importance of the social distinctions of obakan/omo-iya become considerable. Maximal segments of a lineage frequently correspond to omo-iya. Hence, descent among the Kétu takes into consideration the obakan/omo-iya distinction. To lessen the competition between each group of omo-iya within the odede, it is an axiom of the Kétu law of succession that in a title vested in the ídíle:, lineage does not descend the generational ladder in one line. Instead, it rotates among the segments of the lineage founded by each group of the omo-iya of the first generation (Johnson 1921; Lloyd 1962).

There are three categories of property a man may own at his death; inherited property, acquired property, and movable property. The quality of each affects its disposal.

Land inherited as a member of the lineage is retained in the lineage to be exploited by those who remain within the lineage. If quarrels within the group force a member to leave his patrilineage and settle with his maternal patriclan, he automatically loses his right to the exploitation of his father's land. This use of lineage land to enforce lineage cohesion is similar to the practice among the Lozi of Zimbabwe, whose law of land ownership demands membership in the place of residence, for "no one lives elsewhere and cultivates in the village" (Gluckman 1955,50). Land that was acquired through the efforts and personal resources of the deceased passes into the ownership of his children who can dispose of it as best they know without interference from the lineage members.

By tradition, most of the property of the deceased seems to have passed to those members of the omo-iya who were not, because of extreme youth, excluded form inheriting. The conflict created by this manner of inheritance and the threat this conflict posed to lineage unity seem to have necessitated the change in the division of inheritance in favor of the children of the deceased. Johnson's remarks about this change, which spread from Oyo to the rest of Yorubaland in the nineteenth century in the wake of Oyo military supremacy are worth noting.

> At the deliberative council in the year 1858 it was proposed to alter this custom. For whom is a man toiling and saving? The answer comes naturally "For his children". Why then should a brother displace one's children in the succession? If the children are minors, the uncle may act for them until they are of age, otherwise the eldest surviving issue of the founder of a house must succeed as the head of the house in rotation until it comes to the turn of the children of the next generation. (1921,326-7)

Property that the Kétu associate with seniority will not be given to the children of the deceased. These include the voluminous gowns call *gbárìyẹ*, embroidered cow-tails called *Irùkẹrẹ*, and big embroidered caps. These caps were worn only by elders before the money economy broke their monopoly of them by providing the means for their purchase, different from the traditional ones and out of the control of the elders. Such important symbolic items, nonetheless belong to the elders, whom the Kétu consider both wise and great because of their experience.

Conclusion

Analysis of the Kétu lineage system has shown that it insists on collective rather than individual responsibility for the marriage of its members, for its children, and for some of its property. In so doing, it subordinates the roles and the interests of the individual family members to those of the wider kinship group. It also puts a wedge between husband and wife as well as among groups of minors in a polygamous family. From the point of view of marriage and circumcision—the main interest of this work—wives are incorporated into the patrilineage in such a way that the bond between husband and wife does not become so consuming as to threaten the solidarity of the lineage. Circumcision is thought to lessen the pleasure of intercourse for the wife, since such pleasure is thought to reduce the lineage members' intense feeling of loyalty to the lineage by the creation of a strong man/wife bond. Circumcision is also taken as making clear that sexual intercourse is not an end in itself but a means of begetting children who will continue the lineage. Kétu views that associate absence of circumcision with the creation of an intense bond between man and wife is an instance of the case where the facts of ideology have been grafted on to physiology in order to explain the Kétu contention that the intense sexual experience stands in the way of loyalty to the lineage.

Scholars have noticed the tendency of the kinship group in certain societies to employ taboos to divide the family so that members can transfer their loyalty to the larger kinship group. Evans-Pritchard (1945) confirmed the existence of such practices among the Nuer. I. Schapera (1956) maintained that the customary estrangement between the Bechuana husband and wife endears the wife to her immediate affinal relatives. Gluckman stated that such rules and taboos that divide members of the family are also important because:

They introduce divisions—estrangements—into the family and prevent it absorbing the whole-hearted emotional allegiance of its members. Husbands are forced apart from their wives to continue association with their own kin, and children turn to more distant kin and away from their parents. The estrangements in the family are associated with the extension of ties to wider kinship groupings. These groupings support the family, but they are important in building the cohesion of the larger society. (1955,57)

Circumcision among the Kétu corresponds, to some extent, to those practices in other societies that tend to neutralize the wife's influence on her husband.

NOTES

1. The word "office" is used here to connote a lineage chieftaincy title. It does not refer to the "headship" of the *idile* which is assumed by the eldest member. An absorbed member will not qualify for the headship of the segment, his age notwithstanding

2. In this proverb, the in-law is symbolically associated with a bee. The bee makes honey (vital to most Yoruba rituals of life-crises except funerals). The bee also stings. Just as the in-law gives one the greatest treasure—the wife who gives birth to one's children, he can also be so severe as to take one's wife away, thereby cutting off one's chance not only to contribute to lineage population but also the reincarnation of one's dead.

3. To the largely non-literate Kétu, English language (*ede oyinbo*) as opposed to their vernacular, is as strange as Greek. Looked at from the bounded category of Yoruba, English belongs to the group of "non-language." It is a riddle. For one who is expected to cautious, to launch into a stream of riddles is a breach of etiquette.

4. These terms are based on the terminological data provided by Ajisafe (1924), Forde (1951) and on my fieldwork notes.

5. Ajisafe (1924) recorded this now old-fashioned term that offers an insight into the type of relationship that should exist between a child and its grandparents. *Omoloju* is best rendered as "the child who is the apple of my eye" (*oju*-eye). This immediately suggests the privileged position and license children enjoy with grandparents.

6. Longo holds a different view—one open to questioning—stating that "in Yoruba culture a large portion of the family farming is the woman's responsibility" (1964,471).

7. "Lineage" here follows the definitions employed by Fortes and Evans-Pritchard, as a "segmentary system of permanent, unilateral descent group," forming "corporate units with the political functions"(1940,6).

8. The exception to this rule is the royal genealogy, which tradition goes to great lengths to build up and trace back, ultimately, to Oduduwa, the culture hero of all the Yoruba. Connection , either in reality or putatively guarantees high rank to the king and, by extension, to his town.

9. It is a Kétu habit to acquire new cloths only on important occasions, which are not more than three in the year. Thus, quantities of clothing represent annual cycles, and quantities of used clothing represent old age and experience. This proverb corresponds to one that Richards recorded as forming the ideological underpinning of the Bemba girls' nubility rites: "The arm-pit can never be higher than the shoulder".(1956,72)

10. The evaluation of the left hand changes in terms of the context in which it is used. In the context of the sacred, for example, the left hand of the *Ogboni*, an important Yorubal ritual and political cult (Morton-Williams 1960; Biobaku 1952, 1957; Bascom 1944), the left hand is auspicious. It is similarly regarded in reference to the sacred duty of bringing up one's children. In most mundane con texts, it is regarded as inauspicious.

11. This practice of leaving children in the care of their grandparents ensures that members of the FF and MM generation are not left alone. In providing intergenerational care for their grand children, not only are grandparents kept active, there sense of belonging is enhanced as they provide a crucial service of child care, freeing up more time for their own children and their spouses to spend at their business.

12. Bride -service is the husband's obligation to provide free labor to his parents-in-law, over a period of time, as a sign of his indebtedness to them.

13. Fadipe (1970), Bascom(1942), and Schwab call *agbo-ile* the "extended family."

14. Fox (1967) rejects the idea that the nuclear family is the basic unit, favoring instead the mother-child unit as basic. To support this claim, he stated that (a) in a given situation, where the mother can protect and provide for a child, the father is dispensable, and (b) t hat even where a man is indispensable for these tasks, he need not be the genitor of the child.

CHAPTER FOUR

FERTILITY

Introduction

Fertility is a central concern of the Kétu, human fertility being only one aspect of the Kétu complex view of it. Among the Kétu, fertility includes the capacity of all living things to reproduce. This capacity depends not only on certain physical conditions like a suitable climate, copious sunshine, and moderate rainfall but also on expressive or metaphysical forces like the blessings of the ancestors. The fertility of the land and its plants relate directly to the animal world and particularly human fertility. This influence of one type of fertility on another is not necessarily due to the natural dependence of animals on plants. It concerns the expressive use of earth's resources to obtain favors from the divinities and from the ancestors whose goodwill is expressed in the fecundity enjoyed by the lower animals and man. Hence, human fertility is one category within the wider systems of Kétu fertility categories in a context where it acquires its full meaning.

Reactions to drought serve to illustrate the field of interrelated concerns within the Kétu understanding of fertility. Drought strikes at the heart of Kétu society, which is wholly agricultural. The cessation of the rains, coupled with the intensity of sunshine in this tropical area means disaster to the crops as well as to the fish in the streams as they dry up. The resultant scarcity of food crops means not only famine to human beings, but also to the divinities and ancestors because of the dearth of food for feasting. There is a cycle of dependence between the living and the dead. The ancestors as well as their living descendants have an interest in the continuation of fertility, for the cessation of human fertility that results from an interruption of plant and animal fertility threatens the ability of the ancestors to reincarnate. The belief in reincarnation, symbolized in such Yoruba names as *Babátúndé* (father comes back again) and *Yetunde* or *Iyábọ* (mother comes back again) forms the basic dogma of the beliefs of Yoruba traditional religion (Finnegan 1977,15; Ferguson 1970,28). The forfeiture of the right to reincarnation in Yoruba metaphysical thought is not unlike hell in Christian theology. The belief is that the ancestors have as much interest in human fertility and in fertility in general as their living descendants.

The Kétu find it difficult to explain such a misfortune as a drought. Yet it must be explained before they can develop a solution for it. In other circumstances, Yoruba metaphysical thought usually interprets misfortune in terms of the displeasure of the ancestors. In the case of drought, the Kétu know that the ancestors would not be so incensed as to take a step that would result in their own consignment to oblivion. The Kétu extricate themselves from this dilemma by transferring the blame onto those people in the society referred to as witches (*Àjẹ*). These scapegoats are always women—not so surprising in a male-orientated patrilineal society. Peter Morton-Williams has observed the constant tendency of Yoruba men to project their fears onto women (1960, 38). Women who fail to conform to normative roles (or example, women who are barren or who reveal strong masculine tendencies) may be rounded up at the threat of war and

> if the authorities of the town decided to proceed against a woman suspected of witchcraft, they might judicially try her, perhaps compelling her to submit to an ordeal. On conviction she would be publicly executed by an *egungun*. Or instead of a trial, they might order members of the *Oro* cult to seize her and take her to be killed in secrecy of their grove; after which it would be announced that the ancestors had carried her away.(Morton-Williams 1960, 39)

In other words, a scapegoat has to be found to avoid the possibility of blaming the ancestors. There is a close resemblance between the Kétu idea of witchcraft and the Gusii witchcraft beliefs. In reference to the latter, Phillip Mayer has observed:

> The Gusii witchcraft belief helps to maintain their picture
> of the moral universe. By blaming witches they escape
> the need or the temptation to blame spirits[1]. The spirits
> can remain good because the witches are bad (1970:52).

It is the interrelatedness of the diagnosis of this social misfortune and the antidote prescribed for its cure that is expressed in the euphemism that describes the immolation of the victims of the propitiatory acts; "the ancestors have carried them away"(Morton-Williams, 1960,52).

The Kétu express their awareness of this interrelatedness of human fertility with plant and animal fertility in the saying: " As the trees in the forest are affected so are the human beings in the society are" (*Bi oti ṇṣe igi ninu igbo, bẹ lo nṣe enia ninu ilé*). The Kétu annual calendar of festivities illustrates this connection by arranging fertility dances such as "the dance for the cult of the goddess of the farm" (*Orìṣa oko*) (Jones 1946,18-21) and the "stilt dance" (*Ijó gagaló*)[2] to coincide with the period of fruit and crop ripening for the performance of the fertility rites for Kétu girls. Furthermore, even the motifs for Kétu propitiatory prayers for fertility show this relational dimension. The moon (*Oṣupa*), the fish (*Ẹja*) and the kolanut tree (*igi obì*) are but a few of the symbolic objects used in such prayers. A stanza of such a prayer is said for a girl who has completed her rites and is being given in marriage to another lineage:

> May you use your stomach to carry pregnancy,
> and your back to carry children.
> May you have as many children trailing after you
> As the stars trail after the moon.
> May you have many children
> As many as those of the fish in the river.
> May you be as fruitful as the kola tree[3].
>   (Author's translation)

These prayers are intended to operate on the Frazerian homoeopathic principle of "like on like." Kétu folklore identifies the stars as the children of the moon. Thus, just as the fish, the moon, and the kola tree produce many offspring, so the wish is expressed that the girl may be fertile.[4]

The Kétu Notion of Conception

The Kétu take human conception as the practical proof of the fertility of the wife. Conception or pregnancy is expected to take place within the context of marriage. Taking this normal course, the females undergo a change in status from immature girls to mature women. Reproduction is the goal of marriage, the proof of the efficacy of prayer, and the index of the goodwill of the ancestors for their descendants.

The Kétu are aware of the part the parents play in the conception of the child, but they also insist that the final gift of a child does not rest solely on the act of sexual intercourse. Evidence is easily available by reference to the couples who have no children. As the Kétu point out, these couples perform their sexual duties, and so if begetting children depends on sexual intercourse alone, why have the couples not begotten children? The Kétu stress that even "if a couple engages in it (sexual intercourse) without a stop but has not got the blessing of the Supreme Being, the couple is just doing it for nothing" (*Bi ènïa ba se ṣe ṣe di ọtúnlamẹta, bi kòba sí àṣẹ Olódùmarè nibẹ, ókàn nṣiṣẹ sorí òfifo ni*). Thus, the Kétu beliefs concerning pregnancy are overlaid by beliefs of a mystical nature. This overlay expresses the Kétu experience about the existential circumstance surrounding the conception of children; it also confirms for the Kétu the observation made by Victor Uchendu about the Igbo;

> The biological facts of conception are accepted but other factors are also involved in pregnancy and are much more important. These are the consent of the deities and the willingness of the dead lineage members other friendly spirit to reincarnate themselves. The absence of these two agents renders conception impossible. (1965,57)

The additional forces required in procreation, therefore, are the Supreme Being (*Olódùmare*), the divinity entrusted with the molding of the physique (*Ọbàtálá*) and the ancestors (*Awon baba ará ọ̀run*). The Supreme Being as the owner of breath imparts life to the semen (*àtọ̀*). This constitutes the essence of man and the source of his vitality. It is the source of the individual's participation in the divine. The divinity moulds the physique. The ancestor gives the "ancestral spirit" (*Ẹlẹ́da*) (Bascom 1956,9), the second Yoruba soul.[38] This is the reincarnated element in the child which forms his object of worship in the future. All these elements are in the man's semen. Hence, the man's semen contains a miniature child. However, it is at the moment of sexual union that the sacred arm of the Deity sets into operation the actualization of the potency in the semen so that it can, given the conducive conditions of the womb, develop into a proper child.

Two important ideas result from this understanding of conception. The first is that the act of sexual union is sacred, i.e, the couple are participating in the creative power of the Supreme Being. The act involves divine intervention since it is the Deity who sets in motion the process of creation. Thus, there are the taboos about when and where sexual intercourse is suitable. There is also the insistence that it should happen in the context of marriage, the context that determines its normality. Sex, therefore, cannot be casual. The act must be performed with the intention of participating in divine creativity. The second idea is that this understanding of conception allows the Kétu to regard the child as belonging solely to the father. In other words, it supports the patrilineal ideology that vests ownership of the child on the father.

This manner of explaining conception has been given considerable attention by other writers. Helen Callaway (1978) quoted J. Needham as saying that it amounts to the "denial of physiological maternity":

> Joseph Needham calls our attention to ideas held in Greece before the time of Aristotle, ideas which may have had their origin in Egypt, that the father alone was the "author of generation" while the mother provided only the "nidus and nourishment for the foetus" (J. Needham 1959, p.43). He cites a passage from the *Eumenides* of Aeschylus when

Apollo, defending Orestes during the trial from the charge
of matricide, brings forward a philosophical argument.
"The mother of what is called her child", Apollo makes
his case, "is not parent of it, but nurse only of the young
life that is sown in her. The parent is the male and she but
a stranger, a friend who, if fate spares his plant, preserves
it till it puts forth." (Callaway 1978,167-8)

This tendency to underplay, if not to ignore the female contribution
to procreation was not the monopoly of Greek and Kétu societies,
with their strong male-orientation. Isichei has recorded the prevalence of this "denial of physiological maternity" among the Asaba
Igbo;

A good way to think of a man's sperm in order to capture
accurately Asaba notion of it would be to regard it as a
kind of seed ready to germinate in the fallow ground of a
woman's womb. Accordingly, the sperm was a kind of
"miniature baby" and all that a woman did was to develop
it.[39] (1970,90)

Similar ideas have been noted among the Taita of Kenya (Harris
1978,145-56) and the Zulu of South Africa.

Such tendencies to underplay a parent's contribution to the
conception of the child are not only characteristic of patrilineal societies. It has also been observed in matrilineal societies. Among
the matrilineal Ashanti there is the belief that "a human being is
formed from the blood (*mogya*) of the mother and the spirit (*sumsum*)
of the father (Sarpong 1977, 4). The greater contribution of the
mother to the work of creating the child forms the basis of the belief
that the "biological link between one generation and another is provided by the blood transmitted through the mother, hence an Ashanti
traces his physical descent through the female line" (ibid). Yet the
Ashanti appreciate the part of the father, whose recognition, expressed in name-giving, is highly essential.

Other comparisons emerge from these examples. Among the
Ashanti, as well as among the Asaba Igbo, the parent who does not
determine the descent of the child is credited with the "menial" task
of molding the child's personality or kneading the rough matter into
refined form. Thus, for the patrilineal Asaba Igbo, the work of

kneading devolves on the mother; for the matrilineal Ashanti it de-volves on the father. As if to rob the mother of this contributive role in order to establish a stronger case for male-ownership of the child, the Kétu credit the work of moulding the physical features of the child to the creative refraction of the Supreme Being whom they call *Ọbàtálá*. Yet again, the Kétu idea of procreation corresponds with that of the Gonja of northern Ghana who hold the view that

> it is the man who places a child in the mother's womb for warmth and protection, during the early stages of growth—the woman nourishes it, but does not contribute to the actual formation of the foetus. (Goody 1962, 20)

These observations lend themselves to two comments. First, such partial explanations are necessary for establishing claim over a child by a parent whose sex is relevant for tracing descent, for inheriting, and for succeeding to office. These claims will, therefore, exist where unilinearity is overt. Thus, where there is stress on strong patrilineages, such explanations of procreation that either under-play or ignore, where possible, the contribution of women to the child are likely. Second, that such explanations do not express a peoples' ignorance of physiological paternity or maternity as was suggested of the Tully Blacks (Rother 1903, 22/81); of the Trobriand Islanders by Malinowski (1929, 179-85); and of the Aborigines by Kaberry (1939, 43). Rather, they are symbolic statements, express-ing, on the one hand, men's relation to the divinities and, on the other hand, "the relation between the woman's child and the clans-men of the woman's husband stems from public recognition of the bonds of marriage, rather than from the facts of cohabitation, which is a very normal state of affairs" (Leach 1969,87).

Kétu Attitude towards the Sex of a New-born Child

The earlier discussion of Kétu kinship drew attention was drawn to the primary goal of the Kétu patrilineage; to achieve continuity. The Kétu have an ancestor-oriented descent system traced from the father through male ancestors to the common progenitor. The com-bination of the rule of exogamy with patrilocality emphasizes the transfer of female members to their husbands' families. In so doing, the importance of the male members to the continuity of the lineage is heightened.

The Kétu want children and preferably male children. At all ritual and ceremonial gatherings, prayers are said that culminate in the wish for a healthy male child (ọmọkunrin lantilanti).[7] A common Kétu prayer is "Lord, give me a child who will be the centre-pole of the house and who will look after the house" (Olúwá, fun mi lọmọ o, òpómúléró, ọmọ ti yio gbọ ti 'lé). The discriminatory undertone of this prayer is understood through the imagery of the center-pole[8] (òpómúléro), which has two levels of meaning. On the level of function, the traditional Kétu dwelling in the hamlet (as opposed to town) is a circular hut with a central pole. This pole acts as the prop for the skeleton of the roof. If it falls, it brings down the whole structure with it. The Kétu male child occupies an identical place in the structure of the edifice of the lineage. The female child goes out into another family. On another level, the center-pole is a phallic symbol. It is the penis that contributes most to procreation, the Yoruba say.

The Kétu, however, are not satisfied with just any male child. It must be proper (gidi) male child. The criteria for "proper," for the Kétu, are many. The first is that the child be intelligent, resourceful, and healthy (jáfáfá). A common Yoruba proverb makes this point: "the dull, slow-witted, child is no child, the smart one is" (Ọmọ radaràda ọmọ kọ. Ọmọ tójáfáfá lọmọ). Another criterion for the proper child is sensitivity to correction, especially verbal correction. A proper child is one who can interpret both correction by the eyes and by gestures (Ọmọ ti omọ oju ti omọra). The Kétu admire well-trained children. The goal of Kétu and Yoruba child-training is the inculcation of good manners and discipline. The Yoruba believe that children require continual discipline. If it becomes necessary to correct a child in the presence of a stranger, the correction will be made by some bodily gesture expressing impatience or disapproval. The sensitive child picks up such subtle corrections. The ill-mannered child (ọmọ alaigbọran) will, to the embarrassment of all present, ask: Why are you looking at me like that? (Irú ojú wo ni ẹfi nwomi yẹn?). The proper Kétu child must also have respect for his elders. Thus, the Kétu scale of preference is not only in terms of sex but of character as well. Hence, great

84

emphasis is put on this responsibility in the instruction given to the Kétu mother-to-be in the rite of initiation. The most important criterion, in addition to those stipulated, is that the child be able to reproduce. A Kétu proverb states unequivocally the responsibility of the child to procreate: "We have given birth to you, you must also give birth to another" (*Bibi la bíọ, iwọ na gbọdọ bi ènïa*).

The announcement of the birth of a new baby is greeted with the common question: Male or female? (*Ako nbabo?*). If it is male, there is greet jubilation. At times, the booming of guns announces the sex of the child to the community. If the child is female, the celebration, which is not so enthusiastic, often ends with the wish, "next time it is a boy that God will provide" (*Iwoyi bayi igbamiran, ọmọkunrin lantilanti l'Ọlọrun ápèsè*). If, however, it is yet another girl, the attitude of the Kétu tends to oscillate from a very short-lived joy to profound sympathy, couched in such prayers as "May God answer your prayer" (*Ọlọrun a ma gbọ adura rẹ o*). It is worth noting that this prayer is normally reserved for the barren and for those afflicted by "spirit children who are born to die" (*Àbíkú*). This suggests that the Kétu tend to group the barren, the woman whose children die not long after birth, and the mother whose children are all females into the same category.

A woman with only female children knows that her position in her husband's house is not assured. She is aware that in the future, her marks may be cleaned off. She is aware that people will say "her mark is cleaned off" (*ipa rẹ ti parẹ*), an equivalent expression to the Mba-Ise Igbo metaphor—"her door is closed, her path is lost" (Ardener 1954,89). Instead of rejoicing, Kétu mothers may even weep bitterly at the birth of yet another female child. Ardener found similar attitudes among the Mba-Ise Igbo;

> Even if she had had many daughters, neither she nor they could be taken into account in the division. The *omo nne* she had founded would be a transient unit composed of females with no right to hand on ancestral land, and whose claims to land use would be exercised in other local units into which they would marry. The failure of the wife without a son is phrased in the ever-present metaphor of the visible dwelling alignment "her door is closed", and more fully, "her path is lost." (1954, 89).

The position of an impotent young man is equally serious. The Kétu equate impotence with sterility. They recognize only one type of impotence in their males—the failure of the penis to achieve erection. When this occurs, it is regarded as disastrous, and every magical means is sought as a cure. When such cures fail, the case of the afflicted young man is regarded as forlorn. His affliction excludes him from attaining the status of the complete man (*okunrin gidi*) since he is genetically moribund. He is also dead spiritually, since through him the ancestors cannot hope to be reincarnated. The Kétu, therefore, symbolically express the disappointing and pathetic case of a relative's impotence by saying, "He has lost his cutlass" (*Oti so àda rẹ nu*). The imagery of the cutlass fulfils its semantic meaning. At marriage, when the new wife is deflowered, the penis fulfills its role of symbolic association. It is the instrument with which a man deals a blow that causes the blood to flow. In subsequent future acts it will "cut sharply" (*ge*). The phallus of an impotent man cannot do either of these. It has lost its capacity to cut, or to ejaculate the miniature child into a woman's womb.

The Power of the Kétu Female

Despite the preference for boys, the Kétu love their female children. The female child (Ọdọmọbìnrin) as she develops into a young woman (*Omoge*) is a treasure in two ways. She will be an ambassadress of the lineage, making a peaceful extralineage relations possible. She will, through her fertility, exemplify the power of the lineage to aid in the survival of other lineages. The transfer of women provides a second means of reducing the fissile tendencies between the exclusive Kétu lineages. Thus, alliance through marriage supports the office of the oba (king) by encouraging extralineage cooperation in such necessary services as labor for farming, for roof-thatching, and for the provision of goods for ritual feasting.

On the other hand, the Kétu female's failure to have children is a threat to such cooperation. Since the Kétu only recognize one type of impotence in their males, once there is evidence that the male can achieve an erection, it is automatically assumed that the failure of a couple to beget children is due to a sickness in the wife which kills the miniature child deposited in her womb. The lineage of such a woman is faced with the danger of being avoided when young men from other lineages are looking for prospective wives. Thus, again, the fertility of it members, male and female, is the concern of the lineage members.

Kétu females have power and are sometimes ready to use it as a leverage in situations where they find themselves at a disadvantage. Personal control of their virginity as well as good behavior are the two most effective means of expressing this power. It is taken for granted that a girl will remain a virgin until marriage.[9] She is also expected to be of good behavior as this is an index of the lineage's ability to impose discipline on its members. These two expectation go hand in hand. It is not sufficient for a girl to have one without the other. Hence, it is common for mothers of erring young girls to warn them with the Yoruba maxim "Be careful, good manners are better than beauty" (*Şo ara rẹ, ìwà lópé jẹwalọ*). Fajana (1962) testifies to the fact that the Yoruba regard good character as paramount both to success in life and to marital stability. He noted that when one takes

> marriage as an example, there is no doubt that an educated or well trained person has a great advantage over those who are uneducated. For a girl preparing to choose a husband, the possession of beauty is desirable but not essential. In fact, lack of beauty scarcely ever prevents a girl from getting a husband. But lack of good education marks out a girl for criticism and disfavour, within and without the family. (1966,17)

Good character (*ìwà*) is part of the heritage of discipline that a female takes from her lineage. It is not to be infused by the relatives of a woman's husband.

On a point of comparative interest, the difference of opinion on this matter, between the Kétu and another group of Nigerians that Isichei studied is worthy of note. Writing about the Asaba Igbo, Isichei noted:

> The only reliable index of a girl's proper upbringing was her premarital virginity. The care which a mother took to preserve her daughter's virginity was assumed evidence that she could not have neglected in her the other perfections of womanhood in tradition Asaba. *And if in fact a*

particular pre-marital virgin proved not to have learned much else, all was not lost. Such a woman might yet be brought up to a reasonable standard under apprenticeship to her husband's mother (1973,685-6). (Italics for emphasis)

Unlike the Asaba Igbo, the Kétu mother-in-law cannot and is not expected to inculcate good manners into her daughter-in-law for two reasons. The Kétu wife maintains a relationship of respect and avoidance with her husband's kin group. A corollary of this attitude is the tendency to reduce the occasions of meeting between herself and her mother-in-law and father-in-law to the minimum. Hence, there are not many opportunities for such lessons in etiquette. Besides, any attempt by the husband's mother to tutor her son's wife in the art of good manners will be interpreted as an insult to, her daughter-in-law's lineage, whose members have failed in their duty to give sound home training to their young ones.

Moreover, the Kétu, who do not give their daughters in marriage until the age of twenty or more, believe that the character of their daughters is already formed. They will insist that just as "no one uses new tunes to call old dogs" (*Aki fi ïfé titun pe ajá arúgbó*), it is undesirable to teach adults new ways.

If the Kétu girl behaves in a decidedly antisocial manner; if she insults and is quarrelsome with her affinal relatives; if she is uncooperative with her co-wives, she will injure the reputation of her lineage and discourage members of other lineages from agreeing to marry into her own lineage.

If a Kétu girl loses her virginity before marriage, she forfeits her chances of becoming a "proper" woman. She will also injure the reputation of her lineage, whose female members will be regarded as being of loose morals. With the dependence of the lineage on the female resources for alliances, Kétu women definitely have power. They are not just objects or "items of exchange inextricably given tongue" (Levi-Strauss 1949). Such influential roles of the Kétu girls as emerge from this consideration confirm K. Hastrup's observation that the

marginal position of women in most marriage exchanges is rather more powerful than the ideological models would lead us to believe in the first place. Women are not only men's game, they have to play men's game too. They are both persons and currency, as Mary Douglass (1966,152) or, in the words of Levi-Strauss, women have remained both "signs and values." (1978,57)

The Accepted Sexual Roles

The aim of Kétu kinship behavior is to achieve harmonious relations in order to enhance the continuity of the patrilineage. Thus, the socialization of the Kétu child is concerned with certain ways of behavior and thinking to promote such harmony. For example, child rearing aims to reduce differences between the full sibling and the half sibling (*Ọmọ-ìyá/Ọbakan*). After the age of five, children of different mothers are grouped according to their sex. They eat, play, and sleep in a common area of the house together.

There are three phases in the sex role training. These phases correspond to the development periods of five to ten years, ten to fifteen years, and fifteen to twenty years.

Between ages five and ten, boys and girls are trained to be useful in the house. Their chores include fetching water for domestic needs, fetching firewood, sweeping the house, and running errands. They are vested with these first responsibilities through the ceremonial "first trip to the river" (*Odò akọ́kọ́ lọ*), which the young Kétu boy or girl looks forward to eagerly. On the morning of this first trip, the father calls the child and presents him or her with a gourd, saying, "This is a gourd. We use it to fetch water. We do not break it" (*Akérégbe niyi, omi la fii pọn, akii fọ*). Added with this air of solemnity, the trip to the river becomes a test of endurance and carefulness. The child that returns to the house without breaking his gourd is met with jubilation by the womenfolk. After this official beginning, trips to the river to fetch water become an obligation.

Between ages ten and fifteen various duties are allocated in line with the division of labor according to sex. Boys are released from such domestic duties as fetching water and sweeping the house. Girls become more involved with these duties, although they are no longer expected to fetch firewood except in a case of special need. During the preparation of the evening meal, girls are expected to pay attention to and help with the cooking by grinding pepper or any other ingredients needed. Boys who fall asleep before the meal is ready are awakened and fed. Girls who do are not awakened, a punishment for going to sleep when they should have been helping. In addition, to these expectations, girls are made to look after their younger brothers and sisters when the mother is away.

The Kétu girl, at this stage, is under constant pressure to behave like a woman. She must sit like a woman and not carelessly, so that the wrapper around her waist does not reveal that which it should conceal. She is awaiting the onset of menstruation, which usually occurs between fourteen and fifteen years of age. Even when she is energetic she may not engage in such masculine acts as splitting firewood or wrestling. If she does, she will be reprimanded and told to "stop behaving in an unrefined manner like men" (*ye ṣe yarapa-yarapa pa ọkùnrin*). The word *yarapa-yarapa* is an onomatopoeic word depicting manliness in its unrefined, inarticulate form.

On the other hand, boys at this stage are encouraged to assert their evolving manliness by performing their culturally defined manly roles. They replace the domestic roles they had previously performed with roles that cast them in the image of the provider or the bread-winner. They go off into the forest and to the streams for hunting and fishing adventures with elderly men and in bands of their own age group.

In addition to these new activities, boys are given a taste of adult responsibilities. They join their male relatives for farm work; they serve as pages to their fathers at those important meetings that discharge political, economic, and social duties. At the close of such meetings, often on the way home, the father asks his son leading questions to ascertain how much the boy has understood and remembers. If he is found capable, he becomes a regular page. He is also encouraged to discuss matters of interest arising from such meetings. In this way, at an early age he is being prepared for the role of arbiter, since the Kétu say, "The child that will be smart in life shows its smartness very early in life" (*Ọmọ ti oma jẹ Ashamu, lati kékeré ni ati majẹnu shamushamu*).[43] In this way, the Kétu boy, like the Ashanti boy, drifts toward his father and receives some training in adult roles.

> The father treats him sternly, he regards it as his duty to
> prepare the child to shoulder the responsibility of looking
> after his mother, sisters, and future wife and children.
> The father forbids him to engage in what he considers to
> be womanly activities. (Sarpong 1977,10)

The insistence that each sex should keep to its own type is an important aspect of the Kétu division of labor. Boys who acquit themselves in hunting are praised with such greetings as "Well done, you masculine chap" *(Kare ǫmǫ akǫ)*. When the girls cook delicious stews, they are similarly praised. However, if either boy or girl plays a role that does not belong to his or her sexual category, disapproval is vehement, even if what is done is considered a feat when accomplished by the proper sex. Thus, if a girls kills game such as the prized "grass-cutter" *(ǫyǫ)* or antelope *(èsúró)*, an act most laudable in a young boy, she is scolded. In fact, a hunting taboo forbids all hunters and men from eating the meat of game killed by a woman. This taboo expresses two ideas: first, it announces that the girl has defied cherished classification, a very dangerous act (Douglas 1966); second, it refutes the internalized principle of incompetence across sexual categories, which takes for granted that "neither is competent to execute tasks other than those appropriate for his or her sex" (Hirschon 1978, 73). The reactions of commendation and disapproval supported by taboo help to maintain the division of labor between the sexes.

Finally, between the attainment of physical puberty and marriage, Kétu boys and girls take on roles that prepare them for transition. This transitional process involves, for the boys, an initial proof of manliness, after which follows the final attainment of manhood borne out in the birth and naming of first child. At the naming, the young man acquires the right to be addressed by his child's name. This is the prerequisite for adulthood. On the other hand, for the girl, the process involves the strength to remain a virgin for about seven years after the onset of menarche. It also includes circumcision, marriage, and the birth of the first child. Each of these periods in the development cycle of the Kétu child has its own corresponding attitude to sex, which will be explored later in this study.

The Taboos Regarding Fertility

Between the ages of five and ten, children are not segregated in their activities except for sleeping and eating arrangements. The Kétu, who do not normally give their children any sex education, would not, even at this stage, consider that the children have started to think of themselves in terms of their sex. Parents give little importance to the difference that sex plays in their activities. Kétu ethics demand that matters related to sex are not openly discussed and that when they are, they ought not to be discussed in straightforward language before minors. Before minors, such discussions are carried on in a language only intelligible to adults.

If at this stage any Kétu child asks questions relating to sex, he/she is most likely to receive either of two reactions. An impatient parent (and Kétu culture demands that parents be impatient about such matters) tells the child, "Keep your mouth shut" (*Pa ẹnu rẹ mọ*). Other parents would link sex with the inauspicious: paint a gory picture of it in order to frighten the child and convince him that, like the dark with which it is associated, sex and matters relating to it should be avoided. The Kétu child dreads darkness. He is told that it is a time when dangerous snakes, evil spirits, and fearful things prowl about. This fear of the night and anything related to it is reinforced in the mind of the child by the (to him) ominous chirpings and squeakings of insects, certain birds, and animals. In fact, the frequency with which the Kétu child hears the maxim "A well-trained child does not walk about at night" (*Omo abi're ki rin loru*) impresses on his mind the inauspiciousness of night and of sex.

Between the ages of ten and fifteen, both boys and girls are urged to keep to their groups. Boys who, at this stage, constantly seek the company of girls are chided and ridiculed. The terms of the ridicule are related, not with the morality of his action, but with the change in roles that it implies. Thus, jests are made about his desire to become a female. He is derisively called "the child under the control of females" (*Ọmọ abẹ obìnrin*). This abuse connotes weakness, lack of taste and the tendency to fall short of expectations.

The girl who seeks the company of boys is severely reprimanded. She is warned to take care less she may take a short and despicable course to adulthood. The anxious mother of such a girl constantly prods her with sayings such as "Be careful, you do not want to get to the stream before you fetch water" (*Ṣọra ẹ, ikọ fẹ dodò iké pun omi*).

Given this segregated background in daily activities, Kétu boys and girls who, in recent times, have been absorbed into the various coeducational denominational Christian schools with strict segregative principles between the sexes are not undergoing a wholly new experience. If for the purpose of internalizing such principles, the Kétu children are taught the common song that announces the commencement of the time allotted for physical education:

> Boys are to stay apart and girls are to stay apart,
> and we do not want any mixing among them:
>
> Hope you hear me hear me all
> Hope you hear me hear me all

They are not being taught something completely new. The difference between the Kétu process of child training and Western principles of child education lies in the fact that what the former denies the child at one level of existential relationship is provided for at another level. Thus, the Kétu traditional education prohibits a discussion on sex education, but allows children to participate in the "moonlight game," where children can come by some ideas about sex. It is the social significance of the moonlight game that I shall explore below.

The Social Significance of the Moonlight Game

The moonlight game (*eré òsùpa*) is an essential cultural Yoruba pastime. Moonlight offers the only opportunity for the child to reclaim some part of the night from darkness. For children between the ages of ten and fifteen, the game provides tremendous entertainment. Besides its entertaining value, the moonlight game has great social significance. The tenets of the game contravene the rules that regulate the behavior of Kétu minors in the lineage. That is takes place at night points to its inversive role. The Kétu symbolic taxonomy arranges attitudes as well as things into two opposing categories; one auspicious, the other inauspicious. The auspicious category includes notions such concepts as light, work, happiness, progress, good, God, and the ancestors. The inauspicious category includes notions such as laziness, evil, witches, sex, and danger. The auspicious category is associated with the right, while the inauspicious is linked with the left. Thus, the behavior linked with the moonlight game is the reverse of that tolerated during the day. Membership for participation in the game overlooks the strict sexual boundaries maintained within the lineage and ignores the morally exclusive lineage boundaries. Hence, in the course of the game, boys and girls from different lineages mix freely.

This game involves mild competition between representatives of different compounds and households. One such is the "game of covering the face" (*eree bojuboju*)— hide and seek. It is a common occurrence, during this game, that boys from one household tend to pursue and drift along with girls of other households into remote corners of the playground. Immoral excesses are anticipated and checked by the frustrated cries of neglected participants who call individual names and ask such suspicion laden questions as "Imonu (a Yoruba rendition of "Emmanuel") what have you been doing all this time with Shola without coming out?" (*Imọnu, ke ikoiṣe bẹ ati Shọla latoni eyi ikofi jade*). Two of such calls always attracts the attention of an elder, who puts an end to the game for the night.

When the signal sounds for the commencement of the game, all participants should stop whatever they are doing, even if they are talking to their parents, and hasten to the location of the game. O. Daramola and Adebayo Jeje, confirming this aspect of the game, noted:

> When the other children in the locality hear this (signal)
> even if they are eating, they must go out,
> even if they are talking with their mother or father,
> quickly they must get out.

> *Nigbati awọn ọmọ ìyóku ni àdúgbò ba gbọ eleyi,*
> *bi wọn tilẹ njẹun lọwọ, wọn gbọde jade ni,*
> *bi wọn tilẹ mba baba wọn tabi Iyá wọn nsọrọ lọwọ,*
> *kia, wọn ti bẹ sita.* (1968,27)

In ordinary circumstances, for a Kétu child to leave his parents abruptly during a discussion to attend to his playmates amounts to gross rudeness, which is immediately corrected. That a child's de-

94

parture for this game does not meet with the same disapproval points to the accepted inversive role of the game among the Kétu.

It should also be noted that each sibling participant is obliged to inform on other siblings in cases where there are suspicious activities. In such cases, certain individuals are forbidden to take part in the moonlight game. Most of those forbidden to take part are often so close to puberty that it would be in their best interest to stay away.

The final stage, the period between puberty and marriage, is marked by more rigid sexual separation. At this point, the roles are definite, and they prepare the girls for their adult status at marriage and the birth of the first child. It is at marriage that the society acknowledges the right of young people to engage in sexual union. Marriage, therefore, legitimizes sexual intercourse and forms the variable that removes sex from the domain of the "forbidden," from the dark and dangerous to the legitimate, the pure and the useful.

The Essential Moral Contradiction

Between the onset of menarche and the attainment of social puberty the Kétu girl is strongly urged to keep to her type, i.e, her sex. This recommendation is in line with the desire to become a well-trained, mature woman. For the attainment of maturity, the conditions are that she be a virgin until marriage, and that she gives birth.

The preservation of virginity has its individual and collective aspects. The virgin is the epitome of the cultured, the educated. She is a symbol of pure and inaccessible womanhood, the figure of female victory over male machinations. Her natural quality as a virgin becomes translated into a social symbol signifying the victory of one lineage over another. Thus, the acquittal of a Kétu girl as a virgin at marriage is a threefold victory.

Between the attainment of puberty and the time of marriage, the Kétu goal for both boys and girls is the same. It consists in aiding them to take the first step towards wholeness and completeness, towards maturity. Marriage and the birth of the first child put a seal on the achievement of maturity. However, the means to achieve this end is not the same for both sexes. For the girl, the condition is to remain a virgin until marriage. If the Kétu moral code stipulated strict adherence to continence for boys and girls at this stage of development, the task of the girls would be easy, though not as highly regarded. Rather, Kétu social expectations demand that the boys prove their readiness to assume adult role status by having sexual relations with some category of female. They excluded females related through affinal and cognatic ties as well as wives of nonrelatives who are residentially close. This range of exclusions reduces the number of women available for such flirtations and heightens the degree of attention given to those within the touchable category.

This then is the crux of the matter. One young man's food becomes a young girl's social poison. The Kétu, in particular those of them who answer to the nickname "flirting does not make me ashamed" (*Àgbèrè kòti*) expect their young men to flirt to prove their masculine mettle. The girl, on the other hand, is under strong moral obligation to remain intact,[11] elusive, and inaccessible. She should be "the maiden with the cool, pure blood." (*òló ẹlẹ̀jẹ̀ tutù*) This essential contradiction in expectations between Kétu boys and girls provides the dynamics for the continuity of this value within the society.

This contradiction is kept alive by the conspiracy that works against the female. There is a silent agreement that the brother should necessarily protect his sister against the "ravening wolves" (young men from other lineages). In return for this service, the sister undertakes to bring in her friends from other lineages (she is subject to similar treatment!) with whom her brother can "try his luck." The operative principle behind this action is encapsulated in the proverb; "the dog knows how to take care of and suckle its puppies and how to kill the young ones of the gazelle" (*Ajá mọ ọmọ tirẹ fun lọmú, o mọ ti èkùlù ki mólẹ̀*).[12]

Thus, it is sexual intercourse that sets a boy on the road to attaining wholesomeness. It is also sexual intercourse that, at this stage, spoils the purity, the excellence, of the girl and prevents her from becoming a fully respected and complete adult woman. Yet, it is the same sexual intercourse that turns the virgin, pure but not entirely whole, admirable but dangerous, into the complete woman and fertile mother. Hence, no general statement about sex with reference to Kétu boys and girls can be made. The auspiciousness or inauspiciousness of sex changes according to contexts and persons.

There is a practical side to the insistence that the Kétu girl should remain a virgin until marriage, before which they must have taken part in the circumcision rite. For the Kétu girl, premarital sex would defy the Kétu purpose for sexual intercourse, which is solely to beget children. Since premarital sexual experiences are clandestine, they most probably preclude the desire for children. Even when this desire is present, the fact that such experience precedes circumcision offends against Kétu dictates on another level. Such premarital sex serves, the Kétu allege, to create a strong man/woman bond between the two perpetrators, a bond strengthened by sexual enjoyment, still unmitigated by the practice of circumcision. Such a bond, it is feared, may create a formidable barrier to the total control the lineage exercises over its members.[13] The Kétu also believe that pre-marital sex weakens the resistence of the girl and leaves her open to the allegation of infidelity.

A corollary of the essential moral contradiction is the consequence awaiting Kétu boys and girls who do not meet up with the social expectation. If a girl is a virgin at marriage, this quality is publicly attested through symbolic gifts carried before the husband's party as it pays a visit to show the husband's gratitude on the morning after the ritual defloration. If the girl is not a virgin, there is no visit of gratitude because there is nothing to be grateful for. Instead, another symbolic gift expressing incompleteness is sent in the most conspicuous fashion to the parents of the bride. The word soon gets around and people from other lineages tend to associate immorality with the lineage of the wife. If the boys fail to prove their mettle, their lineage could be styled the "segment of eunuchs" (*Idílé òkóbó*). This stigma may cause young men from such lineages some difficulty when they are ready for marriage partners.

With certain reservations, this spectacle of discrimination against young people who fail to meet the cultural expectations may have been responsible for the converted Kétu adherence to the Christian obligation to marry within the Christian community. The bulk of the non-Christian Kétu had no option but to boycott Kétu Christians since the Christian boys would not conform to the traditional expectations of adventurousness, and since their girls would not submit, in certain cases, to circumcision. Having forfeited the right to marry within the larger community, Kétu Christians had no choice but to marry within their new community. As a result, in-group

Christian marriages soared, to the pleasure of the missionaries who interpreted this as expressive of the quality of faith of the Kétu Christians.

Even at this stage, the traditional place of the evening market (ọjà-Alẹ́) provides the opportunity for young men or girls who are not engaged to meet and find partners for themselves. Those who are engaged may use the meetings at the marketplace to reach a deeper understanding. The girls—who have no commercial interests—are, if not engaged, sent to the evening market, ostensibly to sell, but more realistically to create the opportunity for interested young men to make their intention known.

The Absence of an Elaborate Male Initiation

There is no male initiation ceremony for the Kétu boy. He, as has been hinted at above, drifts towards his father and tends to perform minor versions of what his father does. It was confirmed in a recorded message (personal communication) that formerly a father bought a small cutlass proportionate to the size of his son and also makes him "farming clothes" (ẹwu oko). He presents both items to his son on an appointed day in the presence of some elders who offer prayers to the ancestors, seeking their blessing for the child.

The simple Kétu ceremony has its equivalent among the Tiv of northern Nigeria and the Ashanti of Ghana. Among the Tiv, after circumcision, the boy is given a chicken, (Bohannan 1954, 6); which provides the base "on which, by stock-breeding and careful trading, a man is said to build up his fortune" converting his prized chickens up the ladder of the spheres of exchange from chick to pig, from pig to calf, and from calves to wife. Among the Ashanti, a boy is presented with a cutlass (Sarpong 1977). The Kétu boy, like his Ashanti counterpart, is expected to live by the sweat of his brow, like the Tiv boy, who must ingeniously, through labor and diligence, turn his chicken into the medium with which he acquires a wife. Besides this handing-over ceremony, the Kétu boy assumes an adult role only after he has proved himself a man by becoming a father. The teknonymic name he acquires expresses the society's confirmation of his new status.

In explaining the simplicity of the quasi-initiation among the Ashanti, Sarpong has suggested that it is "perhaps partly a reflection of the nonjural aspect of the patrilineal ties" (1977, 11) If Sarpong's suggestion is valid, the female initiation among the patrilineal Kétu should be simpler than that of the male, because of the non-jural aspect of matrilineal ties. Since this is not the case among the Kétu, I would hazard the suggestion that rather than relate the complexity of the rite with the rule of descent, one should look closely at those points of the cultural collective that tend to emphasize rituals of initiation for one sex and not the other.

The Characteristics of Kétu Fertility Rites

The importance of the Kétu female in her society demands that she be well prepared for her adult role; and that when it is time for transition into her new position, it be marked by a series of rites. Yet, it should be noted that Kétu fertility rites are neither as internally well-organized nor as continuous as those of the Bemba (Richards 1966), nor are they as individual in nature as those of the Australian aborigines (Eliade 1958:41) and the Ndembu (Turner 1966). The peculiar feature of the Kétu fertility rites as rites of passage is that microrites succeed each other as components within a spectrum which complete the macrorite of passage that ascribes the status of maturity to the Kétu initiate. Thus, Kétu fertility rites are similar to those of the Bugisu that J. S. la Fontaine studied as a series in a continuum of menstruation rites, marriage rites, and the rites that occur at the birth of the first child (1972).

Conclusion

This chapter has drawn attention to the Kétu understanding of fertility and considered the relationship of dependence alleged to exist between the three types of fertility: (i) the fertility of the land, (ii). the fertility of plants and lower animals, and (iii) human fertility. Land, plant, and animal fertility supports human fertility—the most vital to the three for society's temporal and spiritual survival. It has also been stressed that the exogamous patrilineal Kétu depend upon the fertility of women, who are not relatives, for survival.

The importance of the Kétu woman notwithstanding, the Kétu collective representations about such issues as the notion of conception, their attitude towards the sex of the child, the taboos and fears about sex and fertility and the accepted female roles tend to underplay the importance of the Kétu female. Thus, the Kétu boy is given the freedom to engage in activities that provide food for the household while his sister is cast in the role of one who just prepares that which has been hard-won by the male. The boy is made to witness and to participate in decision-making events at an early age, while his sister is shut off from such participation. His little efforts, over and above what is expected of him, are praiseworthy, while those of his sister, in the domestic sphere, are often taken for granted.[14] On the one hand, there is a recognition of the importance of women. On the other, there is a conscious attempt to underplay this importance in preference for a desire to dominate women. Yet, the Kétu fertility rites leave one without a shade of doubt that women, seen in the context of their roles, are certainly vital to Kétu society. The rites provide an alternative model of perceiving the importance of woman to the society. It is to the ethnography of the rites that I shall now turn.

NOTES

1. If the word "ancestors" is substituted for the word "spirits," Mayer's idea will fit the Ke;tu perfectly.

2. See Peggy Harper (1970, 48-53). She noted that the *gagalo*, "the dance of the stilt dancers" is a harvest festival at which yam must be offered and the stilt-dance be performed before the farmers may harvest their yam crop.

3. The kola tree is famed for its fruitfulness among the Yoruba whose symbolism is replete with prayers that endeavor to transfer the efficacy of fruitfulness to the humans.

4. Gabriel Ojo (1966,174) stated that the Yoruba linked the "waxing of the moon with fecundity because of its being followed, as they believed, by innumerable sons and daughters, namely, the stars!"

5. The third Yoruba soul is "shadow"(*ojiji*). It becomes activated at the moment of death when it makes its appearances to relatives living far away from home, announcing to them the death of the owner.(See Bascom 1956, 1969)

6. The clear way that Isichei tried to make this point seemed to have been compromised when he employed the imagery of the woman as the baker whose role considered of "properly kneading the thick paste of water and flour into a dough." When one recalls a meta phor he used earlier—of the woman as the fallow ground on which the semen germinates—the picture becomes much less clear. Fallow land is worn-out piece of over-worked farmland that requires considerable effort to yield at all. Besides, the kneading of the thick paste into a dough hardly makes the contribution of the woman a small thing. Kneading requires a considerable amount of effort; the kneading of "thick paste" into a dough would seem to require even more effort.

7. The word *lantilanti* is a descriptive onomatopoeic word depicting the sound of a healthy child who is playfully thrown up in the air three times by its mother after it has been bathed.

8. The center-pole is, thus, a symbolic motivation that makes both translations possible(Sperber 1975, 23-24)

9. The relative remoteness of the Kétu area has aided in preserving the strong insistence that is still put on the need for a girl to remain a virgin until marriage. Such insistence is not made nowadays in some areas of Yorubaland.

10. The proverb makes use of a play on like-sounding words; to achieve its meaning *Ashamu* (meaning "name") and *shamushamu* (an ono matopoeia). Ashamu, a boy's name, also stands for smartness and good disposition.

11. J. Turner (1932, 7) noted that virginity was not "regarded as essential except among the Yoruba." N. A. Fadipe (1970, 83) wrote: " In every division of Yorubaland great importance is attached to a bride being found *virgo intacta*, and this was the rule for both high and low alike.

12. The dog (*aja*) is used for hunting game in Yoruba land.

13. This is one of the reasons why the Kétu resisted monogamy. It committed the husband and wife to each other, for better or worse, thus creating a special bond, where none was expected to rival that of the man to his lineage. On the other hand, polygamy aided a man's attachment to his lineage as it creates the difficulty of loving more than one woman with equal intensity.

14. This attitude springs from the Kétu concept of work and nonwork. While farming, hunting, and, in times of friction, warfare, are cons-

idered work, domestic activities are categorized as nonwork. In a paper given to the Research Seminar Class convened by E. Edwin Ardener during Trinity Term 1979, Dr. Parkin of School of African and Oriental Studies(S.O.A.S.) made an interesting exposition of the Kenya coastal Bantu attitude toward duties in terms of the people's concept of work and nonwork.

CHAPTER FIVE

THE SERIES OF FERTILITY RITES

Introduction

In the foregoing chapters, attention has been drawn to certain features of Kétu society in so far as they touch on girls' fertility rites. Emphasis has been placed on the fact that Kétu rites, unlike those of the Ashanti and the Bemba, but similar to those of the Bugisu (La Fontaine 1972), do not form a single, finished sequence of events in such a way that the girl is divested of her childhood roles at the beginning of the rites and, after a liminal period, is invested with adult status. Rather, the Kétu fertility rites form a sequence in a much broader series of rites that begin with betrothal, proceed to circumcision and marriage, and later to the birth and naming of the first child.

Each part in this series of rites displays all the features of rites of passage put forward by van Gennep. Each includes a ritual of separation from an earlier mode of existence, an unclassified period of liminality, and a postliminal period of inclusion. Within the Kétu series of rites, none of these parts alone is sufficient to mark the allocation of the adult role status to the Kétu girl. Instead, the allocation comes from gradual progression through each phase of the ritual ending with the acquisition of a teknonymic appellation at the naming of the first child, which confirms that the young wife and her husband (if it is his first marriage) have become adults. The proverb goes: "They have learned how to wash their hands and they are now admitted to eat in the rank of elders". (*Wọn ti mọ ọwọ wẹ, wọn ti ṣetan lati ba Àgbà jẹun*)

The Betrothal Procedure

Except in certain unusual circumstances, such as a disabling deformity, or a very bad general reputation, a young Kétu man is virtually certain to get a wife. In this male oriented society in which marriage is a sacred duty to one's ancestors as well as to the living, the members of the extended family participate actively in making sure that male members find spouses. Men in different lineages recognize that the rule of exogamy obliges them to cooperate with one another in the Kétu society. Since male elders control rights in the female members of their lineages, cooperation between Kétu men makes the process of finding mates easy. This is to be expected in such a society like that of the Kétu, where

> jural control over an unmarried person is vested primarily in the father. In this situation, marital rights can be established only with the consent of the fathers of a prospective husband and wife; and this is signified by the bridegroom's father when he undertakes to hand over the *Prime Prestation* of the bride price and the bride's father when he agrees to accept it. (Fortes 1962,11)

The Kétu girl, on the other hand, has to struggle to fulfil many stringent social expectations. This phenomenon differentiates Kétu betrothal from that of recorded peoples such as the Arapesh, among whom every female is virtually sure of being married while it is the boy who has to struggle to fulfil the demanding social expectations. With reference to the Arapesh, Mead states:

> The fear of a child's not marrying, the desperate concentration upon marriage as a goal, is transferred in Arapesh society from the parents of the girl to the parents of the

boy. He it is who may get left out altogether, who must be carefully provided for. And one of the chief causes of a son's gratitude is that his father found him a wife while he himself was still a youth and unable to provide for himself. (1935, 87).

A Kétu male may not marry agnatic female relatives (except in the case of widow inheritance). This restriction includes those who, due to residential propinquity, have been absorbed into the kin group. Beyond this circle, the Kétu male can, theoretically, take a wife from any quarter of the town other than his own. In practice, the Kétu man discriminates against females from families of ill repute. He tends to take a wife from communities not too far removed from his own lineage location (*Idílé*), and yet not too near, in order to avoid the complications and demands that may arise from propinquity to affines. The Yoruba proverb that provides a guideline states "Live far off from each other and be popular with each other; live together and know each other's faults" (*Gbe òkèrè ki oníyĭ, ęgbépǫ kię mǫ ęsín ara yin*).

It has been mentioned earlier that the boy and girl meet each other at the evening market, where flirtations may eventually lead to marriage. The age when young boys and girls becomes meticulous about their appearance and frequently pay visits to the evening market is known in Kétu as "the time of being on the look-out" (*ĭgbà ĭfojúsódè*). When a young man meets with a girl who seem agreeable to the idea of marriage, he is obliged to inform his father, who in turn informs the lineage head. His father and the other elders appoint an intermediary or "go-between" who runs errands between the two households involved.

The "Go-Between"

The function of the "go-between"(*Alárenà*) is vital to any marriage in Yorubaland. The choice of the *Alárenà* often devolves on an affinal member of the lineage who has distinguished herself as a good wife and mother. She must be a cheerful person equipped with a tremendous ability to make strangers and visitors comfortable and, and at the same time, possessed unflinching loyalty to the lineage. As an affinal member, the *Alárenà* as an "outsider" to the husband's lineage possesses immunity to carry out some sensitive but crucial enquiries into the credibility and standing of the family of the intended spouse. But the *Alárenà* also serves to integrate the new spouse into the husband's extended family. There develops, through her contact with the spouse, a bond of attachment and companionship vital to alleviating the traumatic experience the girl will undergo through her transfer to the virilocal marriage residence. The position of the *Alárenà*, therefore, serves as a mechanism for effecting the smooth integration of the wife into the polygynous system.[1]

Through the institution of the *Alárenà*, therefore, Kétu culture assures that the new wife, having found an ally and confidante in her senior wife, is not left alone and companionless. The Spindlers brought out this point clearly when they wrote that:

> One of the mechanisms for integrating a new wife into a compound lay in appointing one of the established wives in the compound as an intermediary and "senior wife" of the fiance, thus ensuring her cooperation. She carried instalments of bride wealth to the fiance's house, carried messages back and forth, and often gave presents of her own to the fiancee. Until she had a child, the bride lived with the "senior wife" who often furnished consolation and support of her. (Bascom 1969,viii).

Kétu etiquette lays down preferences that are to be followed in choosing a person to fill this role. The wife, as an outsider to her husband's lineage , is wrapped, to some extent, in the aura of neutrality and detachment. She enjoys considerable cultural immunity in the conduct of her affairs. It would, in the Kétu code of conduct, amount to crass insubordination for an agnatic kinsman of the suitor to conduct an investigation into the history of the lineage of the girl for him to ask questions aimed at unearthing the inauspicious aspects of the bridal lineage. This could incense the relatives of the girl and lead them to terminate the courtship. However, the *Alárenà*,[2] though loyal to her marriage lineage, is nonetheless "foreign" to both the groups in question and is therefore more acceptable to make the preliminary enquiries.

Daramola and Jeje cite the importance of these enquiries:

> When we find out through enquiries that debt is an en-
> demic vice of her lineage members, or that leprosy is rife
> among members of her lineage, or that insanity is com-
> mon in the lineage, or even that the girl is a notorious
> fighter and hater of harmony, it is right that the young
> man forgets the affair and look elsewhere. (1968,26) (
> Author's translation)

Ifá Fǫ´re

If the results of the Alarena's inquiry are positive, the family may
proceed with marriage arrangements. *Ifá fǫ´re*, from the Yoruba
statement *Ifá fǫ ire* means the "oracle divinity approves". The elders of the lineage delegate individuals to consult an oracle concerning the couple's future. This delegation visits the priest of the
Ifá oracle (*Babaláwo*) and presents ritual items for consultation,
which include pairs of goats, domestic fowls, pigeons, tortoises,
and snails. When the oracle has confirmed the auspiciousness of
the intended union, the ritual items are divided in two; one goes to
support the priest and the other "has for its purpose the putting of
the father of the girl and members of her kindred in good humor at
the beginning of a legal relationship between two groups of
people"(Fadipe 1949, 314).

The *Ifá fǫ´re* ritual serves, among other things, to draw the
attention of a wider group to the beginning of a solemn commitment
between the suitor and the girl. It also serves as an occasion for
redistributing wealth in the society. More importantly, since the
items—though symbolic—are regarded as the first instalment of bride-
wealth, they confirm the social character of bride-wealth as one of
the "techniques which employ wealth, by a gift or payment, as a
means of establishing, defining, expressing and evoking social cohesion" (Evan-Pritchard 1965, 182). From this moment onwards,
the manner of approach and behavior towards the relatives of each
party is to be marked by respect and, in the case of the girl, also by
avoidance. Perhaps nothing illustrates better the mode of behavior
of the suitor and the girl towards each other's relatives than the Yor-

uba name applied to one's affines "the people before whom I must feel shy" (*awǫn oníìjú mi*).

Isíhùn

Once engaged, the next step in the marital process is Isihun which literally translates releasing the voice". Although the Kétu boy and girl are allowed to meet frequently after *Ifá fǫ´re* ritual, a peculiarity of such meetings is that the young man is expected to do all the talking while the young girl looks away from suitor.

> It is the custom of the Yoruba that when a man is talking to his fiancee, she should not look him in the face, instead of this, she looks down. And she uses her fingers to search for what she has not lost. This is what the people hint at when they say the fiancee is searching the wall. And it is an indication that she wants to be released to talk, by receiving money from the suitor. (Daramola and Jeje 1968, 27—Author's translation).

This explanation does not exhaust all of the meanings of the practice. It may be seen as another example of the Kétu suitor/spouse ethic. It prepares the mind of the fiancee to accept, in the context of the new relationship, the authority of her husband (who sets in operation her speaking faculty) through the payment of the "money for releasing the voice" (*owó ìsíhùn)*, just as the payment of "virginity price" announces to the society that it was the husband who set in motion her female procreative activities. With this official lifting of the voice, the stage is set for the next step the "pleading for the girl's hand in marriage."

Itǫrǫ

After the lifting of the spouse's voice, and her verbal confirmation of her willingness to marry, the betrothal process commences with Itoro ceremony when members of the lineage of the husband-to-be plead with the elders of the wife-to-be for her hand in marriage for their son. In a pattern set by custom, the suitor makes a solemn declaration of their pledge to get married. He employs symbolic language that says exactly—but in a subtle fashion—what he has in mind. He goes to his father early in the morning, at the second cock-crow, which is between half-past four and five o'clock in the morning, a time of day when the Kétu believe the mind is at its coolest and most ready to absorb. He tells his father "I have seen a very beautiful flower that I would like to pluck" (*Moti rí òdòdò kan ti ólέwà ti osi wunmi ti mofę ja*). The father then proceeds to ask him whether it is a type of flower that they are allowed to pluck. If the answer is in the affirmative, the father then asks for a progress report, at the completion of which, he announces that he look into matter.

On an appointed day after this meeting, the suitor's father in the company of two other elders of the lineage, pay the girl's father an unannounced early morning visit and make known, again in symbolic language, their intention. The girl's father, acting with great caution, thanks them and informs them that the decision about the marriage of his daughter is not his alone, as he has elders whose main business it is to look into such matters. He gives them another appointment. It must be mentioned that it is vital to the whole betrothal process for things to take this shape. The first visit must be unannounced; the girl's father should be "taken aback" at the announcement of the party's intention even when the ritualization of the ifá fǫ´re has already made the intentions clear. Finally, he must, in his reply, go through the motions of showing his loyalty to the lineage, of subordinating his individual view to that of the lineage, by saying that he has nothing against such a union but that the girl is not his, but she belongs to the lineage.

At the next meeting, the major participants are the elders of both lineages as well as the suitor and the would-be spouse. After an exchange of pleasantries, the matter is discussed. An elderly member of the girl's lineage is detailed to ascertain from both the suitor and the girl the veracity of the assertion that they both intend to be committed to each other. When this has been confirmed, the participants set a date for the engagement, called idana ("creating affines").

Idána

Idána is the ritual feast celebrating the transfer of Kétu "prime prestations"—the jural instruments that invest the marital rights of the wife in the lineage of the husband. The Idana ceremony centers around the payment of bride-wealth called 'the money for head' (*owó orí*). Fortes has identified two types of bride-wealth, (a) the prime prestations and (b) the contingent prestation (Fortes 1962, 9-11). The items involved in the Kétu owo-ori belong to Fortes' category of prime prestations, and they feature positionally in other rituals of the Kétu life cycle where they retain the same symbolic function.[3] The items in this category are not negotiable. They have been fixed by tradition, and though they are not necessarily restricted to the context of marriage, they have, in whatever ritual they occur, the same symbolic allusions to the Kétu aim of marriage. As a collection, they form the jural instrument for the transfer of marital rights. They "constitute the *sine qua non* for lawful marriage" (Fortes 1962, 10). They form that part of the bride-wealth that deals with the core of the marital institution—the transfer of the genetricial and sexual rights of the would be spouse to the suitor. They also affirm the solidification of a certain type of relationship of the spouses with their affinal relatives. Their economic worthlessness confirms the misleading nature of its designation, '"money for the head," and corroborates Evans-Pritchard's claim that bride-wealth is "a technique for creating new social relations of durability and frequency between persons. It is the mechanism by which the marriage group comes into being." (1968, 181)

The items in the Kétu prime prestations consist of honey (*oyin*), salt (*iyọ̀*), palm oil (*epo*), kola-nut (*obi;—cola acuminata*) and bitter cola (*orógbo;*). Each of these items serves as a motif for prayers of success for the imminent marital union, in a manner similar to their use in composing prayers at the naming ceremony of the child. Also included in this category are logs of wood, yam tubers, and some quantity of cowries.[4]

These items constitute the core of the Kétu bride-wealth and are equivalent, in the role which they play, to the *Kifu* "womb" cattle of the Taita of Kenya (Harris 1962, 61) and to the *Riso* heads of cattle of the Luo of Kenya (Evans-Pritchard 1965). Through their transfer, a re-ordering in the relationship of the parties to the agreement is effected. They constitute the prestation — the gift that is given that obliges the recipient to give another gift in return.

The contingent prestations are in cash and kind, and they are consequent upon the prime prestations. The first items in the contingent prestations include: (a) the "money compensation for the wives of the lineage"—*Owó aiya ilé*[5] This used to be an unspecified amount of cowries. It was subsequently converted to one guinea, that is, the sum of one pound and one shilling, then to two naira and ten kobo (N2. 10k. local currency in 1979). This amount is taken, I am informed, to compensate, in a small way, for the removal of a member of the female population of the lineage. The second item(b) has also been commuted into monetary payment. It is known as "money for the elders of the house"—*owó àgbà ilé*. In 1979, when the Nigerian local currency was highly valued due to high yields in petroleum it was then ten naira and one kobo (N10.50k, then equivalent to $30.30 cents, which in 1997 exchange rate is one thousand naira, N1030). This money was paid in order to invite the elders of the wife-giving family to relinquish their control over the domestic service of the girl.

The second set of items in this category includes a collection of suitor's obligatory services which, being periodically performed, give continual confirmation of the existence of the special affinal relations between the members of the marriage-group. These obligations include contributions to the affinal coffers to pay for feasting at important ritual ceremonies and to offset debt. They also include raising an adequate labor-force to perform duties ranging from hoeing the farm-plot to thatching the leaking roofs, or to building new walls in the affinal homestead. Substantial contributions to help some member of the affinal lineage to emerge victorious in the competition for a vacant chieftaincy title are also included. These contingent prestations ensure that the ancillary marital values, comprising of the wife's domestic services, will flow in the opposite direction. By its very nature, this second set of contingent prestations admit bargaining, a practice that is taboo to prime prestations. Besides, the contingent prestations in themselves cannot effect a transfer of marital rights, but only help to preserve the goodwill of the spouse's agnates, who have the power to make such a transfer.

It has been suggested, among other things, that bride-wealth helps to preserve marriage and serves as a bond which deters the husband from maltreating his wife (Bascom 1953; 1969, 60) since any evidence of such illtreatment leads to the forfeiture of any refund of bride-wealth. It has also been claimed that it serves as recompense to the parents for the loss of their daughter's services. Besides, it has also been asserted that bride-wealth is a mechanism for reserving wives for older men (Douglas 1967).

The apparent commonness of Yoruba bride-wealth prime prestation items, and the low economic value of the contingent prestations, preclude their becoming an economic lever whereby the bride-wealth's possible refund might motivate those relatives in pressuring her against divorce. Among the Kétu, the economic value of those prime prestations that must be refunded when marriage breaks down is so low that the relatives, having easy access to them, should have, by the same criterion, the contrary effect of encouraging divorce. In this case, parents would be more likely to call off difficult marriages as a first choice and not as the last resort. Again, the meagre economic value of the prestations should not accord them the status of a bond. The husband, in this case, would not be inhibited by the fear of having to suffer any loss in the event of a divorce.

The worth of any Kétu girl cannot be measured in terms of the amount of bride-wealth. It is the symbolic utility of the prime prestations, as motives for forming homoeopathic prayers, that singles them out as features in most rituals of the Kétu life crisis. Because they are common and of little economic value, the elders cannot control their distribution in such a way as to reserve women for themselves. Among the Lele of Kasai, the rafia cloth has become, because of its scarcity and value, the means by which the elders can "distribute" women unevenly through society. Among, the Kétu, on the other hand, the prime prestations are neither of high economic worth nor are they in limited supply. If the sanction of bride-wealth resides in its economic value and the fear of having to make a refund, then the higher the economic value of the bride-wealth is, the more "stable" the marriage should be. In many urban centers in Yorubaland, however, the prestations have recently been commuted to a monetary payment. In these places, the new secularizing tendencies have altered the attitude towards bride-wealth, making it less symbolic and more monetary. This has led to a meteoric rise in bride-wealth, with payments sky-rocketing to as much as N400 ($1200 in 1979) in areas where the annual income *per capita* fluctuates precariously between $400 and $500. Such payments should serve to stabilize marriages. This has not been the case as divorces are on the increase.[6]

If prime prestations of little economic value can confer the capital value of rights in the bride and pave the way for a stable marriage, then their importance must be sought elsewhere. Evans-Pritchard's insight into the nature of bride-wealth stands the test, not only of time but also of the diversity of cultures:

> Indeed, it is evident that the stability of the family is not really a function of economic motives, but of moral and legal norms (from present-day conditions in Zandeland, for in spite of payments, divorce is rife). It is morals that censure divorce, and law that refuses to recognize grounds for divorce which ensure the stability of the union of husband and wife. It derives its stability from the restraints imposed by law and morals and not from economic blackmail (1965, 185).

Therefore, it is the deep sense of moral commitment that the prime prestations generate and the strong tendency of the Kétu to link the importance of the stability of the marital institution to the survival of the Kétu lineage—with all the spiritual sanctions surrounding this—that account, to some extent, for the morals and laws that militate against divorce. The feeling of deep commitment that the prime prestations generate and the sacredness of the duties that they perform for the lineage—duties related to its survival and to belief in the reincarnation of its ancestors—combine to perform the twin duties of censuring divorce and rejecting grounds for it.

As a conclusion to the idana ceremony, reparations are sought and made for past misdemeanors on the part of any of the members of the wife-taking lineage. Allegations about past offences are sought and made in subtle but clear language. Any relative of the suitor's lineage who is made the target for such an attack is not expected to put up a stiff defense of his honor. Rather, with an air of affected humility, he asks for pardon, which he is given only after all the members of his lineage in attendance have pleaded on his behalf. Ostensibly, the reconciliation is made to ensure that old quarrels are eliminated in order to make way for a new, more vigorous relationship. In reality, it is an act designed to streamline the new equivalent of the Indian *Mayu Dama* relationship (Leach 1954), between the "superior" wife-givers and the "inferior" wife-takers. Beattie has succinctly captured the climate of feelings prevalent at such theatrical "reconciliations":

> It is impossible not to be impressed by the manner in which the status difference . . . between the two groups is stressed throughout. On one side, there is an assured, almost aggressive air of superiority; on the other hand, an attitude of humility and subordination. (Beattie 1958, 7)

However, it is in line with Yoruba etiquette that the aggressiveness is not overdone. It is at the completion of this idana ceremony that the date is set for both circumcision (when the surgery is performed on the would be wife) and the celebration of marriage (Bascom 1969, 61-2). It is to this ritual surgery that we now turn.

Ikọlà-Abẹ́ (Circumcision)

Ritual circumcision (Ikọlà-Abẹ́)[7] is performed on Kétu girls who are about the age of twenty. Yoruba men "consider that girls aged 15-16 years are not fit to be mothers" (Turner 1932). The circumcision of Kétu girls is not determined by the onset of menarche because the Kétu make a clear distinction between physical and social puberty. The time for the operation is determined by the near completion of marriage plans. If such plans are not forthcoming in the case of any Kétu girl, members of her immediate social group would impress on her, through subtle verbal nuances, facial grimaces and pointed anecdotes, that it is high time she normalized her state of life. In reality, of course, in this decidedly polygynous society, things are not usually allowed to get to this point, as men are always on the look-out to improve their social standing by adding to their number of wives.

Preparation

Kétu girls marry as late as the age of twenty for several reasons, one of which is that only then do they meet with the expectations of a well-developed young lady. This period in the developmental cycle of the girl brings out the most desirable in females. Manifestations of full development is expressed (a) in the mature appearance of the breasts, which are now dark at the areolae, with the nipples standing defiantly and tantalizingly to the admirer; (b) in the moderate plumpness of the neck and around the arms; and (c) in a certain amount of compact weight at the buttocks (Torday 1930, 237).

An element of moral contradiction, that alluded to earlier, also applies to the Kétu understanding of child development. While some degree of flirting and "conquering" is necessary in the boy, sex is regarded as antithetical to the growth and maturity of the girl. Premarital sex, which is necessarily precircumcision, is said to stunt her growth and to dwarf her breasts, making them undesirable.

Since one characteristic of Kétu circumcision is that it is not individual but collective—embracing all the girls of the same age group in the lineage—consideration is given to selecting the time during which the withdrawal of the services of this cohort of resourceful girls will not impose a great inconvenience on the economic life of the lineage. The high quality of the foodstuff needed for this "fattening period" requires that the time of excision coincides with the end of the harvest season. The taboos imposed on the girls, in line with Kétu folklore understanding of the processes of healing, prohibit such common food items as okra (*ilà*) and fish (*ẹja*). They may not eat okra because its gummy and elastic nature is said to cause a similar type of mucus-coating on the wound. They are also forbidden to eat fish, since their scales could cause homoeopathically the face of the wound to be scaly.[8] This food taboo is avoided by replacing the forbidden foods with delicious chunks of "bush meat" (eran igbe), which can only be obtained in large quantities in the the the dry season, at the end of harvesting, when much bush-burning and hunting is done. This time coincides with the closing ceremonies in the worship of the goddess of the fertility of earth, plants, and animals. In this wise, the timing of the circumcision rites to coincide with the annual worship of the earth-goddess confirms the suggestion made earlier (Chapter Four) regarding the interrelatedness, in the symbolic complex in Kétu culture, of human fertility with nature's fertility.

Finally, two huts (*abà-ìkọlà*) are built in a secluded spot not far from the village and close to a flowing river. They are surrounded by a big circular fence, which leaves ample room around the huts for the activities within the ritual building complex. Bassir corroborates this description when he writes, with reference to the Aku, the freed Yorubas of Sierra Leone, that

> Clitoridectomy is performed on the girls, but not before puberty. Usually it takes place in seclusion, about two months before the marriage ceremony; the girl is away from home for about three weeks. (1954, 252)

It is in the huts that the circumcision takes place.

The Ceremonial Parade

The Kétu ceremonial parade comprises two elements: the parade of the suitors and the parade of the spouses or initiands. Most of the expenses in the seclusion hut are borne by the suitor's lineage and go to publicize "ownership" of the girls as well as the wealth and status of the sponsoring lineage. Preparations reach their climax in the ceremony. Carrying bundles of firewood[9], the company of suitors assemble at an appointed place, then they proceed in a line through the village. There is a great deal of "showing off" and, I am told, it is usual for the group to be led by a pair of drummers, its leader singing the praises of the ideal husband on a "talking-drum" The "talking-drum" —the famous Yoruba drum that is manipulated to emit sounds through the dilation and contraction of the ropes that control the volume of the sound made. Since the starting point of the procession is often the farthest distance from the circumcision hut, many people watch and cheer the suitors along the route. It is common to hear the greeting addressed to the suitors "Praises are due to those who work so hard for the sake of their wives and children, getting married is not a small responsibility" (*Ẹku ọrọ̀ íyáwò, ẹku ọrọ̀ ọmọ,ọrọ̀ íyáwo kò kéré*). The parade suddenly halts at the fence surrounding the huts, and, hurriedly throwing down their bundles of firewood, the husbands-to-be run away as if pursued. At the outskirts of the village, however, they regroup in an orderly fashion and dance through the village until they reach the starting point of the parade, and then they disperse for the day. Custom demands that during the seclusion of their fiancees the suitors are to wait anxiously around the village, meeting each day and waiting for news that all is well with the initiands.

The second parade is that of the initiands, who form the center of the whole ritual activity. Clothed in black *ìró* and *buba*[10], they are led by *Iyá-Àgbà* ("the great mother"), the Kétu equivalent of the Bemba *Nacimbusa* (Richards 1956) and her three helpers to the *Ojú eérì awọn baba nlá* ("the ancestral graveyard"), which always lies within the living quarters of the people. The *Iyá-Àgba* must be an elderly woman from the lineage, that is, a real or classificatory Father's Sister who has distinguished herself as a successful woman, an efficient mother, and one who is well-versed in the customs and expectations of womanhood and motherhood in Kétu society. She must be one whose life represents practical proof that she has combined the virtues of motherhood with those of "motherliness,"[11] because, for the Kétu as for the Ashanti;

> Motherhood is the principal, if not the ultimate end of marriage. Fertility for the girl is crucial . . . as it ensures that the society will not die out. Barrenness then is the greatest calamity that can befall a Ghanaian woman. (Sarpong 1974, 69)

Arranged in a single row according to age, from the *Iyá-Àgba* to the youngest initiand, the group moves out of the compound, paying its respects to every graduand of the rite who is now happily married. At each house that is visited, songs of praise are sung in honor of the lineage for having so many beautiful and cultured girls. Petitions are also made for the success of the operation and for the fast-healing of the wounds. Ancestors are called upon to ward off the evil intentions of witches, who may try to work against the successful completion of the ritual either by causing accidents during the operation or by preventing the wounds from healing. Gifts are then presented to the initiands. Finally, recourse is made to the grave of the ancestor.

The location of the ancestors within the living quarters has intended spiritual and social connotations. The ancestors are the representatives of the lineage before the Supreme Being. It is their duty to mediate for the lineage and to protect its living members from all harm, especially that which may threaten lineage survival. It is in the interest of both the ancestors and their descendants that each party or interest group perform its duties, for if the descendants fail to offer sacrifices and to keep in close spiritual touch with their ancestors, then protection is not guaranteed. If the ancestors fail to keep their part of the bargain, misfortune may befall their descendants, and they in turn will forfeit their right to reincarnation. The location of the ancestral grave in the house serves as a means of social control, sanctioning the authority of the elders, and, in very difficult situations, it is the spot where the immediate and final reconciliation between quarrelsome siblings is effected. The ancestors are people of the "above", close to the major divinities. It is important to secure the help and blessings of the "above" for those of the "below." The ancestors cannot be ignored.

The prayer said at the location of the ancestral grave one Kétu Yoruba informant stated is as follows:

> We worship and entreat you *Ògún* (the god of iron) through the, intercession of our fathers, who are now in the same place as you, to put your power on the ritual razor to be used. Do not let it cut deeper than it is intended. We are doing it as it should be done; let it be as it should be. "Give me, I give you" croaks the toad in the depth of the river. When we excise your children and give the part back to you, blood flows out; in blood flows life, let abundance of life flow back to them.
> Let them use their wombs to conceive children and
> Let them use their backs to carry the children about.
> Let them be able to perform circumcision on their own children too. Drive far from them witches who eat human beings whole.
> Let their wounds heal and let them have mouths to praise you.
> May it be so.

Another Kétu elder provided the following commentary on this translated prayer:

> Our ancestors are our spiritual ambassadors to *Olórun*. Yet they cannot approach the Supreme Being directly, just as we cannot walk up to our *Oba*. No one should jump the queue; it is against Yoruba protocol. Just as we cannot overlook our ancestors and appeal directly to *Ògún*, the divinity worshiped by all who use metal and give facial

marks, so our ancestors are forbidden to overlook *Ògún*, in the abode of the heavens, and walk straight up to *Olódùmarè*. *Ògún* is the one who has been delegated by *Olórun* to take charge of this department of life and so he must not be overlooked. The prayers ask for the safety of the operation. They also state the purpose for which the operation is performed. We give a bit of life back to the giver of life so as to receive more in return. Finally, the prayer asks that witches be driven far away and not be permitted to thwart the success of the ceremony. The manner of eating attributed to the witches is the opposite of what is normal among the Yoruba. Things are not eaten whole and entire. They are to be cut into pieces and shared out. The witches, however, do exactly what should not be done. They are a fearful lot.

We may see at least three important aspects of the ceremony from this commentary:

a. The intense satisfaction with hierarchy and the due process as established by the culture; doing things the way they should be done, going up the ladder to reach the Supreme Being through the ancestors.

b. The purpose, highly spiritual, albeit utilitarian (as most religious acts are), follows the *do ut des* principle, "I give that I may receive," reminiscent of the spirit of the *hau* in Maori prestations.

c. One of the possible images of the witch as inverted, the direct opposite of the image of society.

With the completion of the prayers, one of the containers hanging on the wall above the spot where the head of the ancestor lies buried is opened, and a dry lump of red ochre or camwood is taken out and used to mark the initiands on the forehead. The second container remains closed. It contains white chalk dug, for those who live around the Kétu town of Imękǫ, at a hilly spot called *oke-ęléfun* "the mountain of white substance," situated about three miles from Imękǫ. Similar hilly spots with limestone abound in the Kétu area. Later on, upon the completion of the rites of seclusion, white chalk will be used to mark the initiands on the forehead as a sign of their ritual purity.

The procession then advances amid solemn songs to the *abà ìkọlà* (the secluded hut). At the gate of the hut, the black attire that has been worn up to this point is hurriedly discarded, perhaps melo-dramatically, and the initiands walk, naked, into the seclusion hut where, after a few invocations to the ancestors for protection, they are clad in another set of black buba and iro. The nurses burn the discarded clothes on a mat and collect the ashes. It is believed that unless all the ashes are collected and taken away, the remains can be magically used to bring bad luck on the owners of the clothes.

The Eve of Circumcision

On the eve of the circumcision, which is the first night of their se-clusion, the atmosphere is filled with gaiety. It begins with the cook-ing of the evening meal, as nothing cooked outside the seclusion hut can be brought in for fear of contamination by the failure to main-tain dietary regulations concerning food taboos. One of the marks of adulthood to which girls aspire is lack of dependence on others in performing those tasks—in this case, cooking—which are, in the eyes of the Yoruba, areas of feminine preserve.[12] As will be seen, much of the time of seclusion is given over to streamlining cookery in-structions. This is a vital part of the whole ceremony, and its pur-pose is well brought out in the Yoruba saying; "The woman who cooks the better stew owns the husband" (*Olóbẹ lọ lọkọ*). The girls do not try to excel as individuals but they all cooperate to make the meal a success. Everything used in the cooking must be new; the mud pots, the utensils, etc. Even the ingredients must not be left-overs.

After supper, the assistants of the mistress of ceremonies use improvised drums and sing songs, together with the girls, that de-pict the silent male/female tensions symbolized in the ritual. Since the hut of seclusion is not too far removed from the village, and since noise travels further in the stillness of the night, they try, by their singing, to communicate with the men, who are already wait-ing for this challenge. A typical anti-male song issuing the chal-lenge is:

Wouldn't the father of Ajọkẹ́ come out to dance for Ajọkẹ́?
He is coming to dance.

120

Wouldn't the husband of Ajǫkẹ: come out to dance for
Ajǫkẹ: ?
He is coming to dance,
They look burlesque with their oversized buttocks
and legs stretched out in grotesque fashion,
It is hard to give birth and to marry,
It is very painful, really painful (Author's translation).

Ajǫkẹ: is the name of one of the initiands. In like manner, the names
of the other will be used in the song. Other provocative songs are
sung. When the females pause, the males pick up. One common
way of attacking the females is to sing, with mournful voices and
affected sympathy, about the problems of women, which include
being confined to the bush and cut up "there" (a reference to the
circumcision ritual), enduring the pain of being mounted by heavy
muscular men, and finally going through the difficulties of birth.
The mens' song ends on the note on which it began, a firm avowal
that "if I come back to life again, I will not like to be a woman". Its
text goes like this:

If I come back to life I won't be a woman
So that society won't put me in the bush and cut me up,
So that I do not have to carry heavy musculary men
So that I do not have to experience the pain of birthing
If I come again I will not be a woman.

The songs continue backwards and forwards until late at the night
when the Iya Agba sings the final chorus:

*Fẹ́mú!, fẹ̀mù!!, kẹ́lẹ́nu gbẹnu rẹ dání
Bi alẹ lẹ ki áfi ọmọ ayò fáyò.*

Hush! Hush!! Every mouth must be closed
When night comes we stop playing Ayo.
(Author's translation).

With this solemn announcement, all the nurses and the initiands
retire to the hut for the night. In addition, all the remaining married
female agnates are divided into two groups, each group alternating
in spending the night in the hut.

The Day of Excision

The initiands are awakened just before dawn, a time the Yoruba regard as auspicious because they believe that the night is the "day" when the activities of the evil spirits are at their most destructive. They are, however, powerless during the day, their own "night" period, when they must remain hidden and inactive in weird places such as hollow parts of large trees or caves or shady, dark places in the thick of the forest. The witches are included among the evil spirits and, like the others, will have scuttled back before the dawn to take possession of their empty bodies. This time is regarded as suitable too, because the Kétu hold that the body is still fresh and the blood is not as thin as it is in the heat of the afternoon. Blood is thought to be like oil, warming slowly and then flowing freely. And so, early in the morning at the moment of excision, the blood will be slow and easy to stem.

The initiands are arranged in a circle around the *igi-àgbo* which is at the center of the ritual building complex and which contains protective liquid medicine brought from a pot hanging in the ancestral graveyard. After the Iya-Agba has invoked the names of all the ancestors, and asked for their protection, she scoops a calabash-full of the prophylactic water and passes it around, each initiand using the liquid sparingly to wash her head, her arms and her genital organ. It is essential that the calabash is passed first to the oldest member and then to the next oldest, and so on, down to the youngest.

At the completion of this ritual washing, the initiands, according to tradition, sit down in the same circular form, each with her sponsor chosen from the group of female agnates. At the exclamation "Welcome, my lord!" (*Ma wolẹ, ma rọra olúwa mi*), a male specialist from the lineage of "the mark givers" (*Olóólà*) appears at the gate dressed like a woman, with hair tied in the traditional Yoruba fashion for women and wearing the Yoruba female attire of iro and buba. Without speaking, he sits down with his back resting firmly against the forked-pole holding the ritual liquid of the ancestors. Each sponsor leads her initiand to the place of excision and sits her down as close to the "mark giver" as is conveniently possible. She then sits down opposite her, using her own legs to widen the outstretched legs of the initiand. The senior nurse stands directly behind the initiand, gently holding her arms behind her body. The two other nurses stand by, each one by an outstretched leg. The mistress of ceremonies (Iyá-Àgbà) stands towering over her, exhorting her to be heroic and not to give much fuss or trouble. The marker deftly cuts off the prepuce (Longo 1964, 472). After this, he proceeds to give each initiand three long strokes on the left arm with a ritual razor. These marks are called *ilà-apá*. Informants say that it was to beautify the initiand. In addition, the sponsor is given three strokes on the upper part of the left shoulder with the same razor, which is still covered by the blood of the initiand. This is called "sharing the pain of the razor" (*igbẹnu abẹ)*. Through this mixing of the blood of the initiand with that of her sponsor, a symbolic tie is created between the two women. The younger looks up to the elder as a mother, a confidante and a refuge. When all have received their marks, a basket of live snails is produced. The nurses crack the snails and use the juice both as an antiseptic and as a styptic.

The Iya-Agba leads the way to the river shouting curses on anyone who remains standing on the path after her three warning calls— ago lọna, that is, "clear the road". The initiands are led to the flowing stream, where they are made to stand upriver. In this posture, they are made to wash themselves in a purificatory fashion that symbolically portrays, in the river rushing downstream, the flowing away of childhood, and all its associations. The principle of this ritual is akin to that of Heraclitus' idea that "in a flowing river, no one steps into the same water twice" (quoted in Karl Popper 1945,13). Their childhood is discarded, never again to be resumed. At the end of this ritual bathing, a special medicine associated with the powers of fast healing is applied to the wound. Its ingredients include hyacinth (called in Yoruba *patan mọ* — "close your thighs, your husband is coming") and snails. It is expected to work homoeopathically. Just as the hyacinth closes up on contact, the wounds are expected to close up and heal over; and just as the snail cannot waste blood, because it has none, it is hoped that there will be no excessively long bleeding from the wound. Palm oil, too, is used to help the scar to become smooth. For a second time, the garments of the initiands are burnt, after they have been deposited in the banks of the stream, and a third set of clothing is given to them.

Meanwhile, the specialist mark-giver, who personifies the ancestors and masculine intrusion into the female world of the hut, has gathered up the excised parts and taken them into the ancestral shrine, where they are buried. These immolated parts of the initiands symbolize their personalities which they give back in the hope of receiving abundance of life in return.

The remaining activities of the day include three visits by the group of suitors to the fence surrounding the ritual compound, each of which is announced by the dumping of huge loads of firewood outside the fence. Wordlessly, they slink back, leaving behind them the relative serenity of life in the ritual compound. This thrice daily visit is continued for three days. The chief preoccupation of the next four Yoruba weeks is to allow the wounds to heal quickly. This requires as little movement as possible. Activities are limited to the early morning invocation of the ancestors, the journey to the flowing river, and the telling of tales—which contain a certain amount of sex education. Feeding is given full priority during this period, and it may be justifiably said that this is a period of fattening and of ease for the initiands. The other preoccupation, consequent upon the first, is learning. Through the treatment of the wounds, some rudimentary knowledge of traditional first-aid medicine is learned.

The Last Week of Seclusion

The final Kétu week is hectic, as activities follow each other in quick succession. On the first day of the week (ọjọ́ ajẹ́) the initiands take part in the competition for the best cook. Ingredients are made available from the copious supply provided by the lineages of the prospective husbands given too generously in an attempt to outdo one another. For the competition, a makeshift hearth (ààrò) is built for each participant by placing three stones in a triangle. Dry wood, placed in the intervening spaces, is lit to provide all around heating for the pot.

The competition proceeds through the most difficult preparations of Kétu dishes, including those the initiands are forbidden to eat during the healing period. Bascom, who did field-work among the Kétu, recorded fifty-six dishes and forty-four variants (1951, 126-32). This competition continues into the next day, ending with the activity of extracting palm oil from the fruits of palm trees.

This is a rather tedious job, yet expected of every well-trained wife. It comprises several steps: boiling palm nuts, removing the pericap, from the kernels, extracting the oil from the shaft of the pericap and boiling the oil to kill any impurities.

Kétu men do not take their eating habits lightly, yet they do not cook. They depend on their women to cook for them. Thus, they place high value on their women's cooking skills, one of the important criteria of a good wife. This competition provides the opportunity for their women to show the cooking skills they have acquired. The ability to cook becomes, for the ingenious Kétu woman who wants to have her way on a particular issue, the means of influencing her husband's decisions. As Bascom noted:

> It is the duty of every Yoruba wife to learn the favorite dishes of her husband and to prepare them exactly as he wishes, and in a polygamous family, the favorite wife prepares her husband's food regularly because she can do it best to his liking. (1951,49-50)

The Kétu woman, like most Yoruba women, accepts her duty and wields the power associated with it.

The competition is brought to an end with the processing of oil from palm oil fruits. The sponsors of the initiands choose the girl who has proved to be the best cook. She is called "the wife, the best manipulator of the soup-stirring ladle" (*ìyàwó olówó ṣibi*) and her praises are snug.

On the third day of the last Kétu week (Ojo-Ògún) another competition is held. This is put up ostensibly to pick the girl with the sweetest voice. It is aimed at discovering how much the initiand knows about the history of her bridegroom's lineage. Kétu wives are important sources of history in Kétu society, which is nonliterate but nevertheless retains an impressive repository of remembered history.

There are at least three types of specialists who serve as historians for the Kétu. First in the old kingdom of Kétu and its satellites, there used to be and still is the *Baba Eléégun*. His main function is to recite the list of the kings who have reigned since the inception of the town. In Kétu town itself, where his office was most developed, he recites this list at the enthronement of an *oba*, king. It is said that a single error in recital would cause him to be hanged (Biobaku 1957; Parrinder 1967). Second, there are certain Kétu professional groups that have the responsibility of preserving and rendering some past important events on special occasions. Some of these groups include the hunters who, in their professional songs (*ìjálá*), narrate past events; and the professional mourners (*asunrárà*), who reiterate in their dirges the historic events associated with those for whom they mourn. Third, the wives constitute a special category that preserves lineage history in their praise-songs called *oríkì* are comprised of lists of special events associated with dead members of a lineage. This list includes lyrical songs, songs thought to inspire members of the lineage to maintain the standards set by their progenitors. The recitation of the songs is the sole preserve of women. Special care and attention is taken to ensure that the candidates for marriage are taught the songs. The Kétu attach high value to the learning of these praise-songs. In fact, although only women from the lineage of the initiands are allowed to participate actively in the rituals within the seclusion hut, the only occasion when women from other lineages are invited is connected with the preparation for the competition of the maiden with the sweetest voice. Such "alien" women are those also incorporated into the lineages of the bridegrooms of the initiands. Being acquainted with the praise-songs, they are brought into the ritual hut to prepare the initiands individually for the competition.

During the competition itself, mistakes made by initiands are corrected. Resourcefulness in modulating the voice and innovation on a moderate scale are praised. When the winner is chosen, she is seated in the center and all sing a song to her as "the owner of the sweetest voice" (olówùn Iyò). In this song, she is likened to a bird reputed for good singing called *àwòko*. Her envied prize is to act as the lead-singer at all the gatherings of her age group and of junior groups, and she is to receive all entitlements attached to this position. These entitlements include the rights to have the last say, to take her share of meat and drinks before senior members of her group.

The Last Day

The activities of the six Kétu weeks reach their climax on the last day when, as a mnemonic device and reaffirmation, initiands are made to repeat the major activities. The ostensible purpose for the repetition of cooking is to provide food for the feast to mark the end of seclusion. The feasting is brought to a conclusion with the third ceremonial burning of the initiands' clothes and the wearing of white dresses in their place. The mistress of ceremony (Iyá-Àgbà) then makes a final check of the huts to make sure that nothing is left behind that may be used for sorcery. She goes ahead of the procession, which now moves out amid singing, to be met by well-wishers and drummers who sing congratulatory songs. The procession heads for a ancestral shrine by a long route so as to display the initiands for more people to see.

At the ancestral shrine, only the mistress of ceremonies, her assistants, and the initiands go in to express their gratitude to the deity, through the ancestors, for the success of the excision. The ashes of the burnt clothes are later mixed with cow dung and used to decorate the ancestral room. The Iyá-Àgba then proceeds to mark each initiand on the forehead with white chalk. From this day until the day of the "dance of departure to the house of the husband"(*ijo bọlọjọ ajo rele ọkọ*) which is ideally a fortnight, the girls stay at home to get ready for marriage. This ends that phase of excision in the ritual series of fertility rites.

The Dance of Departure

The dance of departure *(Ijo-Igbéyawó)* serves several purposes for the Kétu. It is the last opportunity for the initiands to act together as members of an age-group before departing to their respective marital homes. It affords the chance for the lineage to display its precious wordly goods. The lineage expects, in return, admiration from other lineages for the success of the initiands. The dance also provides the chance for members of the lineages of the bridegrooms to display their wealth.

While the initiands were in seclusion, negotiations were already in progress with the lineage of drummers called *Ilé Elegbèdé*. The consulting fee, which is paid collectively by the initiands' families, consists of two gourds of palm wine[13]and two kegs of locally brewed spirits called *ṣongiro*.[14] The date of the dance is agreed upon and payment is made for services to be rendered by a specific amount of foodstuff and drinks. It is not unusual nowadays to include a fee of ten naira (N10). The same arrangement is made with the head of the guild of musicians called *Aláwòrò*, who compose special songs for the girls.

On the appointed day, the entertainment begins just before noon, which is indicated by the vertical position of the sun. The Kétu gauge this time as being "when the sun stands straight to the head" (*oòrun kan àtàrí*). The initiands are decked in the most expensive Yoruba ceremonial clothes called *aṣọ-òkè*. The dance procession goes right though the town with pauses for special displays in front of each bridegroom's house. These special stops provide the relatives of the bridegroom with the opportunity to display their wealth. Several people from the lineage, representing the different age groups, line up and go into the crowd of dancers and approach the bride who will be married into their lineage. Then, one after another, they put currency notes or coins on her forehead. It is essential that the display be prolonged as well as ostentatious, because the longer it lasts, the greater the impression on the spectators and the higher the rating given to the lineage. The dance procession terminates in the evening at the same place from which it begun.

Preparations for removal of each initiand to her marital home is heightened after this dance. Three Kétu weeks after this dance, the lineage releases the initiands at intervals of two Kétu weeks. The release of the initiand to the "wife-taker" group is made in the ceremony of "carrying wife"(*ìgbeyàwó*).

Marriage

On the day of the marriage ceremony (*ìgbeyàwo*), there is much feasting, both in the house of the bride and the bridegroom. Large rounded containers called *bẹmbẹ́,* containing the clothes and personal effects of the bride, are set out in conspicuous places, producing another opportunity for the family to display its wealth. The process of "carrying" the wife is complicated. About midnight, a group of the bridegroom's family (*àjọ ìyàwó*) call to take the bride away. The members of the bride's lineage pretend ignorance as to the mission of the *àjọ ìyàwo*, which is received cordially. The leader of the group states their intention in the most polite manner. The leader of the females of the bridal lineage then pretends to understand. She states that she will fulfil the wish of the mission promptly. She enters the inner room with some assistants and brings out an imposter bride who is presented to the *àjọ ìyàwo*. The leader of the group takes a close look at the imposter and consults with other members of her entourage. After the consultation, she informs—with extreme courtesy—the relatives of the bride, that the bride they are seeking is much finer and that she would be most indebted if the bride is brought forward. When after a period, the real bride is not brought forward, the leader makes a restrained appeal to the elders of the bride's lineage, some of whom are customarily within easy reach. With equal cordiality, the elders make it clear that, as much as they would like to help, they are in no position to do so. The ajo-iyawo then goes back home to return after an interval with more gifts for the bridal lineage.

The *àjọ ìyàwo* is cordially received at the second call. The bride's relatives make a show of complying with the wish of the mission. They go into another room and, amid rejoicing, present yet another imposter. The joy of the *àjọ ìyàwo* is short-lived when it is "discovered" that the girl brought forward is not the bride. This time, a most vigorous attempt is made to get the elders to come to their aid, but it is turned down in a disarmingly cautious manner.

The *àjọ ìyàwo* makes a third attempt after the first cockcrow, and this time the bride is brought out amid jubilation. Songs are sung in praise of her beauty and culture. The bridal train anxiously tries to speed up her departure after special prayers have been said, offered by the elders, that she may be fertile. However, just as the ajo iyawo group is about to proceed, the mood of the female relatives of the bride lineage changes. They insist that the bride will not be allowed to leave until some exorbitant fee is paid. This delay takes some time and agreement is reached only after some part of the fee is paid. The wife is then handed over to the *àjọ ìyàwo* while she weeps passionately. After this classical display of privileged obstruction of marriage, the bride is taken to her marital home amid jubilation. The last few paces to the bridal house, she is carried shoulder high and then set down on the doorstep. It is from this act that the ceremony of marriage derives its Yoruba name *ìgbéyàwó* "the act of carrying the wife." After the pouring of cold water on her legs and the saying of prayers, she is led into the house with her face veiled and then taken into a special room. The husband, who is not allowed to watch these proceedings, is sent to join the bride to consummate the marriage. This takes place on the bridal bed consisting of two thick mats, laid over each other, and a covering white cloth.

Both sets of relatives of the bride and the bridegroom wait anxiously around the bridal room for the completion of the test, the success sign of which is the blood-spattered garment. The proof is important since virginity is an index of culture and of home-training as well as a mark of the respectable wife. Bassir gives the reaction of the relatives of an Aku Yoruba to the outcome of the test:

> Later...an announcement will be made regarding the bride's premarital virginity. If her husband has found her to be a virgin, her relatives will go about beating a metal drum and singing that a mother has looked after her children well and there is no shame in the family. If the girl was not *virgo intacta* at marriage, her parents go home quietly, and it is considered bad form to speak about it. (Bassir 1955, 255)

The reaction observed by Bassir is very mild considering the premium put on virginity among the Kétu. After the consummation of marriage, some female members of the bridegroom's lineage go into the room to inspect the bed. If the white cloth is found to be smeared with blood, there is a great burst of jubilation, and it is taken and displayed for all to see. If not, there is at first an unusual quiet followed by a burst of unarticulated protest from various members of the groom's family, who feel they have been cheated. It does not stop at this, and Fadipe (1949) confirmed the violent excesses into which it can degenerate when he stated that, at the announcement, those representatives of the bride's lineage who had escorted her to her new home, must take to the forest or stand the risk of being roughly treated.

When the test of virginity is positive, the festivities continue into the next morning, when the groom and his age-mates make a ceremonial visit to the bridal home, carrying with them brimming kegs of palm wine and other symbolic gifts, whose completeness indicate the completeness of the most precious gift of the bride's lineage to the groom's. If, however, the proof of virginity was negative, and the groom's lineage bring themselves around to sending gifts, whatever items are sent are sent in halves, thereby narrating the state of incompleteness in which the bride was found. After the sending of these symbolic gifts to confirm the state in which the bride was found to be, she is left in the care of the senior wife.

When the new wife discovers that she is pregnant, she tells her husband, who reports this to his father. The husband's father in turn, reports the news to the eldest member of the compound. The eldest man prescribes certain prenatal observances for the wife. These observances fall into three categories. The first has to do with the maintenance of lineage taboos (*eèwǫ*). It is thought that this will encourage the ancestors to protect the vulnerable foetus adequately. The second category of observances has to do with occasional ritual baths for the mother-to-be. The medicinal contents of the herbal liquid (*àgbo*) thought to possess the power to scare away malevolent forces from the pregnant woman. The Kétu believe that a pregnant woman is also vulnerable to the attacks of jealous, destructive mystical forces. They also hold the belief that when a pregnant woman walks around in the heat of a tropical afternoon, or later at night, she is most likely to be attacked by evil spirits. The pregnant woman then, is forbidden to walk about in the early part of the afternoon or late at night. The third prenatal observance has to do with ensuring quick and easy delivery. This is related to the preparation of what the Kétu take as a more vigorous medicinal bath. The bath is prepared by boiling the bark of certain trees along with herbs in a large earthen pot.

The Birth and Naming of the First Child

Among the Kétu, delivery takes place in the ancestral shrine of a compound. This assures the protection of the ancestors and their help to secure a safe delivery. It also expresses the three-dimensional perspective of the Kétu. The future represented in the child is brought into contact with the past through the present. This location of delivery also sets the seal of ownership on the *pater* who cements his claim by being the one to dispose of the placenta.[15]

The expectant woman is taken to the shrine at the beginning of labor. There she is joined by a medicine man, the lineage "midwife" (*agbẹbí*) and three other female elders. To strengthen her against the ordeal of giving birth, she is given another medicinal bath. When the birth-throes increase in intensity, the medicine man, in order to aid delivery and to lessen pain, recites the incantation:

> The goats have no midwives
> The sheep have no midwives
> When the goat is pregnant, she is safely delivered,
> When the sheep is pregnant, she is safely delivered,
> You, in this state of pregnancy will be safely
> delivered. (Longo 1964, 471)

The Kétu woman in labor is not forbidden to cry out. She is expected to, and later on in life, she may beseech her son to change his mind on a particular issue by reminding him of the pains endured at his birth. She will say "Remember the kneeling of the woman in labor" (*Ranti ìkúnlẹ̀ abiamọ*).

Upon the delivery of the child and its placenta, the booming of a dane gun informs the lineage members that the delivery has been successful. The umbilical cord (*ìdodo*) is severed with a ritual knife. Then the child is handed over to the eldest male member who welcomes it to the lineage, and prays for it, saying:

> May you be a true and healthy person. We have
> given birth to you, you should give birth to
> another. Listen to your father and mother and
> take care of them. Welcome to our midst.

With this prayer concluded, the child is handed over to the mother, and they both go into seclusion until the day of the naming ceremony.

On the day of the naming ceremony, the members and the representatives of the lineages of both parents assemble in the house of the father of the new child. The mother and the child are welcomed into the assembly, thus making their first public appearance. They both wear a considerable amount of red ochre (camwood). Once in the assembly, the young mother is reminded of the fact that the child belongs to her husband and his lineage. This is done by the dramatic taking-away of the baby by an elderly female who is either the child's father's sister or classificatory father's sister. Only then does the ceremony of naming begin.

The ritual items for the ceremony include bitter kola (*orógbó*), salt (*iyò*), kola-nut (*obì*), red palm (*epo pupa*) and, nowadays, money (*owó*). These items have already features as part of the prime presentations of bride-wealth. The eldest male member of the husband's lineage serves as the master of ceremonies. He begins by thanking the ancestors for the gift of the child, and he employs them to speak favorably on the baby's behalf before the Supreme Being. He then holds each ritual item, using its symbol to form a prayer for the child. The format of the prayers is straightforward, although each prayer specifically brings special blessings of its own to the child.

A list of the prayers in translation is provided below followed by an analysis of the meanings derived from each and the wishes they evoke for the child.

1. This is salt. May your life be sweet
   (*Iyò niyi. Ki aiye rę níyò*)
2. This is bitter kola. It lasts long. May you too live to old age
   (*Orógbó niyi. Gbígbó ni orógbó ígbó. Ki ogbó Ki otó*)
3. This is kolanut. The kolanut tree bears fruit in plenty. May you increase and multiply
   (*Obì niyi. Fófófó ni ori óobi kun. Ki obí si, ki oręsi*)
4. This is palm oil, it has a cooling effect on sauce, may your life be cool
   (*Epo niyi, Epo lęlęrǫ obę. Ki aiye rę rǫ*)

The first prayer, built on the symbol of salt, makes an explicit wish for the child's happiness. The Kétu understand the qualities of salt. They know that it flavors and that it preserves. The wish is that the child enjoys a healthy and happy life. A happy life is, in metaphoric Kétu usage, a flavored life.

The translation of the second prayer suppresses the meaning derived from the root of the Yoruba word for bitter kola. *Orógbó* is a combination of two words—*òro* and *gbo*. *Òro* is a fruit that takes a notoriously long time to ripen; *gbo* is a verb meaning "to mature." The prayer expresses two wishes. The first wish is that the child matures; the second is that the child may live to a very old age.

The third prayer is rich in symbolic meaning. There are two levels at which meaning can be teased out of this prayer. On the level of sensory reflection, the kola-nut tree bears fruit in abundance. There is, therefore, a symbolic association between the fertility of the tree and the implied fertility of the child. The wish is that the child be fruitful and become the father of many children. This is the *summum bonum*—the highest good—of the Yoruba value system. Although there is no equivalent of the public ceremony of congratulations, performed for a couple with ten living children, as practiced among the Ashanti in Ghana (Fortes 1954, 265), there is no doubt that Kétu parents of many children are blessed and privileged. Implicit in the same wish for fertility are the wishes for economic prosperity and spiritual salvation. The size of the family, to some extent, determines the extent of human labor available for the intensive and unmechanized system of farming on which the Kétu build their wealth and status. Besides, the larger the size of the family, the greater the chance for one to receive, at death, the standard burial that the Kétu believe will bestow admittance into the ranks of the ancestors. On the second level, there is a play on words in order to reach a deeper meaning. *Bi*, the last two letters of *obi,* when standing alone with the right accent, also become the verb "to give birth." This second meaning supports the former wish that the ability to give birth may not remain unactuated.

The Kétu, who take a good quantity of pepper in their sauce, use palm oil to down its searing effect. The fourth prayer, using oil as the symbol, includes the wish that the baby live a gentle, happy life.

At the conclusion of this prayer, each member present comes forward to give the child a name. He drops some money into the bowl of cold water in front of the assembly and pronounces the name he gives to the child, each pronouncement being echoed by the assembly. If the eldest member's given name is *Akanbi* — one who is very special, one in a thousand, one who is deliberately born—the members of the assembly call the parents of the baby by adding "father" (baba) or "mother" (ìyá) to Akanbi (Akanbi's father—*baba Àkànbí*, Akanbi's mother—*ìyáÀkànbí*) Then, and only then, has maturity been achieved

Notes

1. N. A. Fadipe, whose ethnographic account of Yoruba marriage is outstanding and who rightly makes much of the traumatic experience that the spouse undergoes because of the residential change at marriage, seems to have overlooked the vital integrating role of the *alarena* and her alleviating effect on the trauma during the transition.

2. The Osage Indians(Laflesche 1912) and the Etsako, an Edo speaking group in Nigeria (Imokhai 1979) have institutions similar to the alarena. Among the Osage Indians, the role is known as *nigka do he* and its functions are performed by four elderly men. Among the Etsako the role is known as *okhiukhu* and is performed by a person.

3. Fortes 1962, 9-11. The positional level is the third Turner level of ritual meaning. It is elicited by comparing the use that is made of the same symbolic items in different ritual situations in an attempt to identify their meaning in relation to each other. The other two l evels are the exegetical and the operational. (See Turner 1962, 1967.)

4. Cowries were once the medium of exchange before the introduction of money-currency. If, as Bascom (1969, 60) recorded, cowries were still in use in 1937 at Ile- Ife, the culture center of Yorubaland, and hence the first city in the hinterland to receive full attention from the British, this medium of exchange must still have been in use in outlying districts much later.

5. Nigeria currency is naira (N) and kobo (k).

6. There is no attempt here to reduce the reasons for the relatively high divorce rates prevalent in some Yoruba areas to explanations about a change of emphasis in bride-wealth prestations. The increasing tendency to make marriage an individual contract between two persons instead of the collective responsibility of two lineages, and the decreasing control exercised by the lineages over the affairs of the individual, are two of the other reasons. What I wish to emphasize is the weakness of the argument that advances bride-wealth as payment or economic blackmail for marital stability.

7. It may be noted that the Kétu ìkolà-abẹ: is simple in comparison with the elaborate genital operations of the Sudan (cf. Zanootelli

1970) and those of some East African communities. It is, however, similar to that of the Gikuyu girls of Kenya, performed by the female specialist Norwithia, who "with a stroke... cut off the tip of the clitoriis"(rong'otho). As no other parts of the girl's sexual organ's interfered with, this completes the girl's operation"(Kenyatta, 1953, 140)

8. It is worth noting that these taboos about healing also prevail among the Tiv of Nigeria. Bohanna wrote: "they could not eat fish with scales for fear that the wound would be scaly . . .. They were not allowed any food which contained small seeds such as okra, tomatoes, and gourd seeds (*ingishii*) as the small seeds would affect the healing and source of the scar. (1954, 5)

9. The Yoruba use dry sticks or firewood called *igi ida'na*—"the wood for making fires"—as the chief source of their heating. Even in the big towns, where it has become a status symbol to purchase a gas cooker, the Yoruba place heavy reliance is put on firewood, which is scarce, and yet its supply is neither as irregular nor as expensive as gas.

10. Iro and buba are the traditional clothes that every Yoruba woman wears. Buba is an upper piece not unlike a blouse; iro is a larger piece of cloth that is wrapped around the lower part of the body.

11. For more on the difference between "motherhood" and "motherlines" see Sarpong (1974), especially Chapter Nine, Ghanaian Values.

12. Bascom observed that "Yoruba men do not cook for themselves for fear of gossip and ritual; it would be assumed that they were either so bad that their wives and close relatives refused to cook for them, or that they were so miserly that they were trying to save a little that their wives might waste" (1950, 50).

13. The Yoruba have a "tree-culture." They exploit ordinary palm trees for both the reddish palm oil and for the grayish kernel oil extracted from palm kernel. They also extract a brand of palm wine from raffia trees and kola-nut from kola trees. Palm wine is the rough equivalent of corn-beer, which people in "grain cultures" use to repay labor debts. It must be said that palm wine alone does not suffice as payment for labor.

14. *Songiro* is an important intoxicant locally brewed from palm wine. Its sale was proscribed despite its popularity. The drink is called

by different nicknames so as to outwit law enforcement agents who, despite drinking it themselves, are only too happy to arrest other drinkers. These nicknames include "sobida," "Sapele water," "404," and "push-me-I-push-you."

15. This practice is not peculiar to the Kétu. It seems to be wide spread among the different Yoruba subgroups. (See Callaway 1978,166). Among the Kétu, the social significance of disposing of the placenta was one of the reasons that made delivery at clinics unpopular.

CHAPTER SIX

INTERPRETATION OF THE FERTILITY RITES

Introduction

Many Kétu would find this description of the ritual series satisfactory. This chapter will analyze fertility rites to elicit the meanings they convey and the alternative values they present in Kétu society, whose dominant structures are male-orientated. Efforts have been made to adhere closely to the main outline of Audrey Richards' model, the contents of which I have noted in chapter Three on models for the study of initiation rites.

While the reasons for choosing Richards' model as the main guide of this interpretation of the Kétu series of rites were clearly stated, two instances have necessitated recourse to the ideas of other models: first, when the meaning of certain aspects of the ritual could be illustrated more clearly by ideas of models other than Richards'; and second, when certain features of the ritual could not be accommodated by Richards' model. Thus, Ardener's model of "the wild" will be employed to illustrate and illuminate the different reasons advanced for circumcision by males and females. In addition, Marcel Mauss' idea of counterprestation will clarify the purpose of circumcision.

The rites will be treated in relation to Kétu dogma and values. This will involve showing the link of dependence between such institutions as kinship and practice such as hunting and funerary rites and the institution of marriage, to which the fertility rites belong. Although, *prima facie*, those practices appear unrelated to the fertility rites, their relatedness will demonstrate the interdependence between Kétu cultural practices and institutions. The tensions and conflicts inherent within the society will be thrown into relief since it is being suggested that such tensions find expression and temporary resolution in the series of rites. The analysis will conclude with a treatment of color and numerical symbolism and will show how these contribute to the meaning communicated by the rites.

Richard's Model

Expressed Purpose
Much of the material preceding this chapter stands for the expressed purpose derived from asking the ritual actors what they think they are achieving and from accurately summarizing the different views of participants on those ritual features (Richards 1956, 112). However, some streamlining is necessary to clarify which expressed purpose is primary and which is secondary.

Expressed Purpose - Primary
The Kétu emphasize that the purpose of the series of rites is to transform Kétu girls into (a) "proper women" (*obĭnrin òtítọ́*); (b) "decent women" (*obĭnrin àtàtà*); and (c) "to bring their learning to conclusion" (*lati parí ẹkọ wọn*).

The Concept of "Proper Women"
The Yoruba adjective for "proper" (*òtítọ*) is used to discriminate between females who are women and those whom the Kétu do not see as such. The concept of proper includes the desire for growth because when the Kétu are pressed to explain what is meant by becoming "proper" women, they would often answer, "to make them develop" (*onjẹ ki wọn dàgbà*). The verb *dàgbà* is a compound of two words; the verb "to become"—*di*, and the word for elder—(*àgbà*). *Dàgba* connotes, therefore, both physical and

mental growth as well as a quasimagical qualitative change necessary for the assumption of the trying role as mother. The distinguishing characteristic of maturity (àgbà) is not a physical growth, for the Yoruba proverb says: "Big clothes do not make a man great" (*Aṣọ nla kọ ni ènìa nlá*). Wisdom singles out the elder. Making the girls mature through the performance of the rites implies imparting wisdom to them. The amount of wisdom imparted is measured in reference to how one's behavior is guided by the values of the society.

On the eve of the ritual excision, Kétu girls are set apart from the society. They remain in the seclusion of the hut for the duration of the healing of the excision wound. In the evening of their first day in the hut, they taunt the larger society with a verbal challenge as if to express their independence of it, their temporary inaccessibility to it, and also their capacity to survive without it. This period of seclusion is marked by a temporary halt in normal activities. The girls wear black clothes, which the larger society associates with mourning. Their isolation is shared not only by the custodians of the ceremony, the Iya agba and her assistants, but also by many in the larger society. Their sponsors are females who have married into other lineages and who have to leave their duties at frequent intervals to attend to the girls in the hut. The ceremonial, thrice-daily fetching of firewood by the suitors expresses male concern for, as well as cooperation with, what was going on within the hut. The ban placed on using the stream when it is in ritual use and the curse placed on men who may try to invade the privacy of the hut are instances of the involvement of the larger society in the experience of transition that it has set for its girls. The test of maturity that marks this phase includes learning lengthy complicated songs and enduring the excision.

The rites of this phase include those aimed at seeking supernatural protection for the girls. This appeal to the metaphysical is not peculiar among the Kétu to the fertility rites alone. It also features in the ritual of installation. For the girl to become a proper woman, just as for the king to become invested with the essence of kingship, there must be a qualitative change, magically made possible either through the sacrifice of a part of the initiand as prestation or, as in the case of the king, through the ritual of eating an excised part of his predecessor. This special appeal is aimed at removing the fear attendant the change, thereby ensuring that the role assumption is made with confidence. Such fears are nursed by the girls' mothers about the possibility of their daughters' indulgence in premarital sex, which is precircumcision sex. It is believed that for such a defaulter the operation will be difficult and dangerous. Although this belief may be seen as a social lever to make the girl conform to certain expectations, it cannot be doubted that the potent force of such fears confer, on a successful endurance of excision, a magic protection against danger.

Going hand in hand with the magic of warding-off dangers is that of guaranteeing fertility. The prayers said at the ancestral graveyard refer to the ideal woman who gives birth to many children and carries them on her back. The ritual washing of the excision wound in the river has an element of the magical cause of fertility. It also confirms the polysemous quality of the ritual item. Thus, in reference to ritual item, i.e., fish, it is clear that "it is the nature of symbols ... to become the center of a cluster of different associations" (Richard 1956, 164), and that the symbol can at one and the same time represent the thing that must be done and the thing that must not be done (Richards 1956,165). It is taboo for the girl to eat fish during the period of convalescence for fear that the scales on the fish may homeopathically cause the wound to be scaly and perpetually fresh like the fish in the river. Yet, the early morning ritual bath in the river is performed in the hope that just as the fish reproduces prolifically, the girl, too, may be blessed.

The Concept of a "Decent Woman"
The second discrimination made by the Kétu is between "decent women" (*obìnrin àtàtà*) and "nondecent women" (*obìnrin búburú*). It is an ethnocentric artificial category erected to distinguish "our women" from "their women." Our women are, necessarily, the decent women, while their women are indecent. The mark of decency is the willingness to live according to Kétu mores, with interdictions against bearing children before one's incorporation as wife, elopment, precircumcision sex. The basic tenets of Kétu mores for females include the obligation of respect for elders and the achievement of the status of maturity through enduring the pains inherent in the maturation ritual series. The end product of

this painstakingly gradual process could not be anything other than "our women," the decent women.

On the contrary, "their women" are of two categories; the aliens who do not practice circumcision and those few Kétu girls who have independently given themselves to men before the rites. Therefore, inherent in this discriminatory exercise is the tendency to classify the society into the two categories of "we and our women" and "they and their women." The former category is associated with the "village" and in corollary with "culture" while the latter is linked with "the wild" and hence with nature. The domain of culture is auspicious, while that of nature is inauspicious. Three points are worth noting about this arbitrary classification:

(a) that it is designed to perpetuate the efforts of one group to regard itself as superior to another;

(b) that the boundaries of such classification shift from one homogeneous group to another ("the wild") of the dominant group may include the sphere of culture of the "muted" group - Ardener 1972, 143-5);

(c) that it is conformity to the values dictated by the dominant group that qualifies the Kétu girl to be regarded as mature.

To become a "decent woman," therefore, the Kétu girl must conform to the role expectations for women set up by the male-orientated society.

To "Teach Them"
The third expressed purpose of the ritual series is the desire to instruct the maidens. Their instructions are twofold: (a) learning of the praise songs (*oríkì*) of the suitor's lineage and (b) the reaffirming female role expectations. The competition for the best cook (*Ìyàwó olowó ṣibi*), ostensibly aimed at finding the best cook among the initiands, has the more pragmatic purpose of showing that the girls can cook and confirming them as graduates in this vital area. The stimulating atmosphere of mild rivalry inspires each initiand to defend her "honor" against the others. The fear of shame that greets poor cooking combined with the

urge to score marks associated with the mature and well-trained woman, accelerate the capacity of the initiand to show that she can cook better than others.

The competition for the *olóhùn iyò*— the sweet-voiced maiden —provides the initiands with some knowledge of the history of the house into which they are marrying and makes them veritable sources of history in this nonliterate society, probably without any awareness of their vital import. Great preparations go into this competition, as the best senior wife soloist is invited into the seclusion hut both to instruct and sometimes to sing with the initiand. The stern warning given to the initiands to pay particular attention to their instructors shows the importance attached to this wifely duty.

The consideration of these two competitions reveals certain important differences between the Kétu fertility rites and those of the Bemba. While the instructions that take place and the manner in which they are conducted in the Kétu hut of circumcision (*abà ïkolà abę*) should not conjure up the mental picture of girls sitting in rows and listening with forced or voluntary attention to some whip-waving instructress who takes them through the gamut of life experiences and the role expectations of a wife, it should be said that instructions are given and received about what should have been learnt but was not. Here, in contrast with the Bemba, where initiands are "shoved away in the corner of the initiation hut and sometimes given direct orders not to look at what was going on" (Richards 1956,126), the Kétu girls are exhorted to pay attention to what is being done and even during the competitive segments, to excel at it.

There are no secret terms to learn, though it was common to initiate the maidens into a special kind of phraseology that is the prerogative of adults. The deep structures of this adult language generate meanings other than that apparent in the surface structure. In this way, they—along with other adults—can "talk above the heads" of the immature about such matters as sex and yet be speaking in an apparently "normal" manner.

In these rites, emphasis appears to be placed on wifely duties geared to pleasing the husband and to meeting the goals of Kétu marriage. Hence, the rites place emphasis upon socially approved attitudes. It is worth noting that the high premium placed on women sacral cultural duties buttresses the patrilineal male-orientated ideology. In making those duties sacred and their performance the yardstick that measures or distinguishes the "woman of culture" from the woman of nature, great importance is placed on them by women who wish to excel. In Richards' terms, "the rite not only consecrates the woman's duties in the sense of making them seem honorable, but it is an occasion for the public affirmation of the legal obligations of the marriage" (1956, 128). Thus, the rite establishes that the only way open to women is through obedience to rules that perpetuate their control by men.

Implied in the rites is the confirmation of status change. As the penultimate step towards marriage, the series of rites do not transfer the Kétu girl from the unmarriageable to the marriageable category. Rather, they confirm the imminence of marriage and ensure the status change takes place in a manner that is not traumatic for the maiden. Hence, through such functionaries as the "go-between" (*alárenà*) and the senior wife, who acts as the suitor's lineage song instructress, and the relationship that the initiand has with them, the new connection engendered by marriage is highlighted, and the smooth integration of the initiand as a new wife into a new environment caused by the practice of virilocal marital residence is effected. The observable mark of the new wife is the *ilà apá*, the three long marks on the left arm that show conspicuously under the short-sleeved *bùbá*. In public places, the marks express their state and remove these women from the category of those females who can be wooed. Hence, these marks symbolize both their state of commitment and, in corollary, their inaccessibility.

Expressed Purpose - Secondary
As indicated in Chapter Five the responsibility of making provisions for the women in the seclusion hut devolves on the suitor's lineage. This responsibility offers opportunity for two kinds of display: (a) the display of the lineage's social standing; and (b) the ceremonial expression of kinship ties and obligations through the contributions made by the suitor's relatives to off-set the costs. Since the initiation is collective and not individual, Kétu female rites have an inherent element of competition. The different lineages into which the initiands are to be incorporated at marriage compete to outdo one another by providing lavishly for

their prospective spouses. To accomplish this honor-ascribing task, kinship obligations are enforced. Even minor lineages that have broken away for some reason or another but still maintain some tenuous links with their major branch feel compelled to make contributions that will put their ancestral roots in a good light, which will eventually reflect on themselves. Hence, this attempt to pull status over other lineages necessitates the prestation of kinship obligations.

Deduced Attitudes

In the succession of rites, three occasions give rise to a heightened sense of apprehension; namely, the ordeal of circumcision, the test for virginity and the throes of childbirth. In the first two cases, fears multiply among relatives that the girl will prove worthy and therefore able to proceed to the next phase of the series of rites. The crux of the matter here is not just apprehension about her ability to endure pain, but rather the apprehension that springs from the belief that if the girl is no longer a virgin, then some supernatural force will be invoked during the excision that will appear on the sharp point of the ritual knife and render it blunt. This force will cause the ritual knife to inflict a wound deeper than intended as an expression of ancestral wrath. It is only the timely application of propitiatory medication that acts on the extrasensory force to prevent further harm. The belief in *confessio parturientis*, very strong among the Yoruba, teaches that an adulterous expectant mother will suffer prolonged birth throes as long as she refuses to confess to her illicit affair. It is believed that as soon as she confesses her lapse, her suffering comes to an end. It is said that the shame of having to make such a confession serves as a deterrent for Kétu females.

The test of virginity also puts a great deal of pressure on the relatives. The ultimate test of their worth as a disciplined and cultured household depends on the success or acquittal of their maidens. The proof of virginity as well as the successful endurance of the pains of circumcision and childbirth effect the transition from girlhood to motherhood. Incidentally, the modern tendency to omit or shorten certain features of the rites has left these three instances untouched. Where circumcision is still practiced, and it is rare, the quasi magical belief pertaining to the suffering to be endured by initiands who have had precircumcision sex is still strong. It is, therefore, particularly appealing to suggest along with Richards (1956, 139) citing Schapera's view, that "magic rites tend to survive in contact with Europeanism, while religious ceremonies associated with moral values or prayers to ancestral spirits tend to be abandoned." However, I suggest that one should hesitate to draw this conclusion in reference to the Kétu. These three rites—the test of virginity, the endurance of the pains of circumcision and childbirth—promote the patrilineal ideology, loyalty to which is taken for granted in every Kétu who must subordinate his wishes to those of the lineage for his personal survival as well as that of the lineage. Here one is not dealing with the survival of a magic rite *per se*, as opposed to those other aspects of the ritual such as the liturgical or petitional. One is, instead, dealing with those elements that are bound to survive where the Kétu still perform the initiations that spring out of a body of beliefs that subordinate all lineage activities and values to the fundamental duty of survival.

Ikola-Abe in Relation to Kétu Dogma and Values
Kétu society—a conglomerate of quasiautonomous, exogamous lineages (Lloyd 1959), vertically united by the institution of kingship and horizontally linked together by marriage alliances, aims at achieving its survival. Thus, the *summum bonum* of the Kétu value system is procreation. The females who cooperate with lineage men to make procreation possible are given considerable preparation in order to ensure that they measure up to the standards expected of them.

Seniority is the first rule of ordering in Kétu society. Respect for elders is, therefore, the first canon of Kétu dogma. If they are to instil respect into their children, the females, who are their children's first teachers must show respect for their elders. Thus, in the ritual hut, it is important to discover to what extent the initiands are imbued with respect. Such a practice as passing the bowl containing ritual water from the eldest to the youngest initiand, or the constant repetition of a proverb, e.g., "A child cannot have more used clothes than his parents"—stresses the importance of showing deference for age.

Along with the circumcision rites, the rituals of installation of the king, the burial of an elder, as well as beliefs connected with hunting, form the basis of Kétu dogma and values. Such cultural practices and beliefs are the product of an essentially homogeneous body of beliefs. They all aim for the same goal.

The rites of installation end with a wish for the continued fertility of the soil, of animals, and of human beings. The king confirms his desire for fertility by joining the *gèlèdé* society, a cult devoted to the worship of the earth-goddess, the source of fertility. In the *gèlèdé* cult, the king, the chiefs, and all who wish to be protected from the destructive power of women, as well as all who seek children, come under the authority of the priestess of the earth goddess and her council of female elders. This priestess (*Iyáláshe*) offers sacrifices to propitiate the goddess and to induce her to bestow her blessings on their society. As a conclusion to her annual propitiation, Kétu men perform the transvestite *gèlèdé* dance to appease Kétu women.

The priestess of the earth goddess gives her approval to every lineage's desire to perform fertility rites for its girls and offers prayers on behalf of the girls. Also, in the context of installation, through her role handing the excised portion of the deceased king to his successor, the priestess shows Kétu women approval of the king-elect. Her refusal to perform the ritual would cause a constitutional crisis, as the king-elect would not be invested with the essence of kingship symbolized by the eating of the ritual portion. The other link between the kingship and the fertility rites is that the Kétu measure the success of a king's reign in terms of the blessings of fertility.

There is an equally strong link between a successful burial and fertility rites. After the announcement of a death by the booming of a gun, feasting begins, although not yet lavishly. The corpse is washed and treated medicinally to prevent immediate decomposition. The children and the relatives of the deceased come together to bury the corpse within the living quarters. As of the moment of burial, the deceased is in a precarious state of non-classification. He remains in this state until the children have indulged in prodigious feasting. Then, and only then, it is believed, will he be incorporated into the abode of the ancestors and have the opportunity to reincarnate. Hence, it is desirable that a Kétu have many children to discharge the socio-spiritual duty needed for his redemption.

There is an equally strong link between the Kétu hunter (as most men are) and his marriage. The Kétu believe that if a hunter is unfaithful to his wives, his hunting labors will not be required. They also hold the belief that if the wives engage in extramarital sex, their hunter-husband will be adversely affected. His wanderings will not be blessed with game, and when he does find game, his accuracy hitting the target will be impaired. Hunters who experience such setbacks offer sacrifices to propitiate the divinity of hunting (*Ògún*). It is believed that when next the husband goes hunting he will meet a mating pair of quarry, and the sex of the animal killed will indicate which of the human couples is responsible for the previous hunting failure. Amends are made by offering more sacrifices and by the offending partner's public confession.

What is the relevance of the recapitulation of Kétu beliefs and practices connected with rituals of kingship installation, burial, and hunting taboos to female fertility rites? The relevance has to do with the importance of women's cooperation of women for the proper performance of these acts and also for the smooth maintenance of the Kétu social order. Here, a premium is placed on a worldview that links survival of the group with the power of its members to procreate with the cooperation of women from other lineages. But the emphasis is not just on procreation, but on keeping the blood of the group pure by ensuring the extramarital sex, for the wife, is completely discouraged. This is achieved by placing both supernatural and natural sanctions against such acts. It is also achieved by making such an act represent a threat to the whole social fabric of Kétu society. Hunting and farming are the mainstays of life in this society. Yoruba food is regarded as neither complete nor satisfactory if it does not include meat, especially delicious portions of game. Also the credibility of the king's authority, based on ancestral sanctions, equally depends on fidelity in marriage and hence upon the cooperation of the royal wife for if the king-elect were to be the product of marital infidelity, not only would his bloodline be impure, but the essence of kingship and the qualities of the former king taken in through the instance of ritual cannibalism would be transmitted into the wrong body, an empty shell. This would spell doom for the group.

The second level of importance lies not in the need for a Kétu wife to keep the blood pure, but rather in her ability to procreate. Prayers, on most occasions, are concluded with

Olodumare do not let us see the debacle of famine,

> The king of the sky put away the danger of barrenness,
> Let the pregnant give birth to children,
> And let the sterile put their fingers in camwood (Abimbola 1976,5-6).(Author's translation)

The success of a king's reign is measured not solely in terms of the reactive peace of the society, but also in terms of the birth rate among his subjects. The qualifying spiritual test of the deceased lies in the great volume of feasting and sacrifices made on his behalf by his many children. The proper successor to the king as well as the hunter or the mark-giver should be the real son of the lineage. If an unfaithful wife deceptively introduced foreign blood into a lineage, she would undermine the wellbeing of all.

Seen against the backdrop of the source and motivation of such homogeneous beliefs, it becomes clear why the Kétu ìkolà-abę rites emphasize the desire to ensure, and to enhance, fertility. It also becomes clear why the rites place such emphasis on the need to remain a virgin if a maiden is to achieve social maturity. It also becomes clear why the lineage has such a stronghold on the family unit, and why it reduces the movement of its "wives" virtually to the circle of "the wives of the house"—*aya ìdílé*.

Kétu women have a strong contribution and a great influence on Kétu social order. To ensure the survival of the lineage, based as it is on cooperation with married females, the wives must be kept, controlled, and made to remain "pure." Excision distinguishes them from other women, the initiates having overcome the danger of impurity by not succumbing to premarital sex. They are then "our women," women who are pure, as opposed to the noncircumcised non-Kétu women, women who are impure. The test of virginity not only testifies to their purity but also glorifies them for subjecting themselves to men's control. Through this test Kétu men are able to set in motion the procreative capacity of their women, the only controllable natural aspect of the female (as compared with giving birth). In this way, the Kétu female is given the impression that that aspect of her being, which is so completely under her control, which makes her so indispensable to Kétu men, is made operative only through an appropriate Kétu male. This reduces the male feeling of gratitude and dependence on the female, making fertility, instead, the gift of the male to the female.

The Kétu ikola-abe and the other rites in the series provide an opportunity for the increase socialization of the Kétu girl. By ensuring that she lives up to her role expectations as wife and mother, the society procures the continuation of her special contribution, which is indispensable to the stability of the society. The process of socialization itself is built on the desire to pass on to coming generations the values, beliefs, expectations, and roles of the culture of any given group. Hence, if education is taken as "a process that attempts to ensure the cultural continuation of the group, race or nation ... transmitting skills, knowledge, modes of enquiry and values from the mature to the immature" (Gutek 1972, 11), then the Kétu rites of maturation are an example of a didactic cultural mechanism for exactly that transmission. The importance of marriage and procreation to the success of a king's reign, to the ascent of the dead to the privileged position of the ancestors, to the possibility of reincarnation, to success in hunting, and to successful communication with the ancestors only points to the importance of women in Kétu society.

The relationship and the social function of the ìkolà-abe:Ù to the institution of marriage itself appear to be clear. Ìkolà-abę occurs as a penultimate step to marriage. However, what is of more importance is the fact that the series of rites themselves express marriage ethics. The emphasis of such phrases as owo isíhùn—"payment for lifting the voice of the spouse"—as well as the customary behavior of the marriageable girl before the suitor are those of submission to the husband. The effective performance of her wifely roles is made the yardstick for measuring the calibre, and worth, not only of herself but also of her lineage. There surfaces then a "co-operation" of the men in all lineages to socialize their females in those roles that give the impression of subordination.

The rites also have undertones symbolically demonstrating the husband's duties. The suitors' ceremonial parade through the town, where they carry heavy bundles of firewood, does not merely announce the identity of would-be husbands of the initiands, but also confirms the obligations of the husband to the wife. The Kétu wife is a complete housewife. It is not her duty to till the land to support the family. It does not devolve on her even to fetch the firewood she will use as fuel. This used to be the task of the husband or the young boys until recently, when commercial advances relieved the husband of it and free primary education program absolved young boys of it. The duty of a wife was special and consisted in raising up the new members of the lineage in whose veins the pure blood of the ancestral line would flow. It is proof of the importance that Kétu culture gives to this role that guarantees the Kétu wife such a tremendous amount of time. This may also explain the resourcefulness of Yoruba women in petty trading as well as in other new ways of self-expression. It is this phenomenon that has led other writers to agree with Kenneth Little's conclusion that "the stereotype image of the African woman, as the down-trodden and oppressed does not fit Nigerian women" (Little 1979, 1760).

Unconscious Tensions and Conflicts

The patrilineal, virilocal Kétu society reveals certain tensions and paradoxes arising out of the characteristic features of its social structure. For a society committed to the patrilineal ideology, yet heavily reliant on females to make the working of the institutions possible, these tensions cannot fail to exist. The patrilineal ideology regards the male as the relevant sex for tracing descent and for the transmission of the rights of succession and inheritance. The implication is that only the birth of male children can ensure patrilineage survival. Yet female children are needed to create lineage alliances. Again, the natural impossibility of men to beget children on their own necessitates reliance on women to procreate. But the rule of exogamy compounds this masculine dependence powerlessness by putting a ban on female lineage members as possible spouses. This situation compels the Kétu male to look outside his lineage for a partner and also to carry out obligations designed to impress upon him his indebtedness to his wife-givers. In an effort to underplay this dependence and to make Kétu females feel privileged to have a husband, Kétu collective representations evolved a set of rites for maturation. In spite of efforts to conceal it, tension arising from the paradox of male dependence on females, and female subordination, have their overtones in the seclusion of the ritual hut where, surely, albeit temporarily, the female will triumph, shutting off, except for the one instance of "male" intrusion, the domineering world of the male. In the peace of the ritual hut, the female symbolic representation predominates.

The circular boundaries of the seclusion hut, women confirmed to my informant, offers the demarcating line of the point of refuge for females. In this sense—under the third property of symbol (the polarization of meaning), the hut possesses those two qualities of the symbolic motivation that Turner highlighted as the properties of ritual symbol.[1] It has both the sensory and the ideological poles. In terms of the sensory pole, it is a stockade of protection, a haven for weary women seeking solace from the taxing male domination within the larger society. From this vantage point, the Kétu ikola-abe transforms the girls into mothers who, in turn, act as sources of solace and refuge to their own children. The Yoruba make this an essential quality of motherhood and express it in a proverb that compares the conscientious mother to the hen protecting her chicks—"The good mother shelters her children as the hen covers up her children" (*Iyá òtító ràgà bo ọmọ rẹ bi ẹdiẹ ti nràgà bo awọn ọmọ rẹ*). The refuge quality of the ritual fence implies that the initiands are the source of refuge to their children.

At the ideological pole, the hut highlights the domain of the female as against the male. The sexual opposition and boycott implied in this is heightened by the ceremonial dumping of the firewood at the precincts of the hut. The thrice-repeated performance of fetching firewood signifies the intense struggle of the males to break into the female preserve. Their nonacceptance and the manner of their exit symbolizes male rejection and frustration and female triumph, however temporary, from the fact that the only male intrusion permitted is on female terms, the intruder slotting himself temporarily through transvestism into the female category. This point becomes clearer if it is known that mark-givers do not normally put on a female attire in order to perform their duties. The only instance of this practice is when they go into the female hut.

Yet shadows of the male linger, and male influences are felt within the hut. The ritual complex was built by male labor. The copious supplies of foodstuff were made available through male efforts. The center of the ritual activities is the *igi àgbo*—the tree on which is placed the medicinal pot from the ancestral shrine. The mark-giver, though temporarily and superficially "changed" remains in essence, a man. The excised parts of the initiands are buried on the ancestral grave site—the proximate sanctioning force of male domination. Even the contents of the fertility rites are heavily orientated toward pleasing the male. The salient features of its structure provide in effect, for the periodic cooperation of men in order to "boost" the maiden from one phase to another. Men initiate marriage and, when they meet with cooperation, remove Kétu girls from their prior state of asexuality. Once involved in the rites, the girls need men to gain access to a vigorous sexual life by being made "pure" through success in the test for virginity. Then through sexual union, they are made to conceive and become mothers.

In spite of these undertones of masculine presence in feminine affairs, there is an interesting paradox that comes out in the obligations of men in the ritual. They cluster together and wait anxiously for news about their maidens, as one male informant was reported to have said "like women." They are snubbed at the precincts of the hut instead of being allowed into it to receive praise for their dutiful concern. Finally, they retreat from the seclusion area with tremendous "loss of face." Such treatment, it is said, is associated in Kétu society with women not men. There is, then, the contrast, on the one hand, between the subordinate and unrewarding role of the husband as portrayed in the ritual, and, on the other hand, his commanding, controlling, and confident role and position in real life. On the one hand, there is the husband submitting to the pressures of his spouse's affinal relatives in the comfort of whose protection she is ensconced; on the other hand, there is in real life, a not-so-comfortable or protected wife in the foreign milieu of her husband's lineage. Again, on the one hand, there is a submissive husband working without reward and accepting the fact of frustration, while there is, in real life, the over-bearing husband.

Perhaps these paradoxes originate from an attempt by Kétu culture to redress the balance, at least in the sphere of symbolism, by drawing attention to and giving recognition to male reliance on the female. Kétu culture gives prominence to the diligent mother, but denies her claim to the ownership of the child in order to strengthen the tenuous male claim to ownership. This denial is necessary because, try as man may to claim complete ownership, the woman naturally feels a stronger sense of social immortality and ownership of her children in a way a man cannot. Morton-Williams has put this point clearly in reference to the Yoruba stress on the cult of *egúngún*—representatives of the ancestral spirit—when he wrote:

Men may have *egungun* which guarantee them a social immortality. Women do not. Ordinarily, a woman is assured of a form of immortality through her children. She sees her pattern of life repeated in that of her daughters. In this patrilineal society children belong to the father's and not the mother's lineage; but the mother has experienced both the continuity of her own identity (in spite of changes of residences) and also the recurrence of motherhood however many begetters her several children may have had. I think it is true that a mother sees her immortality in this during her own life-time, while the Yoruba man needs the assurance that grandsons will perpetuate his memory. (1960, 37)

Cultural attempts to establish that guarantee coincides with those aimed at corroding the naturally felt strong sense of assurance of the female. This attempt to unseat female assurance so as to establish that of the male reaches its climax among the Kétu and some groups of the Yoruba with the rite performed after the death of an elderly woman. This rite requires

the dead woman's eldest daughter to lead her other children to a part of the open country outside the town, there to take a last farewell of their mother's *egungun* which, after this single encounter, will never appear again. Socially, this ensures that the male ancestors dominate, at the cost of denying to women the assurance of distinctively

tively individual immortality in any form, except that of
reincarnation in a descendant (ibid, 37)

Perhaps it is to make up for this stern treatment meted out to women
that the paradoxes are not underplayed but remain striking in the
ritual series.

Sex hostility shows clearly in the ìkolà-abẹ́. The boundary
lines of the ìkolà-abẹ ritual hut creates a group within a group,
with the females in the hut representing the female militant. The
hut reverses the normal order of things. It posits the importance
of the female sex, as against the unimportance of the male, as the
proximate source of authority and a certain type of inner knowledge, superior because no equivalent maturing rite of seclusion is
available to Kétu young men. The females in the hut are so
strong as to afford to be independent of men, temporarily rejecting their overt control and instituting norms of self-regulation to
which all must submit, whatever their sex, if they are to be considered at all for participation in the special life of the hut. The
hostile line comes out clearly in the challenge of songs in which
the representatives of both sexes trade abuse and cynical statements. The challenge ends with no victor, a silent cultural testimony that neither side can stand alone, but each needs the cooperation of the other.

Pragmatic Effects
Besides the expressed aims, primary and secondary, verbalized
by the actors, Kétu rites produce certain effects both in the mind
of the individual as well as on the group. In the mind of the girl,
who until now has been sheltered from any great experiences of
fear, save the fear arising from small transgressions, the strong
apprehensions and fear concerning the dangers associated with
going through the ritual form quite a new experience. For, while
she may be confident, if she has observed Kétu sexual mores,
about the outcome of the test of virginity, she has no such assurance for the accurate and successful performance of the other
tasks that are important to the transition. Fears about her capacity to master the art of cookery and to remember the tortuously long
oriki songs may set her mind in turmoil. These fears are characteristic of "the marked stage" (Richards 1956, 162). For the girl, this

stage points to the fact that things are no longer the same. There is a gradual change from the old stage of dependence, from sheltered security to a new, not yet defined stage. This marked stage prepares her mind to appreciate privileges that will accrue and to believe that she is no longer what she used to be—a girl.

The ordeals of endurance at excision and of giving birth are part of the ritual acts that enhance the growth and introduce a sort of qualitative change in her life. These acts also convince the Kétu that the change in her life has really taken place, and that the initiands have proved themselves to be not only productive, but to have also shown positive tendencies for coping with the strains of married life in the future. The successful completion of such acts infuses a considerable amount of confidence into the initiand, who is now able to count her successes and look to the future with more fortitude and willpower. The feeling of confidence she gains is akin to that of one who has newly acquired a driving license. She goes agitatedly to the testing ground with a driving instructor at her side and, once in the car, nervously clutches the steering wheel with both hands. When successful, she insists on driving back confidently steering the vehicle with only one hand.

The parade of the initiands to the female kin's house on the day of seclusion announces to the community the imminence of marriage, which is also a sign of readiness for motherhood. The similar parade by the men makes an institutional claim on the maidens. The Kétu, unlike the Ashanti, do not wait until the completion of the nubility rites to display their girls in the hope of gaining recognition of their marriageability as well as attracting possible suitors. The lateness of the Kétu rites has given ample opportunity for this. The rites confirm the advanced stage of the marriage negotiations. Also the "dance of departure" (*bolojo*) gives Kétu society the chance to admire as well as to praise and reward Kétu girls for their endurance and good character. This praise spills over to the lineage and finally develops into a profession of faith in the ancestors for keeping the girls safe, that is, by replenishing their sources of inner strength that has prevented them from submitting to the wishes of young men who would have destroyed their chances of going through the ritual successfully. In aiding the lineage daughters in this way, the ancestors have prevented them from dragging the name of the lineage into the mud. What is more important, of course, is that by becoming mothers, the daughters have confirmed the power of fertility inherent in the lineage and infused by the ancestors. Through the daughters, the ancestors continue to bestow on the lineage the power to aid other lineages in their struggle for survival.

The Importance of Ikolà-Abẹ: to Kétu Fertility Rites

The restricted form of the ritual activities connected with *ikolá-abẹ́* (circumcision) in the whole series of rites would suggest to observers that it has probably been given an importance beyond its worth or due. While observers may well feel justification in focusing on circumcision itself in isolation, they definitely would not have acquired an understanding of motive that leads the Kétu to see it as the center of the rites. Until this is done, if the observers are ethnographers, they cannot be regarded as having made an adequate study of the ritual.

The Kétu look on the *ikolá-abẹ́* as standing for something other than itself. It may be described as the metaphysic, the essence of an institution central to all the aspects of Kétu social structure, and basic to all other institutions of Kétu society. In this way, the meaning of ikolà-abẹ́ cannot be obtained by focussing simply on the circumcision alone. In the foregoing, an attempt has been made to show its many ramifications—religious, moral, and political, i.e. as an instrument of social control—as well as its enormous importance as a didactic mechanism responsible for the transmission of the group's history and values. Seen in this structural relationship to the religious, political and moral institutions of the Kétu, it becomes clear that ikolà-abẹ́ is a simple, tangible act that points to something not tangible, not visible, yet real and highly valuable. Like an important feature of the emblem mechanism in Bemba *chisungu*, it provides a fixed form, a model that points to the multiple tenets of the various institutions of Kétu society. As Kenyatta wrote, "clitoridectomy, like Jewish circumcision, is a mere bodily mutilation, however, is regarded as the *conditio sine qua non* of the whole teaching of tribal law, religion and morality" (1932, 128).

But why clitoridectomy and not emblems like those of the *mbusa* of the Bemba? The answer to this question will involve not only a consideration of the different opinions about *ìkolá-abẹ́* but also a look at the Kétu idea of sacrifice. The reasons given for the practice of excision vary widely. Some men, claimed my informant, stated that it was a practice ordained by the ancestors, hence is was the right thing to do; and that no well-bred Kétu would take to wife a maiden who has not had her excision. Other men stated that it was dangerous not to have the excision because it is taboo for the head of the baby to touch the part of the clitoris that is not excised at childbirth. Other men, tending not to be as subtle as the as those in the first two groups, said rather bluntly: "We do it to prevent our girls from flirting" (*Aṣe ki awọn obìnrin wa ma ba jẹ oníṣekúṣe*).

The first statement hardly amounts to a convincing argument, but is the subjective evaluation of men who believe that only ordination from the ancestors can transform a young female into a woman. The second statement, which stresses the taboo, is as fastidious as the taboo that warns a Kétu child that holding knives too close to his teeth will cause the growth of two many teeth. This second taboo is a charter of security to the playful child to stop him from hurting himself, just as the first taboo is a charter for male control over female erotic desires; hence, it is akin to the blunt reply "We do it to stop them from flirting." These do not constitute positive reasons; for those we must look elsewhere.

An informant, Papa Alao, stated that all the women he interviewed, together with a few elders, agreed that the excision is done so as to give back to the source of life a bit of that part of the human body that stands for fertility, hence, ensuring an abundance of fertility in return. It is, therefore, an immolative prestation to the giver of fertility. Among the Kétu, sacrifices abound, and as Talbot confirmed:

> They are made on every conceivable occasion and for almost every imaginable purpose, but chiefly in connection with the production of fertility in man, flocks and fields and with the worship of the forefathers who themselves are however perhaps mainly placated on account of that control over the reproduction forces of nature.

But for those sacrifices made to placate Esu (the trickster chief-constable of the divinities), sacrifices like the piacular ones with their characteristic prophylactic and apotropaic features, so well documented among the Nuer by Evans-Pritchard (1956, 275), are made in thanksgiving, in propitiation, in transvaluation—e.g, the exchange of the life of the victim for the life of the man (Lienhardt, 1961, 239) as well as one man dying vicariously on behalf of the whole society. The motives of Kétu sacrifice are so varied that they are difficult to summarize up in a nutshell. Evans Pritchard's remark regarding the Nuer may fit the Kétu;

> to sum up the meaning of Nuer piacular sacrfices in a simple word scarcely does justice to the very complex set of ideals they express. We have found it necessary to use a variety of words in speaking of them; communion gift, apotropaic rite, bargain, exchange, ransom, elimination, expulsion, purification, expiation, substitution, abnegation, homage and others. According to situation and particular purpose, one element in this complex of meaning may be stressed in one rite and another element in another rite, or there are shifts in emphasis from one part of the sacrificial rite to another. (1956,282)

The motive for the sacrificial prestation, made in the context of fertility, aims at producing fertility in abundance. The very fact that no social event is complete without including a wish for the abundance of fertility for human, animal, and plant life is only an indication of its importance to the Kétu. Just as the "ox and more particularly the bull, are for the Dinka creatures in which vitality is especially abundant" (Lienhardt 1961, 56)—hence, making them the most suitable animals to sacrifice in petitioning for fertility—female genitalia are, for the Kétu, the ultimate source of life and symbol of fertility. The immolation of a part of female genitalia is, therefore, seen as ideal prestation for the abundance of fertility. The intended result of such prestation is the abundance of fertility in the females whose parts have been excised and immolated. The principle of the operation of this sacrificial prestation is built on that of Marcel Mauss' notion of prestation and counterprestation. Mauss corrected the idea of counter prestation[2] in which a Maori hunting ritual practice ordains the ceremonial return of certain game birds to *mauri*, housing the *hau* of the forest, which causes game birds to proliferate, in the hope that the birds will reproduce in abundance in the future for the hunters. Hau is a metaphysical sanction against the recipient of a gift who fails to reciprocate. This operative principle is applicable to the Kétu idea of immolation of the excised part. Ellis who confirmed this principle (even before Mauss popularized the Maori concept of *hau*), wrote:

> Circumcision among the Yorubas, as among the Ewes, is connected with the worship of Elegba, and appears to be a sacrifice of a portion of the organ which the god inspires to ensure the well-being of the remainder. (1893, 66)

If one were to consider only the views and reasons advanced by Kétu men as the sole motivating factors for circumcision, one would be left with a poor, uninspiring, and negative understanding of the practice. One would have concluded, with some justification, that it is only a means concocted and supported by men for social control of females. However, the female- orientated explanation of circumcision as a sacrificial prestation lifts the ritual practice from the merely political and mundane to the spiritual, and accords it a mark of positivity.

The tendency to shed a small amount of blood and offer up a part of the living body to the source of life in order to receive the blessing of abundance of life in return is not peculiar to the rites alone. It is a feature of other Kétu practices. The practice of putting marks on the face, quite apart from its use as a means of classification in the society, much in line with the totem, also includes this sacrificial overtone. At the on-set of life a child sheds a part of himself and some of his blood so demonstrating that as life flows in blood to the ancestors, more life returns in abundance to the donor. Facial marks are important partly for this reason. Yoruba who did not have marks were ridiculed as either too poor to pay for the mark-giver's services or too sickly to withstand the risk of the slightest bloodshed.

This phenomenon constitutes a significant point of difference between the Kétu and the Ashanti, who consider circumcision and tooth extraction physical deformities that deplete the personality of the individual and disqualify the individual from taking traditional office. (Sarpong 1977, 12) Among the Kétu, the royal family has its distinctive marks, and not having marks is a sign of uncertain origin, which disqualifies people who may aspire to traditional office.

Color Symbolism

Three colors feature prominently in the rites; white, red, and black. Initiands wear black garments in the seclusion hut. Their foreheads are marked in red with a lump of camwood at the completion of the period of seclusion, after which the initiands change from black to white attire.

The point of interest about Kétu color symbolism is that none of these colors can be said to be completely inauspicious or completely good, as each color exhibits both positive and negative associations. It is the context of association that determines their value in any given ritual. Normally, the Kétu associate the color white with the Supreme Being whom they refer to as the "King who spreads to all the corners of the earth and who is the essence of the whiteness of the above (*Ọba atẹ́rẹ̀rẹ̀ kaiye, alálà funfun òkè*). In this context, it symbolizes purity, power, and honesty. The Yoruba way of attesting to honesty in another is to say: *Inu re mọ* (*mọ* being another word for *funfun*), that is, "his mind is clean" or "white." When they say that one is a good man, they mean that one is begotten by God, that is a "child of God" (*Ọmọluwàbí*). Hence, the red chalk mark on the forehead together with the white clothes worn after the completion of the seclusion period symbolize the new state of purity-yet-to-be-made-complete, that is, purity in potency and also the power deriving from the support of the ancestors.

The milky-white color has different symbolic import. It can be taken to symbolize sperm—*àtọ*—which, Kétu understanding contains the miniature child injected into the woman, where—given the right conditions—it grows to its normal size. In this context it is still auspicious. But milky-white can also be associated with palm-wine, a beverage tapped from raffia and palm oil trees, that is notorious for its intoxicating power. In Yoruba mythology, it is accursed as the cause of ill luck. This is related to the legend about the creation of the universe in which Ọbàtálá (*Òrìṣà nlá*), the divinity delegated to create the earth, became intoxicated as a result of drinking palm-wine, proving himself unworthy to perform this noble task, whereupon it was accomplished by his younger brother.

In the context of giving birth, red is auspicious; it is the source of life. Yet in the context of war (and the Yoruba saw a great deal of it in the nineteenth century), it is the sign of death, since as blood flows from the wounds, life flows out with it. Black stands for the inauspicious and is associated with the night, with the dark, and with death. But black, too can stand for positivity. It is again associated with sex, as it is only at night that the Kétu who are mostly farmers, believe it should take place. Through sexual intercourse new life is born. These, then, are the symbolic associations of color for the Kétu. In the rites, all these aspects are present, including that built on the milky-white color of palm-wine, always in great demand at marriage feasts and at the naming ceremonies.

Perhaps nothing gives a better testimony to the complimentarity of colors in Kétu symbolism than the Yoruba maxim *Ninu ikòkò dudu ni ẹkọ funfun ti njáde*—It is from the black pot that the white corn porridge comes out (i.e., cooks).

Numerical Symbolism

Ever since Durkheim and Mauss drew attention to the numerous symbolic classification of ethnic groups and societies into moieties as marriage and totemic classes (1963, trans.), interest has grown in studying the symbolism of numbers. Rodney Needham wrote an influential study (1979) along this line. Using a comparative cultural context, he showed the symbolic ways in which societies are partitioned among other such classificatory categories: into dualism—with the instances of the Chinese *Ying* and *Yang*, and the North American Miwok Indians' water and land; into triadic or tripartite division—based on dualistic categories separated by an ambiguous marginal zone, an instance of which is found among the Kaguru (living persons/ ghosts/God); and into four—with the Kariera of western Australia as a case in point. A study of Kétu numeral symbolism is equally revealing.

Kétu numerical symbolism is basically triadic. The suitors bring their heavy bundles of firewood near the seclusion hut thrice daily for the first three days after the operation of excision. The maidens change their black dresses three times. The wife-taking entourage makes two attempts before succeeding on the third. Kétu cosmology is tripartite with two basic categories; the sky, "the abode of the divinities, the Deity and the ancestors" separated from the earth, "the home of the living" by a third, ambiguous intervening state, where the not-to-be-integrated (the damned, in Kétu view) as well as the yet-to-be-integrated deceased roam permanently or temporarily as the case may be.

Since hierarchy is the abiding feature of Kétu social order and respect for it the dogma of Kétu spiritual and mundane behavior, Needham's suggestions that "the partition into opposites is maintained and given expression by interposition of an ambiguous type of category (1979, 9) carry illuminating weight. Among the Kétu, this partitioning is done to attest to the superiority of the abode of divinities to the abode of the living. This is not surprising because

> a further point of interest in this form of dual classification is that in each pair, one category is defined in some respect as superior to the other. The conceptual unity of the contextual genus is expressed . . through the mode of dual inequality. The dual division thus not only classifies; it also provides for a ranking of categories. (1979, 8-9)

But the symbolic associations of the number three are not reduced to streamlining, and the ranking of the categories that it separates is a basically dualistic system. In Judaism it signifies infinitude, hence the meaning of a biblical extract like: "For the three crimes of Damascus . . .for the three crimes of Gaza . . ."(Amos, Chapter 1) is that "for the many sins of Damascus and Gaza." For the Kétu, three stands for finality. Every hardship should be given three trials of endurance, after which it may be abandoned without any loss of face. This also accounts for the tendency among Kétu to resolve very serious marital difficulties until after the third break-up. Then the Kétu say that there can be no amends made, because *òrò na ti gun igi kòjá ewé* "the matter has climbed the tree up to the leaves and beyond".

Here, then, is the semantic symbolic field of the Kétu use of the number three. It ranks the two basic categories of the Kétu worldview in the superior and inferior order, thereby highlighting the need for the respect shown to the "above" separated from the "below." On the other hand, it teaches the lessons of endurance and courage to the Kétu, provided that courage does not degenerate into foolhardiness.

The Adequacy of Richards' Model

Richards' model has proved useful for the interpretation of the series of rites. An attempt has been made to keep to the main outline of the model as far as the Kétu data and the unique circumstances surrounding them permit. The fact that Bemba society is matrilineal, while Kétu is patrilineal introduces a strong element of difference. Strains peculiar to each ideology (matrilineal and patrilineal) emerge. This vital difference provokes two questions of theoretical interest: (a) Applying the premises of analysis Richards' model to the series of rites, what conclusions emerge? (b) How do these conclusions agree or disagree with those of Richards? Before answering these questions, it will improve analysis to briefly state the similarities and dissimilarities between the Bemba chisungu and the Kétu *ikolá-abé*.

The Chisungu and the Kétu Fertility Rites

The differences in certain aspects of the social structures notwithstanding, chisungu and Kétu *ikolá-abé* stress some identical social expectations. They both point to the importance and the goal of marriage for which they prepare their candidates. For their initiates, symbolic tests, which, successfully performed, certify that the transition from the immature asexuality of childhood to the mature sexuality of adulthood has been made. The rites convince their societies that the candidates are ready to be invested with adult responsibilities and, thus, to be accepted into the adult category. Both ceremonies focus on the socially approved roles of the adult female and insist, for different reasons, that the wife show respect for her husband. On the one hand, for the Bemba, this insistence is an act aimed at placating the husband, forced to live in "foreign" marital surroundings and deprived of the right of ownership of his children. On the other hand, for the Kétu, the ritual is, it is suggested, a subtle means of turning the "giver" into the "recipient," the strong

165

into the "weak," in order to reduce the level of gratitude due to the female whose cooperation is vital to lineage survival. Among the exogamous, matrilineal, matrilocal/uxorilocal Bemba, a man from another lineage is needed to help in procreation; among the exogamous patrilineal, patrilocal/virilocal Kétu, a female from another lineage is required. Yet, neither the Bemba husband nor the Kétu wife can make claims of ownership to the child.

CONCLUSION

The preceding chapters have shown the importance of Kétu girls' fertility rites to that society's social institutions. This study has necessitated the exploration of Kétu kinship practices and beliefs connected with fertility, as well as the explanation of Kétu ideas concerning sacrifice. The ceremonies that characterize these rites have a symbolic structure peculiar to the rites of passage. Some relevant key elements of Richards' model have provided a guide for the interpretation of the series of Kétu fertility rites. In line with the categories of that model, the explicit purpose expressed in Richards' terms, the "primary purpose" of the rites was to enhance fertility in the Kétu girl, such fertility being vital to the survival of the society.

As shown, men and women have a different understanding of the meaning of circumcision, an operation that is central to the fertility rites. The procedure of understanding the persistence of circumcision in many African societies has taxed the imagination of many scholars, as well as observers in other professions (Worsley 1948; Hills-Young 1949; Butt-Thompson 1929; Schultz 1975; Hosken 1979; Ogunmodede 1979; Matherson 1979). The operation itself dates back about two thousand years to the Coptic female circumcision practice (Lane 1944, 60; Briffault 1927, 323; Hansen 1972, 2). Some centuries later, conflict arose within the ranks of the then influential Coptic (Catholic) church between the strong Egyptian desire for the continuation of the practice of clitoridectomy among the Coptic Christians and the equally great desire of the missionaries to suppress it. In an attempt to resolve the issue, Rome commissioned representatives to look closely into the background of the practice and make their recommendations. These people came to the conclusion that:

> The heat of the climate, or some other natural cause, did
> in that particular nation, invariably alter the formation, so
> as to make a difference from what was ordinary in the sex
> in other countries; and that the difference did occasion a
> disgust, which must impede the consequences for which
> matrimony was instituted. (Bruce, HRAF, 5, quoted by
> Johns 1975,8)

As a result of their consideration, the Church ruled that "the imperfection was, by all means to be removed" (ibid). Thus, this ancient ruling seemed to have outlined the official attitude of the Catholic Church to the practice of circumcision.[3]

Among those societies that practice circumcision, there is a great deal of variation in the type and the time of the operation. The Igbo circumcise their female babies between the third and eighth day (Taylor 1970, 10). The Yoruba circumcise girls shortly before marriage (Bascom 1969, 61). Arabs circumcise girls in the first few weeks after birth (Worsley 1938, 691). Sudanese groups perform the operation between the ages of four and ten (Hills-Young 1949, 13). In old Egypt, circumcision was performed between the ages of three and eight, and in modern Egypt, between six and eight years (Worsley 1938, 691). The Somali practice two types of operations on the female genitals; they perform the clitoridectomy at three years and the other, more extreme operation, infibulation, at ten years (Worsley 1938, 691; Kennedy 1970, 175; Zanotelli 1971, 53-4).

The degree of severity of the operation varies from society to society. For example, the Kétu remove the prepuce. The Gikuyu excise the clitoris and cut away part of the *labia minora*, while others—like the Somalis—perform a more extreme type of operation, infibulation. But, however minor the operation, it is clear that it involves intense suffering and considerable medical risk (Hills-Young 1949; Laycock 1950, 446; Bunch 1990, Rosenthal 1992, 1993). The task of the observer is to discover why, in the twentieth century and in societies where some traditional practices or customs seem to have given way in the face of social change, that such operations still continue to be performed.

The answer, at least among the Kétu, is to be found in the meaning of these rites for the participants. It is not sufficient to explain the continued practice of clitoridectomy from the point of view of a society where females are subordinate and act as coagents of their own suppression. As we have seen, Kétu society has an ideology of male dominance although females are equally prominent in specific areas. Since there is a rigid division of labor accorded to the sexes, the female position is not one of inferiority because the separation of roles creates the need for mutual dependence and respect. The evidence suggests that the Kétu continue this practice because it satisfies certain powerful motives in the experience of both men and women.

Most anthropologists who have interested themselves in this topic have been men. Those who were not were fed with data provided by male informants. Kétu men, like men in most societies that have been studied, explain clitoridectomy as a means of controlling women's sexual behavior, and certain female observers seem to echo this view (Ogunmodede 1979, 30; Taylor 1970, 15; Johns 1975, 9). The generality of this interpretation throughout the literature only partly explains the persistence of the practice. The data on the Kétu, however, suggest that we can only understand it by learning how women justify the practice. Kétu women see circumcision (ìkolá-abẹ́) on the deeper ritual level that is best explained in terms of Mauss' idea of counterprestation. They explain that the excised part was given back to the "source of fertility" in order that the giver may receive, in return, blessings that would make her fertile. Thus, in the case of the Kétu initiate, the testimony of counterprestation is the birth of the child. This event decidedly alters her status from an unclassified asexual youth to the ensconced sexual adult and a complete woman.

Although emphasis in African development programs has, among other things, been placed on population control, the fear of infertility is, in fact, a more serious concern in most African societies and numbers of authorities have commented on the fear of impotence and infertility (Richards 1956; Ardener 1962; Harrell-Bond 1972; Liell, Okedeji, Trowt and Vlachos 1965; Okedeji and Okedeji 1966; Okedeji 1967, 1968; Olusanya 1967, 1968, 1970). It is natural that in a society whose collective representations force a link between fertility and the practice of circumcision, people who are desperate for children will submit themselves to the risks and intense pain implied in having the operation.

It should be recalled that the excised part is given as sacrifice to the ancestral shrine in the belief that the ancestor will present them to the source of fertility so as to obtain blessings of fertility for the initiates. I am reliably informed that in Sierra Leone, the excised part is ritually cooked and served in a sacrificial meal to the initiates upon graduation, and that a small quantity of the meal is served to certain favored men as a protection against infertility. Thus, even today, the practice of circumcision continues not only among the Yoruba in the rural areas, but also among those in urban centers and among people with a fair amount of formal education (Ogunmodede 1979, 31). The only variation being in the age at which it tends to be performed; for those in more urban centers, about the age of fifteen when schoolgirls tend to drift away from home in search of jobs.

Besides studying the reasons provided for the continuation of the practice of circumcision, effort has been made in this work to examine the functions the series of rites perform. While looking at these functions (keeping to the guideline provided by Richards' model), the intention was not to treat the rites in terms of status change alone. To paraphrase Levi-Strauss, an ethnographer who stops with the enumeration of such features is like Moses standing at the point where he could take a good look at the promised land of deep ritual analysis but never actually getting there (1966, 37). Accordingly, different meanings have been deduced by considering the rites from a varying number of viewpoints.

The rites involve the instruction of the initiates. They affirm the accepted standards of morality and good behavior. They stress the duties of a husband to his wife and those of the wife to her husband. The function of the go-between (*alárenà*) and her special relationship with the initiate may be seen as a means of integrating the young wife into her new home. Thus, the rites emphasize that the socialization of the girls for their new roles as wives is a continuing process.

The series of rites also provide entertainment and the means for re-ordering the rank of the families in the society. Each phase of the series concludes with feasting, together with much dancing and eating, characteristic of Yoruba ceremonies. The feasting has direct bearing on the allocation of rank in the society. When opulent provisions are provided for the feeding of those in seclusion, the mistress of ceremonies and her assistants spread the news of the wealth of the particular patrilineages sponsoring the feasts. Publicity of this kind enhances the rating of the lineages concerned. Feasting occurs on the day of the "dance of departure", on the day of the marriage, and on the day of the naming ceremony for the first child. If those feasts are regarded as good, that is, if participants had an abundance to eat and to drink, the lineages that hosted those feasts gain more prestige. If the feasts are poor, there is a decline in the prestige of the lineage involved.

In terms of political control, certain aspects of the rites have been related to the lineage need for survival and its dependence on females from their lineages. Through the transfer of females, alliance relationships occur. Such alliances give rise to extralineage cooperative activities that support the rather weak, over-arching authority of the king (ǫba) over the intensely exclusive Kétu lineages. Thus, Kétu women form a means for articulating political control. The existence of such alliances, and the obligations they entail, are given expression in the rites through the involvement of all graduands of former rites as sponsors of the girls in seclusion. To perform their services from their lineage, the married graduands temporarily withdraw their services to the lineages of their husbands. Such withdrawal leads to a temporary but accepted paralysis of activities within the lineages of the "wife-takers." In this way, the obligations of affinal relatives are underlined, and the members of the larger society associate themselves with the aspirations of the initiates. Through this involvement, people outside the seclusion hut are drawn into the ceremony. Thus, as social categories, those men and women not directly related to the initiates act in organized groupings within the realm of the ritual to achieve the rebirth of their daughters or wives through the rites enacted in the seclusion hut. Their participation may be in the form of active involvement symbolized in the thrice-daily dumping of firewood bundles close to the seclusion hut, or it may be expressed in the unquestioned acceptance of the withdrawal of their wives' services.[4]

The series of rites have also given an insight into the tensions and conflicts inherent in the society. Thus sexual hostility is expressed in the form of female resistance to male domination. In the ritual continuum, the dominant place of women as against the "muted" place of men is a feature that contrasts with the position of the sexes in a real-life situation. Yet such a dominant position is not restricted to the fertility rites alone but finds correspondence in some other Kétu rituals that are performed either to placate women considered to be powerful or to neutralize the efficacy of the power of those women considered to be witches. Thus, the *gèlèdè* ritual dance is performed to appease women beyond menopause who are regarded by the Yoruba as having potentially dangerous powers. It is implied that, having been placated, such elderly women will use their powers for the good of the society. Also, the *Orò* cult performs rites aimed at giving public correction to erring women. When such public corrections fail, the cult members carry off the suspected women and put them to death. Morton-Williams has drawn attention to the tendency of Yoruba men, at moments of crisis, to vent their frustration on some marginal female figures in the community.

The symbolic field of the Kétu is dominated by women, either actively or passively. It is, I suggested, in agreement with Audrey Richards, that in the fertility rites, the paradox of female importance to the Kétu social structure and female muteness finds expression and temporary resolution. To appreciate the depth of analysis that explains this resolution between the Kétu male/female relationship, I refer to Ardener's model of the "wild."

Ardener used his model of "the wild" to demonstrate the technical and analytical problems inherent in the anthropologist's tendency to "crack the code of a vast range of societies without any direct reference to the female group" even when studying matters pertaining to females. Because of their dominance in certain societies, men band themselves and their females in the group of culture. Everything outside this category (including roles unique to females) is looked upon by men as belonging to 'the wild' and classified with nature. With this classification, men inadvertently place their women ambiguously in the margins of their own society. Once placed in that margin, women become—in terms of Douglas' *Purity and Danger* (1966)—both sacred and polluting. Yet women feel differently about what men take their views to be. It is in symbolism that the female view finds uninhibited expression. Figure 1 serves as an illustration of this.

Figure 1

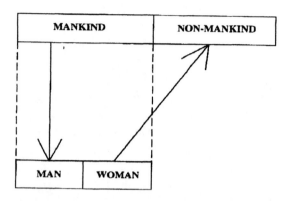

Edwin Ardener's Model of the "Wild" in Belief and the Problem of Women. See M. Chapman Edwin Ardener: *The Voice of Prophecy. Oxford*: Blackwell 1989.

Kétu men, who are dominant in this patrilineal society, assume the right to enunciate their views as representative of those of Kétu society. They speak for Kétu women, who are expected to be seen and not heard. Thus, as wives, they are bound together with the males in the category of culture since it is the men who determine what is the norm. As mothers, though they are "muted," they appear as central to the male-bounded world. As dominant figures in rituals, however, Kétu females belong to the wild and are, on that account, dangerous—targets of the defensive ritual activities of males. It is in the ritual activities such as in the *gèlèdè* and the fertility rites, that Kétu women become the dominant figures, while their men accept the muted position. Thus, from the bounded world of female domination, expressed as *matrifocality*, the "wild" of men becomes the preserve of women (James 1979). As Ardener suggests, the "totality of symbolism" of any given society is the sum total of the symbolic representations contributed by the different classes of male and female as groups of all ages and sexes.

In Figure 2, the larger circle surrounding the two smaller ones shows the totality of the symbolic representation of the Kétu society. The largely unshaded small circle represent that of Kétu males.

Figure 2

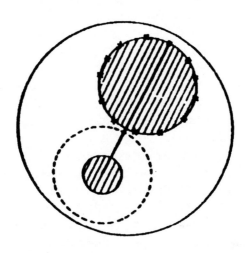

_____Population considered in models based on observation

--------- -Population considered in models based on talking about observation from men's viewpoint

x x x x x Population considered in models based on talking about observation from a matrifocal view

/ / / / / / The place occupied and dominated by females

Concentric with the circle, representing the male worldview is a central shaded area occupied by the Kétu female as a mother. In this location, the role of the Kétu female is essential to the desire of the Kétu male to effect the continuity of his lineage. It is a sacred place set out to acknowledge the genetricial resources of the female and within this sphere, also linked with the domestic, female power is felt. The place of the female Kétu after menopause or as a witch, is in "the wild" of the male-bounded world.

The shaded smaller circle within the larger one stands for the female symbolic representation. It is the area of female dominance and male mutedness. It is revealed in symbolism and on ritual occasions when the male-generated views are temporarily ignored. It is the area of female preserve to which men are admitted on female terms. The line drawn to connect the areas of female preponderance easily shows that the power of women is not restricted to the female area of dominance. It is also felt in the domestic and genetricial spheres of the male world. Of course, both the shaded and unshaded circles form the sum total of the symbolic world of the adult Kétu sexes. The crux of the matter is not, Which model is dominant? Rather, the germane question is: "How do both models contribute to resolve the conflict arising from different views about the world?" The answer to this question may be obtained from the use of another paradigm.

Examined in terms of the paradigm of Yoruba kingship, the relation of the sexes to resolve conflicts becomes interesting. A unique feature of the Yoruba kingship is that the king (*oba*) is not an absolute ruler (Atanda 1973; Morton-Williams 1962, 1964). Ruling is in the hands of the chiefs. Yoruba tradition hedges the king with taboos and places the administration of the towns on the chiefs. The chiefs rule in a way that gives the impression that the king is the all-powerful ruler—and not his chiefs. In the same way, Kétu women know that certain specific areas of activities in Kétu society are virtually controlled by them. They give birth to and raise their children, who carry on the names of the lineages. Kétu women are the chiefs, while their husbands are in the position of the king. Perhaps, in self-defense at the perceived power of women, Kétu men treat their women as if they were subordinate and perform many rituals to counteract the magical power of women. Kétu women know that their men believe that they (the women) are subordinate and powerless. Kétu women allow their men to bask in this belief because they know that power in certain spheres is in their hands. If this power is to be retained, it will be in the interests of Kétu women to make their men believe that they (men) are dominant. Thus, the idea of male dominance becomes a mythical charter proffered by females in order to retain their power. This attitude receives confirmation in Susan Carol Rogers' study of a Guatemalan community (1975, 727). Summarizing the latest studies on women's status, Quinn quoted Rogers as saying:

> Male dominance myths, far from reflecting women's over-
> all low status, arise precisely because women have con-
> siderable economic importance, personal autonomy and
> domestic influence (1977, 219).

Theoretical Interests
Seen against the backdrop of its religious, economic, political, and socializing functions, Kétu ìkolà-abẹ is an example of what Marcel Mass terms the "total social phenomenon." Since Richards' model has been used as the basis to interpret the Kétu fertility rites, it is of theoretical interest to note how far her conclusions are applicable to the Kétu.

> 1. Much of the magical and petitioning acts in the rites as
> well as the immolative principle behind excision, which
> aims at ensuring the fertility of the graduands, find corre-
> spondence in the Bemba Casing. This correspondence
> supports Richards' idea that in tribal societies women were
> taken as being responsible for failure to bear children. This
> point is buttressed by the fact that Kétu boy circumcision
> takes place when they are three weeks old, and not in the
> context of marriage. No magical rites of fertility are per-
> formed for the boys, as they are considered to be naturally
> fertile.

> 2. If the imputation of infertility goes in the opposite di-
> rection as the rule of descent (i.e., if, in patrilineal societ-
> ies, it is female who are accused of being infertile), it would
> have been natural for the Bemba to put the blame of infer-
> tility on their young men. This is not the case, as the
> Bemba young man is considered potent and fertile in so
> far as he can effect an erection of the penis.

> 3. Applied to the Kétu, Richards' conclusive agreement
> with Schapera's hypothesis, that in a situation of contact
> with Europeans, magical rites tend to survive, needs some
> modification. The survival of the magical rites in the Kétu
> series of rites is not because they are magical *per se*, but
> because they are expressive charters of the patrilineal ide-

ology. Of themselves, I suggest, they would not survive, but as charters of lineage interests, they will survive as long as the lineage goals remain feasible and its control operative.

4. Kétu stress on the fertility of the graduands seems to suggest, contrary to Richards' hypothesis, that such emphases are not peculiar to matrilineal societies. Rather, it is to be found in any nonindustrial society, whatever its descent rule, because it is the fundamental function of every lineage to seek its own survival (Fortes 1945, 32).

5. Premarital pregnancy among the Kétu is considered inauspicious as preinitiation pregnancy is regarded among the Bemba. Both societies condemn such pregnancy for different reasons. The Bemba regard it as inauspicious because the offender did not submit herself to the qualifying rites of purification and endurance of initiation trials before arrogating to herself the status of a "woman." Thus, she has a polluting effect on the society. On the other hand, the Kétu disaffection with the offending girl hinges on the fact that she has contravened two regulations. Among Kétu, premarital sex is necessarily precircumcision. Circumcision highlights the Kétu emphasis that the goal of marriage is procreation and that the purpose of sex is not personal sexual pleasure but the means to the end, i.e., bearing children to continue the lineage. Precircumcision sex undermines this emphasis by making it possible to achieve maximum sexual pleasure since the prepuce, the erotic tip of the clitoris, has not been excised. In so doing, it creates the chance for the formation of a strong man-woman bond, which may threaten the Kétu man's total loyalty to his lineage. The existence and the spread of such individualistic tendencies within the lineage may work against lineage tendencies to unite all interests so as to survive. The Kétu lineage cannot afford this contravention. Although the Kétu do not believe that the perpetrators of such a crime be "driven out into the bush ... to save the community from danger" (Richards 1956:33), through the use of gossip and jests, life is made unbearable for the Kétu couple, who, to save face, may make a shift in residence.

In summation, the foregoing expresses the points of theoretical interest emerging from the application of Richards' model to the Kétu girls' fertility rites.

Finally, should it appear to the reader that this treatment of the rites has tilted the "balance of power" in favor of Kétu females, that impression would be contrary to the reality of the relationship of mutual dependence existing between men and women in Kétu society. It became necessary to highlight areas of female prominence in order to effect the otherwise nonapparent balance between the sexes in a society that is male oriented. In doing so, I have made it clear that, among the Kétu and, indeed, the Yoruba, the question to ask about the status of the sexes is not which sex is dominant?, but rather, over which areas do the sexes enjoy prominence? The prominence that one sex enjoys in a particular area of human activity does not make the people of that sexual category independent of those of the other. It is in cooperation that the sexes effect the continuity of the group. The Yoruba people themselves recognize this fact of mutual dependence, expressing it in the maxim "It is when the right hand washes the left and the left washes the right that both hands become clean" (*Ọtun wẹ òsïn, òsïn wẹ ọtun ni ọwọ fi nmọ*).

Notes

1. Turner (1967, 27-30) talks about the three properties of ritual symbol: (a) condensation, (b) unification of disparate significata, and (c) polarization of meaning that branches off to the sensory and ideological poles.
2. See M. Sahlins, *Stone Age Economics* 1972 (London: Tavistock) Chapter Four, especially pages 157-159.
3. In the absence of adequate medical evidence or support for the biological irregularities mentioned, it is suggested that the reason was given, not because it was practical but to justify the continuation of this practice to an influentioan Catholic group.
4. Max Gluckman records a similar manner of involving the sexes as social groupings acting in an organized way to effect the transition of initiates (1949, 145).

CHAPTER SEVEN

POLICY ISSUES:
THE NEED TO TAKE A BROADER
VIEW OF AFRICAN CULTURAL
PRACTICES

As a Nigerian anthropologist trained in England and working now in America, I have watched with fascination and concern the efforts to curb the sad practice of clitoridectomy in my home continent.

In this country genital mutilation has become a hot issue in newspapers, magazines, the talk show circuit and was even featured recently on *Nightline*. Some have advocated granting asylum to women trying to escape this practice in their own countries.

To me, this outpouring of Western concern over genital mutilation offers a case study in how the well-intentioned efforts of Americans to improve the lot of oppressed people elsewhere in the world can have precisely the opposite effect intended. In at least some of the societies targeted by this movement, the practice has increased.

Concerned Americans have a tendency to place issues in a context which they understand, but which may have little relevance to Africa. In this case, feminists have interpreted genital mutilation as a simple expression of male domination. They have created a perception in America that the only reason why this practice continues is to reduce a woman's pleasure in the hope of ensuring against promiscuity.

Instead of making an effort to understand why this evil practice continues, Americans express surprise and dismay and then unleash strategies which have proven effective in forcing change here, but which can have the opposite effect there.

So there is no misunderstanding, let me say here that I understand and share the outrage over clitoridectomy. Cultural differences are not excuses for violations of human rights.

When a military tyrant hangs a dissenting poet in Nigeria, or a religious bigot kills a female who ignores orthodox restrictions on attire in Saudi Arabia, or teenage girls bleed to death in Egypt after having a portion of their clitoris removed, there ought to be international expressions of dismay.

Anyone interested in helping individuals of both genders reach their full potential should be horrified that clitoridectomy endures. But reducing the practice to a bizarre expression of male chauvinism just limits the wider cultural understanding needed to stop it.

Cultural practices endure because they make sense to individuals in a society. Sacrifices are made willingly only when individuals believe their loss is offset by some greater gain.

In Western society, the supreme value is personal freedom, and the opportunity to excel at one's chosen career. To others, particularly in nonindustrial societies, the highest good is procreation and nurture.

The freedom-loving Westerner's emphasis on things like achieving full sexual satisfaction or personal individual growth and professional achievement are secondary goals in these societies. The greatest measure of happiness and success is not how much pleasure one achieves, how much money one earns, or how much professional status one attains, but how many healthy children one has. Even as these societies change and become more modern, traditional values often remain rock solid underneath.

Since health-care delivery is notoriously poor in these parts of the world, infant mortality and maternal morbidity is usually quite high. At the same time, the main occupations people depend on for subsistence—farming, fishing and hunting—are still carried out in labor-intensive ways.

The most valuable resource for survival in these countries is human labor, and a family with many strong members is wealthy indeed. So is it any surprise that the cultural ethos of such societies demands procreation as a measure of human worth?

Barring North Africa and some other areas of Islamic influence around the Horn of Africa where extreme forms of infibulation (fastening the female genitals with a pin or clamp) are performed, sub-Saharan Africa generally has very mild forms of excision (no form is acceptable).

The logic of the practice is couched in the anthropological term of prestation, a gift that you give under pain of sanction, for which you receive a greater gift in return. The logic of clitoridectomy is that by taking a tiny bit of the sacred instrument of fertility as an offering, the god of fertility will bless you with more children and easier childbirth.

This is quite different from the way clitoridectomy is presented in Alice Walker's popular novel, *Possessing the Secrets of Joy*. The protagonist, Tashi, also known as Evelyn, is a native of Sierra Leone in West Africa. She is married to Adam, an African American pastor. The couple move to America, where Tashi is tormented by the memory of her sister, Dura, a hemophiliac who died after undergoing a clitoridectomy.

Tashi subsequently returns to Africa on a pilgrimage of revenge. She kills the elderly woman who performed the excision on herself, Dura, and countless other girls. Before Tashi is executed for the crime, she finds her "secret of joy" in resisting the historical brutalization by men.

The best-selling book helped make genital mutilation a hot topic, arousing indignation and protest in America, but also creating a siege mentality in societies where it is still practiced. The feeling that "they" are "attacking our way of life" has led to a communal regrouping, and a renewed determination that no young female should escape the blade.

The damage that clitoridectomy does to women suffices to make it alone the object of attack. Making it part of a larger feminist and Western agenda has just widened the practice and stiffened resistance of change.

Any effective strategy should include efforts to improve health-care delivery in countries where infant mortality and maternal morbidity are high. It is only when more babies and mothers survive that the value placed on bearing many children will be reduced, and families will become more concerned about best caring the ones they have—which will quickly lead to having fewer of them.

In 1980, when Nigeria's earlier investment of oil resources began to pay off in improved health care, the social emphasis on procreation quickly changed. Women asked, "Shouldn't we have fewer children, who then can excel?" Most Nigerian families have the same goals and hopes for their children as Americans do.

This approach will end clitoridectomy a lot faster than Tashi's murderous missions, or great gusts of feminist outrage. It is built on a sound understanding of the cultural logic which sustains the practice. As more infants survive, the link between fertility, human worth and genital mutilation will slowly but surely be broken.

YORUBA MYTHS OF ORIGIN AND MIGRATION: A TESTIMONY OF FEMALE PROMINENCE

Aspects of Kétu beliefs that contribute to our understanding of the motivations lying behind the Kétu fertility rites will be discussed here. Some Yoruba myths will be analyzed on the pattern Leach provided in his work on the story of creation (1969) in the Book of Genesis. The method adopted by Leach in that work was based on that of Claude Levi-Strauss (who had himself been inspired by writers such as Dumezil, Vladimir Propp and Ferdinand de Saussure). I will also discuss the Kétu idea of time so that references to time in the presentation of the ethnography will be readily understood.

The Myths of Origin

The Kétu share with other Yoruba subgroups the myths that attempt to explain the origin of the Yoruba. These fall into two categories: migration and creation.[1] Myths of migration recount the story of how the group left Ile Ife, the Yoruba culture center, its experiences while on the move and how it came to settle in its present location. Myths of creation tell the story of the group existence by placing the group at the center of the world. These myths state that the work of creating the world and all that is in it began in Yorubalan., The popular version of the Yoruba myth of creation follows.

By a sheer act of divine initiative, *Olódùmarè*—the supreme being in the Yoruba spiritual universe—decided to create the world. He assigned the fundamental tasks to his senior son *Ọbàtálá* (a.k.a *Òrìshá-nlá*) whom he exhorted to carry out this work with utmost commitment. On his way, *Ọbàtál*a become thirsty and helped himself to copious amounts of palm-wine. He became intoxicated and fell into a deep sleep. When he did not return to the heavens at the appointed time, Olodumare sent down the archdivinity's junior brother, *Odùduwà*, to find out if all was well with him. *Odùduw*à came upon the drunken *Ọbàtál*a, took stock of the situation, and quietly proceeded to carry out the work of creation. He descended into the void by a chain, threw a quantity of loose earth onto the water and set the five-toed hen loose upon it. The hen scratched the earth and spread it to the end of the world. Then *Odùduw*à let down the chameleon to test the firmness of the earth. The chameleon, because of its the delicate movements had been chosen to carry out this test. It gave its approval. The spot where the creation took place was called "spreading " (*ifẹ*) in commemoration of the event.

Ọbàtála appeared not long after only to discover his junior brother had completed the task and in so doing, usurping his right as the creator of the earth. He quarreled with *Odùduw*à for his impertinence. The quarrel was reported to Olódùmarè, who effected a reconciliation between the two estranged brothers. In compensation, he commissioned Òrìshà-nlá to perform the special duty of molding the human physique. He confirmed *Odùduwà*'s right to own and rule the earth on his behalf from Ife, the sacred city. *Odùduwà* later gave birth to several children who moved away from Ife to establish kingdoms of their own. His second child, a female, gave birth to *Alákétu* whose offspring are the Kétu.

A second myth, collected by Ellis (1893), asserts that Yoruba originated from a series of incestuous dealings among the divinities. In this myth, *Odùduwà* is presented as a female, the earth goddess.[2] *Ọbàtálá* the arch-divinity belonged to the heavens. He married *Odùduwà* and they had two children; "the land" (*Aganjù*) and "water" (*Yemaja*). These engaged in sibling marriage and" gave birth to the "air" (*Òrùngan*), that is, the region between the solid earth and the edge of the heavens. *Òrùngan* brought the incestuous relationships to a head when he ravished his mother *Yemaja*, who in an attempt to escape further humiliation, purposely fell and burst open, whereupon a number of minor divinities emerged from her gaping body.

A third myth of creation shows the link between these two myths of origin. It also bears out a message of the myths that emphasize the important position of women in Yoruba society. This third myth recounts the great escapades of a virtuous Yoruba woman of great beauty, Morẹmi. She contrived and succeeded to free her people from the attacks of a neighboring group called the Igbos (these have connection with the Igbo major sociolinguistic group). On previous raids, the Ife warriors, all male, would not defend themselves against their attackers who dressed as if they were superhuman. Morẹmi vowed to the river goddess *Esinmerin* that if the goddess helped her to overcome the attackers, she would sacrifice her dearest possession to the goddess. At the next Igbo raid she allowed herself to be captured. Being a woman of great beauty, she was given as wife to the Igbo king into whose favors she endeared herself. During her captivity, she discovered that the dreaded enemies were mere human beings who dressed in grasslike garments that made them look like spirits. She escaped, went back to her people, and revealed the Igbo warriors' secrets. The attackers were met at the next incursion with lighted torches. The Ife victory was decisive. In fulfillment of her vow Morẹmi made great sacrifices to the river goddess, who refused everything save Morẹmi's only child, *Olúorogbo*. Morẹmi complied and her loss was mourned by all people. *Olúorogbo* rose up and later ascended to heaven on a rope.

As myths, these stories cannot be taken as an accurate record of events, and several scholars working among the Yoruba cautioned that the stories should not be taken at face value (Lloyd 1959, 217). Among the conservative Yoruba (Simpson 1937, 5), they served as charters for social action aiming to accommodate new experiences that should be presented as part of existing traditional practices. Thus, they projected current social issues, perspectives, and aspirations into the past to accord them the authority of the ancestors. The sanction of the ancestors was vital to the acceptance of any new idea by a people who lived in the belief that their social order and values were ancient, unchanging, and continuous, having been handed down from one generation to the next, untouched.

Contrary to the foregoing usage, the myths may also serve as a charter to counterfeit history by a people who struggle to blur, if not erase, the contents of recent traumatic experiences in the life of the group. Such stories become vital as the group attempts to unify after a period of internal division. Such stories endeavor to put an end to the recurring dialectic of segmentary fission and fusion by building up an elaborate genealogy specifying the common origin of all subgroups. The implication is that the desire to unite is of ancestral origin. Such myths of origin, according to Fortes, "become intelligible when it is realized that they are nothing more than formulations of the contemporary scheme of political and ceremonial relationships" (1948, 23).

In the structural tradition, however, myths have been shown to express the contradictions in the basic premises of culture. When they do, they show the gap between what the cultural institutions try to achieve and what they actually succeed in achieving. Although such myths are related to given empirical facts and reality, they are not a clear reflection of reality. One must analyze such myths to identify the contradictions that they mediate if one is to get at the message they convey. It is in this light that I shall now examine these Yoruba myths, following the example of Leach's analysis of the story of Creation in Genesis.

The antimonies of "Heaven" and "Earth," "good" and "bad," "strong" and "weak," are built into the structure of each of these myths. In the first myth, there is clear discrimination between the deity and humans. Thus Olódùmarè in the heavens above delegated the archdivinity to create men below. In addition to the sets of oppositions given, two other sets appear; "heaven" and "earth," "God" and "man". These sets imply another set; "above" and "below." The link between the sets of oppositions comes in the divinities, Ọbàtálá and Odùduwà—who symbolize the opposition in their final act of separation with one going to the heavens and the other becoming the ruler on earth. Yet Odùduwà on earth is heavenbound having originated there; while the archdivinity is earthbound, having been assigned the duty of molding the figure of humans who inhabit the earth.

The characters of the archdivinity and Odùduwà develop the theme of opposition. Thus, the "good"and "strong-willed" Odùduwa resisted the temptation to drink and succeeded in accomplishing the task of the "bad" and "weak" Ọbàtálá. In the second story, the "bad" *Òrùngan* had an incestuous relationship with his "good" mother (the permitted act of incest among the divinities being between brother/sister and not child/parent), who demonstrated a considerable measure of strength by attempting to escape. In the third story, the "good" and "strong" Morẹmi found the solution to her people's predicament, while the scared, "weak" and cowardly Ife men failed to defend them. The sets of oppositions that emerge from the relationships may be rendered as:

heaven: good: strong; above :: earth: bad; weak; below.

When we add the set of sexual opposition to the sets above, on the merits of the characters in the stories, we will assign woman to the column of strength and man to that of weakness. This addition anticipates the suggestion that underlies this work; that Kétu women are powerful, and that the instances of overt expression of male domination are a mechanism of male defense against the perceived power of females.

At the level of discrimination in sexual relations, the analysis offers a more interesting insight. Most societies recognize some rules of incest (in whatever way it is defined[3]) and exogamy. In the second myth, although the divinities regarded sibling incest as "normal" they viewed child/parent incest differently. Yemaja's attempted escape and subsequent death expresses disapproval of child/parent incest. In Morẹmi's story, the marriage of the heroine to the Igbo king, no matter how brief, exemplifies the exogamous marriage of alliance as opposed to the practice of marriage within the group. The contrasting point of interest is that while the incestuous assault of *Yemaja* by Orungan led to the death of *Yemaja*, the exogamous liaison of Morẹmi led to the survival of her people. This is an example of transformation where the end result of the second set is a reversal of the first. On the one hand, coercive endogamy led to death; on the other hand, exogamy (albeit temporary) led to life.

In the myths about Morẹmi and the incestuous relationships of the divinities, women play very active, positive parts. The fact that there is no complete agreement on the sex of Odùdúwà, who is, in most areas of Yorubaland, regarded as female, it is clear that women are imbued with characteristics such as strength, life, fertility and courage. The same myths associate the opposing characteristics of weakness, death, and lack of courage with men.

There are three dominant themes in myths.

1. They emphasize the insistence on marriage within the group, so maintaining the purity of the group.

2. They speak of the consequent change necessitated by practical political considerations that suggest the wisdom in creating a peaceful link with neighboring groups through exogamous marriages.

3. They speak of the powerlessness of the Kétu (Yoruba) men who realized that they depend on the goodwill of their females to effect these extra group alliances. The powerlessness of the men is masked by the ideology of male dominance and by the socialization of women which encourages them to accept such dominance.

The Yoruba tradition insists that people marry within the group so as to keep the blood of the group pure. Although this praçtice created a sense of exclusiveness and unity within the group in relation to others, in the Morèmi affair it shows the price of maintaining such exclusiveness. To the conservative elements within the society, the overture to relate with the neighboring groups was construed as a complete break with tradition. The myths of Morèmi and the incest of the divinities, with their end results, provide the ideological underpinning and charter for the change. In so doing, they help the ordinary Kétu man to absorb the new practice as being traditionally ordained; thus avoiding the conflict that may accompany social change.

The compromise in tradition implied in the transfer of females had another effect on the relations between the sexes in the society. To the Yoruba man who always wanted to exude an aura of superiority over the Yoruba female, the realization that he depended on females for survival weakened his feeling of dominance. Thus, these myths portray the contradiction inherent in the patrilineally oriented world of the Yoruba, where the male asserts his dominance over the female on whom he depended for survival. This paradox runs through the relationship between the sexes. I suggest that it explains the one-sided training of the Yoruba girls in the art of pleasing their men as part of the fertility rites.

The Story of Kétu Migration: A Confirmation

The story of the westward migration of the Kétu from Ile-Ife shows the importance of women to the surival of the Kétu both during and after the migration. The role of Kétu women in speeding the progress of Kétu migration and in effecting a comfortable settlement was significant. Women's courage and initiative made the integration of the Kétu back to a normal cultured existence possible. These facts support the main thrust of the interpretation of the significance of women in Yoruba myths of origin.

The story, recorded by Crowther (1852) and Parrinder (1956) and summarized by Smith (1969), relates that the Kétu subgroup migrated from Ile-Ife under the leadership of an Ife prince—a grandson of Oduduwa—named Ṣopàṣán. Having crossed the Ògùn river, the migrants split into three divisions. The first division continued westward under the leadership of Ṣopàṣán and his nephew Ọwẹ́ the second turned to the northwest and then to the south, finding the cognate subgroup of Save; and the third moved northwards and founded by Ọwẹ, where the migrants stayed longer and broke camp during the reign of the seventh king, Ẹdẹ, who revived the westward migrations. Here again, the party split into three divisions. The first division founded a village called Idòfá the second settled at Igbó-Ọrá and the third Ẹde group—the largest of the three—moved westward guided by the hunter *Alalumon*.

Eventually, the Ẹdẹ group ran out of water at a place not far from the actual site where Kétu town was founded. They were saved from dying of thirst by the kindness of a woman, a lonely old sorceress called *Ya Mepéré*, who would later fulfill a promise she made to Ede by building a powerful charm to protect Kétu town. The migrants continued their westward movement until they came to the site of Kétu. On their first night they had no fire for cooking. *Alalumon*, the hunter, went in search of fire, finding a place called *Panku*, inhabited by an autochthonous group. At Panku, an old woman, Ya Panku, gave him a brand from her fire. In remembrance of this, all lights are extinguished at the death of a Kétu king and Alalumon, one of the leading chiefs, goes to Panku to light a ritual fire (Parrinder 1956, 20).

The main outline of this story exhibits the features of a rite of passage; separation, transition and aggregation. The migrant group left the larger Ife group, and under the leadership of Sopason went to found a town of their own. From the moment the migrants separated from the Ife group to the moment they were incorporated back into the society by the symbolic gesture of the gift of fire, they lived the unclassified, marginal life of the semi-nomad. They lived in "the wild" of normal Yoruba society. Although they tried to keep a semblance of the civilized Yoruba cultural way of life by preserving their kingship, they did not belong to the larger Yoruba society. Contrary to the sedentary, agricultural Yoruba, they were on the move and lived largely by hunting. They lacked two important elements that support human survival, water and fire. Fire, in particular, is associated with culture as against the raw nature. In asking for fire, the Kétu group was, in effect, putting a definitive end to their near natural state at the transitional period.

The migrants, in their efforts to survive and to be integrated into the cultural society, were aided by women who, as marginal figures, mediated their transition. Both women were old, one of them a declared sorceress who lived alone. Old women who have passed the age of menopause are regarded as potentially dangerous by the Yoruba. The sorceress gave them water to quench their thirst and a magical charm to boost their morale, and to enable them to gain the confidence to ask for integration into normal society. The gift of fire had both practical and symbolic implications. It effectively ended their transitional state of nature, and it also symbolized a welcoming acceptance by the group who already lived in that area.

The myths of Yemaja, *Morèmi*, and Kétu migration demonstrate instances of female power in the face of male weakness. *Morèmi*, the heroine, volunteered to move into the unknown in order to free her people at a time when the Ife male population had lost the will-power to defend its people. *Yemaja* restrained herself from her son's incestuous advances, preferring to die in protest. The old women, Ya Mepere and Ya Panku, radiate strength. The former saved the Kétu from death and restored their confidence by boosting their morale with a powerful magic charm. The latter retrieved, through her gift of fire, the Kétu from the anonymity of the marginal natural state and elevated them back to the cultural plane.

In Kétu history, women have held important political positions, and they still do. There is, for example, the case of Queen Ida of the royal house of Kétu who encouraged the Kétu in exile at Abomey and its environs, to return to the old site of Kétu and rebuild it. She was the chef de canton (district head) from 1911 to 1919. Today there is the post of *ìyálaṣẹ* in every Kétu town. The iyalase is the priestess of *Iyánlá* and the mediator between her society and Iyanla —the earth goddess who serves as the source of fertility. She wields considerable influence and is consulted in the selection of a candidate for the office of kingship.

NOTES

1. Lloyd classified the myths of Yoruba origin into two, creation stories and stories of conquest. He drew attention to a third type; town myths that sanction the position of the king by creating a link between him and Ile-Ife and its first king, Oduduwa. Under this category come the lineage myths that fix them into the social structure of the town (Lloyd 1959, 21-4).

2. There is disagreement over the sex of Oduduwa. Ajisafe (1924,10) asserts that he was a man who married *Omonide* who gave birth, among others, to Alakétu. Parrinder (1967)noted a Kétu tradition that claimed Oduduwa to be female. Idowu (1962, 24-27) said that the historical personality of Oduduwa, the deified ancestor of the

Yoruba, was grafted onto that of the earth goddess Oduduwa, whose cults flourish at Ado and Imeôkoô in Yorubaland.

3.   For a comparative approach to incest, see Goody (1956).

BIBLIOGRAPHY

Abayomi, S.O. "Ife Myth Revisited". 1978, Unpublished seminar
    paper, University of Ibadan.
Abdullahi, A. An-Na' im. 1994 State Responsibility under International
    Human Rights Law to Change Religious and Customary Law. In
    Human Rights of Women, ed. R. J. Cook.
Abimbola, W. 1976 *Ifa; An Exposition of Ifa Literary Corpus*. Oxford:
    O.U.P.
Abraham, R.C. 1958 *Dictionary of Modern Yoruba*. London: London
    University Press.
Abu Shamma, A. O. 1949 Female Circumcision in the Sudan. *The
    Lancet* (26 March), 544.
Adedeji, Adebayo (ed.) 1966 *An Introduction to Western Nigeria; Its
    People, Culture and System of Government*. Ife: Institute of
    Administration, University of Ife.
Adesanya, Adebayo. 1958 Yoruba Metaphysical Thinking. *ODU* 5: 36-
    41.
Afigbo, A.E. 1967 The Warrant Chief System in Eastern Nigeria;
    Direct and Indirect Rule? *JHSN*, 111: 683 - 701.
Ajayi, J.F.A. and R. Smith. 1964 *Yoruba Warfare in the Nineteenth
    Century*, Cambridge: CUP.
Ajisafe, A.K. 1924 *The Laws and Customs of the Yoruba People*.
    London, Lagos: C.M.S. Bookshop.
Akinjogbin, I. A. 1966 "Western Nigeria, Its people and its culture" in
    Adebayo Adedeji (ed.) *An Introduction to Western Nigeria; Its
    People, Culture and System of Government*. Ife: University of Ife
    Press.
Ardener, E.W. 1954 The Kinship Terminology of a Group of Southern
    Ibo. *Africa* 24: 85-99.
_____. 1959 Lineage and Locality among the Mba-Ise Ibo. *Africa*
    29:113-32.

_____. 1962 *Divorce and Fertility: An African Study*. London: OUP/ NISER.

_____. 1971 *Social Anthropology and Language*. Association of Social Anthropologists monograph 10.

_____. 1972 "Belief and the Problem of Women." In *Interpretation of Ritual*, (ed.) La Fontaine London:Tavistock.

Ardener, S. 1973 Sexual Insult and Female Militancy. In *Man* 8: 422.

Ardener, S. (ed.) 1977 *Perceiving Women*. London: Dent and Sons.

_____. 1978 *Defining Females: The Nature of Women in Society*. London, Croom Helm

Armstrong, R. 1964 *The Study of West African Languages*. Ibadan: IUP.

Asiwaju, A.I. 1970 "The AlaKétu of Kétu and the Onimeko of Meko; The Changing Status of Two Yoruba Rulers under French and British Rule. In *West African Chiefs: Their Changing Status under Colonial Rule and Independence*, ed. Michael Crowther and Obaro Ikime, New York: African Publishing Corporation. 34-60.

_____.1974 Anti-French Resistance Movements in Ohori-Ije (Dahomey) 1895-1960. *JHSN* 7.

_____.1976 *Western Yorubaland Under European Rule 1889-1945*. London: Longman.

_____.1979 The Aja-Speaking Peoples of Nigeria; A Note on Their Origins, Settlement and Cultural Adaptation up to 1945. *Africa* 49:15-28.

_____.1984 *Partitioned Africans*. Lagos: LUP

Atanda, J. A. 1973 *The New Oyo Empire*. London: Longman.

_____. 1973 Yoruba Sacrificial Practice. *Journal of Religion in Africa*, 5, 2:81-93.

Awori, Thelma. 1975 For African Women Equal Rights Are Not Enough: The Real Task Is to Rethink the Role of Men in Present Day Society. UNESCO *Courier* 5: 21-5.

Aydelotte, W.O. 1937 *Bismark and British Colonial Policy: The Problem of South-West Africa*. Philadelphia.

Bassir, T.A. 1977 Psychological Aspects of Female Circumcision. *5th W.H.O. Congress of Obstetrics and Gynecological Society of Sudan*, Khartoum.

Babalola, S.A. 1966 *The Content and Form of Ijala*. Oxford: Clarendon Press.

Babatunde, E. D. 1983 Kétu Myths and the Status of Women: A Structural Interpretation of Some Yoruba Myths of Origin. *Journal of the Anthropological Society of Oxford*. 14.

_____.1983b   Kinship Behavior and Patrilineal Ideology: A Case Study of the Kétu Yoruba", *Journal of Business and Social Studies*. N.s. 6.

_____.1984 Methodologies In Comparative Education: In Search of an Appropriate Model for Developing Countries. *Ilorin Journal of Education*. 4.

_____. 1985   An African Concept of Penance. *Shalom* 3.

_____. 1986 The Missionary, the Yoruba and the Baconian Idols:The Problems of Education for Evangelisation", *Insight, Journal of World Faiths*. n.s., 13

_____. 1988a "Marriage in Contemporary African Society."In *Introduction to Sociology*.,O. Olusanya and L. Olurode eds. Ikeja; John West.

_____.1988b "Religion and the problem of Order." In *Introduction to Sociology*, O. Olusanya and Lai Olurode eds. Ikeja; John West.

_____.1988c   "The *gèlèdè* Masked Dance and Kétu Society: The Role of the Transvestite Masquerade in Placating Powerful Women While Maintaining the Patrilineal Ideology." In *West African Masks and Cultural Systems*, S.Kasfir ed. Tervuran: Musee Rajal De L'Afrique Central.

_____.1991 The Status of Women in Kétu Myths and its Sociological Ramifications. *Women's Research Program Publication Review*, (National Taiwan University).

_____.1989 "Urban Marginality's Perception of Self, Preliminary Comparative Notes on Ilubirin Apeja (Lagos) and 35-47 Street, Southside of Chicago, Illinois." In *Borderline Issues* A.I. Asiwaju ed. University of Lagos Press.

_____.1992 *A Critical Study of Bini and Yoruba Value Systems of Nigeria In Change: Culture, Religion and the Self.* Lewiston: The Edwin Mellen Press, 1992.

_____.1994 "Marginality's perception of Self: The Kétu astride the Nigeria/Benin Border." In A. I. Asiwaju and O .J Igue eds. *The Nigerian/Benin Transborder Relations*. Lagos: University of Lagos, 1994.

_____.1996   "Cultural Diferrences and Marital Crises Among Africans and African-Americans: Case Study of Some Immigrants." In *Exploring the African-American Experience*, Sudarkasa and N. L. Nwachuku (eds.) Lincoln: Lincoln University Press.

_____. 1996 Healing the Wound between Africans and the Diaspora. In *Visions* 1.

_____. 1996   The Need to take a Broader View of African Cultural Practices. In *The Philadelphia Inquirer* 26 October.

_____. 1997 The need for Values. In *The Philadelphia Inquirer* 11 March.

_____.1997 Why it is valuable to value our elders. In *The Philadelphia Inquirer* 2nd April.

_____.1997 Strengthen bonds to stay grounded. In *The Philadelphia Inquirer* 11 May.

Bamgbose, A. 1966 *A Grammar of Yoruba*. London: CUP.

_____.1972 The Meaning of Olodumare: An Etymology of the Name of the Yoruba High God, *African Notes* 7: 25-52.

Bascom, W. 1942 The Principle of Seniority in the Social Structure of the Yoruba. *Am. Anthr.* 44.

_____.1951 Social Status, Wealth and Individual Differences Among the Yoruba. *Am. Anthr.* 53: 490-505.

_____.1951 Yoruba Cooking. *Africa* 21:125-37.

_____.1951 Yoruba Food. *Africa* 21: 41-53.

_____.1953 African Culture and the Missionary. *Civilizations*, 3: 4.

_____.1955 Organization Among the Yoruba *Am. J. Soc.* 65: 5.

_____.1956 "Yoruba Concepts of the Soul." Paper presented at *5th International Congress of Anthropology and Ethnographical Sciences*, 1-9.

_____.1969 *The Yoruba of South-Western Nigeria*. New York: Holt, Rinehart and Winston.

_____.1973 "The Early Historical Evidence of Yoruba Urbanism," in *Social Change and Economic Development in Nigeria*, eds. Ukendi G. Damachi and Hans Dieter Sebel 11-39. New York: Praeger Publications.

Bassher, T. A. 1977 "Psychological Aspects of Female Circumcision." Paper presented at the 5th W.H.O. Congress of Obstetrics and Gynecological Society of Sudan, Khartoum.

Bassir, O. 1954 Marriage Rites Among the Aku (Yoruba) of Freetown. *Africa*, 24: 251-55.

Beattie, J. H. M. 1951 "Checks on the Abuse of Political Power: A Comparative Study of the Social Factors Acting in Restraint of the Abuse of Such Power by Indigenous Political Authorities in Certain Native Societies of Africa. B. Litt., Oxford University Thesis.

_____.1958 "Nyoro Marriage and Affinity." *Africa* 28: I.

_____.1966a *Other Cultures*. London: Routledge and Kegan Paul.

_____.1966b "Ritual and Social Change" (The Malinowski Memorial Lectures, 1965). *Man* 1 (1): 60-74.

Beier, H.U. 1955 The Presence of Yoruba Women. *Presence Africaine*. n.s. 1-2: 39-46.

_____.1958 The Egungun Cult Among the Yoruba. *Presence Africaine*, n.s. 17-18: 33-6.

_____.1960 Obatala; Five Myths about the Yoruba Greater God. *Black Orpheus* 7:34-5.

Bettleheim, S. O. 1955 *Symbolic Wounds*. London: Thames and Hudson.

Biobaku, S.O. 1955 The Use and Interpretation of Myths. *ODU*, 1: 12-25.

_____.1958 An Historical Sketch of Egba Traditional Authorities. *Africa* 32: 35-49.

Blair, A.H. 1940 "Intelligence Report on Meko, Ilaro" (*Western Region Survey File.*)

Bohannan, L. 1952 A Genealogical Charter. *Africa* 22: 300-315.

Bohannan, P. 1954 Circumcision among the Tiv. *Man*, 54: 2-6.

_____. 1964 *African Outline*. London: Penguin Books.

Boulware-Miller, K. 1985 Female Circumcision: Challenges to the Practice as Human Rights Violation. *Harvard Women's Legal Journal 155, 170n; 89*

Brown, J.K. 1963 A Cross-Cultural Study of Female Initiation Rites. *Am. Anthr.*:837-53.

Bunch, C. 1990 Women's Rights as Human Rights: Toward a Re-Vision of Human Rights. *Human Rights Quarterly* 486.

Burton, R.F. 1863 *Abeokuta and the Cameroons Mountains*. London: Tinsley Brothers.

Butt-Thompson, F.W. 1929 *West African Secret Societies*. London: H.F. and G. Whetherby.

Callaway, H. 1978 "The Most Essentially Female Function of All: Giving Birth." In ed. S. Ardener *Defining Females*, London: Croom Helm.

Carroll, K.F. 1967 *Yoruba Religious Carving*. London: Geoffrey Chapman.

Chapman, M. (ed.) 1989 Edwin Ardener: *The Voice of Prophecy and Other Essays*. Oxford: Blackwell.

Charlesworth, et al 1991 Feminist Approaches to International Law, 85 American Journal of International Law 613: 625-640.

Clapperton, H. 1829 *Journal of a Second Expedition into the Interior of Africa from the Bight of Benin to Soccatoo*, Philadelphia; Carey, Lea and Carey.

Clarke, J. Digby 1944 Three Yoruba Fertility Ceremonies. *Journal of the Royal Anthropological Institute*, 74:91-96.

Cloudsley, A. 1984 *Women of Omdurman: Life, Love and the Cult of Virginity*. New York: St. Martin's.

Comhaire-Sylvain, S. 1949 The Status of Women in Lagos, Nigeria, *Pi Lambda Theta Journal*, 27: 158-63.

Cook, R. J. 1994 State Responsibility for Violations of Women's Human Rights, 7 *Harvard Human Rights Journal* 125.

Courlander, H. 1973 *Tales of Yoruba Gods and Heroes*. Connecticut: Fawcett Publications.

Crowe, S.E. 1942 *The Berlin West African Conference, 1884-1885*. London.

Dallmeyer, D.G. 1993 Reconceiving Reality. *Woman and International Law* 93-170

Dalzel, A. 1793 *The History of Dahomey. An Inland Kingdom of Africa*. London: Frank Cass.

Daramola, O. and A. Jeje (eds.) 1968 *Awon Asa Ati Orisa Ile Yoruba*. Ibadan: Onibonoje Press.

Diels, H. 1956 Fragmente der Versokratika 91.1:171, line 9.

Douglas, M. 1966 *Purity and Danger*. London: Routledge and Kegan Paul.

Drewal, H. J. and Drewal, M. T.(eds.) 1990 *Gẹ̀lẹ̀dẹ́ : Art and Female Power among the Yoruba*. Bloomington: Indiana University Press.

Durkheim, E. 1947 *The Elementary Forms of the Religious Life* Glencoe: The Free Press.

_____.1964 *The Division of Labor in Society*, trans. G. Simpson New York: The Free Press.

Duze, M. 1963 *A Primary Geography Course for the Western Regions in Nigeria*. London: Macmillan.

Eighmy, T.H. 1968 *Problems of Census Interpretation in Developing Countries: The Western Nigeria Case*. Lund: C.W.K. Glerup.

Eliade, M. 1958 *Birth and Rebirth: The Religious Meanings of Initiation in Human Culture*. London: Harvill.

Ellis, A.B. 1894 *The Yoruba-Speaking Peoples of the Slave Coast of West Africa*. London: Chapman and Hall.

Ellis, W.B. n.d. "Age of Puberty in the Tropics." *Mss Afr. S. 1323*, Rhodes House, Oxford.

Evans-Pritchard, E.E. 1934 Social Character of Bride-wealth with Special Reference to the Azande, *Man* 34:172.

Evans-Pritchard, E.E. and M. Fortes (eds.) 1940a *African Political Systems*. London: OUP.

_____.1940b *The Nuer*. Oxford: Clarendon Press.

_____. 1945 "Some Aspects of Marriage and the Family among the Nuer," *Rhodes-Livingstone Paper, II*.

_____.1965 *The Position of Women in Primitive Societies and other Essays in Social Anthropology*. London: Faber and Faber.

Fadipe, N.A. 1970 *The Sociology of the Yoruba*. Ibadan: UIP.

Fajana, A. 1966 Some Aspects of Yoruba Traditional Education. *ODU*, 3:16-26.

Farrow, S.S. 1926 *Faith, Fancies and Fetich*. London: Society for Promoting Christian Knowledge.

Feierman, S. 1974 *The Shambaa Kingdom, A History*. Madison: University of Wisconsin Press.

Ferguson, J. 1970 *The Yorubas of Nigeria*. Bletchley: Open University Press.

Finnegan, R. 1977 *Aspects of African Religion*. Milton Keynes: Open University Press.

Finnegan, R. (ed.) 1978 *Oral Poetry*. Thetford: Fowe and Brydone.

Forde, D. 1951 *The Yoruba-Speaking Peoples of South-Western Nigeria, Ethnographic Survey*. London: IAI.

Forde, D. and P.M. Kaberry (eds.) 1967 *West African Kingdoms in the Nineteenth Century*. London: OUP/IAI.

Fortes, M. 1945 *The Dynamics of Clanship Among the Tallensi*. London: OUP.

_____.1954 "A Demographic Field Study in Ashanti," in *Culture and Human Fertility*. Paris:UNESCO.

_____.1962 *Marriage in Tribal Societies*. Cambridge: CUP.

_____.1962 "Ritual and Office in Tribal Society." In ed. M. Gluckman *Essays of the Rituals of Social Relations*. Manchester: M.U.P.

Fox, R. 1967 *Kinship and Marriage*. Harmondsworth: C. Nicholls.

Frazer, Sir J.G. 1911 *The Golden Bough*. London:

Freud, S. 1933 *New Introductory Lectures on Psychoanalysis*. New York: W. W. North.

_____.1938 "Three Contributions to the Theory of Sex." In *The Basic Writings of Sigmund Freud*. New York: The Modern Library.

_____.1949 *An Outline of Psychoanalysis*. New York: W.W. Norton.

_____.1950 *Some Psychological Consequences of the Anatomical Distinction Between the Sexes, Collected Papers*. London: The Hogarth Press.

_____.1952 *An Autobiographical Study*. New York: W.W. Norton.

Fried, M. H. 1968 On the Concepts of 'Tribe' and 'Tribal' Society. In ed. J. Helm *Essays on the Problem of Tribe*, Proc. of the 1967 Meetings of the American Ethnological Society, Seattle and London.

Frobenius, L. 1913 *The Voice of Africa*, trans. R. Blind. London: Hutchinson.

Garigue, P. 1954 "Changing Political Leadership in West Africa." *Africa*, 24: 220-232.

Gbadamosi, B. and H.U. Beier, 1959 *Yoruba Poetry*. Ibadan: Nigerian Printing and Publishing Company.

Gluckman, M. 1950 "Kinship and Marriage among the Lozi of Northern Rhodesia and the Zulu of Natal." in *African Systems of Kinship and Marriage*.

_____.1955a *The Judicial Process Among the Barotse of Northern Rhodesia*. Manchester: Manchester University Press.

_____.1955b *Custom and Conflict in Africa*. Oxford: Basil Blackwell.

Gluckman, M. (ed.) 1962 *Essays on the Ritual of Social Relations*, Manchester: Manchester University Press.

Goldberg, J. 1997 "Our African Problem." *The New York Times Magazine*, March 2nd.

Goody, J. 1961 "The Classification of Double Descent." *Current Anthropology*. vol 2: 3-25.

Greenberg, K. 1963 "The Languages of Africa." *International Journal of American Linguistics*. 34: 1.

Gutek, G.L. 1972 *A History of Western Educational Experience*. New York: Random House.

Hans, N. 1949. *Comparative Education*. London: Routledge and Kegan. Paul.

Hargreaves, J. (ed.) 1919 *France and west Africa*. London.

Harper, P. 1970 The Role of the dance in the *gèlèdè* Ceremonies of the Village of Ijio. *ODU*. 4:67-94.

_____.1970 A Festival of Nigerian Dances. *African Arts*. vol. 3: 48-53.

Harrell-Bond, B.E. 1972 *Some Factors Influencing Attitudes Towards Family Limitation and the Use of Contraceptives Among the Professional Group in Sierra Leone*. Leiden: Afrika-Studiecentrum.

Harrell-Bond, B.E. *et. al.* 1978 *Community Leadership and the Transformation of Freetown (1801-1976)*. The Hague: Mouton.

Harris, J. S. 1940 The Position of Women in Nigerian Society. *Transactions of the New York Academy of Sciences* 2, 5.

Harris, G. 1962 "Taita Bridwealth and Affinal Relationships". In *Marriage in Tribal Societies*, ed. M. Fortes. Cambridge: CUP.

_____. 1973 "Furies, Witches and Mothers." In *The Character of Kinship*, ed. J. Goody. Cambridge: CUP.

Hastrup, K. 1978 "The Semantics of Biology: Virginity." In *Defining Females*, S. Ardener ed. London: Croom Helm.

Henry, J. 1949 Agricultural Practices in Relation to Soil Conservation. *Empire Cotton Growing Review*, 24: 12.

Hills-Young, E. 1949 Female Circumcision in the Sudan. *Anti-Slavery Reporter and Aborigine Friend* Series 6, vol.5:1

Hoch-Smith, J. and A. Spring (eds.) 1978 *Women in Ritual and Symbolic Roles.* New York: Plenum.

Horton, R. 1962 The High God: A Comment on Fr. O'Connell's Paper. *Man*, 62:137-140.

_____.1966 Conference of the High God in Africa. *ODU*, 2: 87-95.

Hosken, F.P. 1979 *The Female Report: Genital and Sexual Mutilation of Females.* WIN: Lexington.

Howard, R. 1984 Women's Rights in English-Speaking Sub-Saharan Africa. In *Human Rights and Development in Africa*, eds. C. E. Welch, Jr. & R. I. Meltzer 46, 66.

Huddleston, C. 1949 Female Circumcision in the Sudan. *The Lancet.* 62.

Idowu, E.B. 1962 *Olodumare: God in Yoruba Belief.* London: Green.

Imohkai, C. 1979 "The Missionization of Uzairue: A Study of Missionary Impact on traditional Marriage." Ph.D. dissertain: Columbia University.

Isichei, P.C. 1970 "Marriage and Family in Traditional Asaba." B. Litt. Thesis, Oxford University.

_____.1973 Sex in Traditional Asaba. *Cahiers D'Etudes Africaines* 3, vol.13.

James, W. 1978 "Matrifocus on African Women." In *Defining Females*, S. Ardener ed. London:Croom Helm.

Jeffreys, M. D. W. 1957 Palm-Wine Among the Ibibio. *Nigerian Field* 13:1.

Johnson, S. 1921 *The History of the Yorubas from the Earliest Times to the Beginning of the British Protectorate.* Lagos: C.M.S. Bookshop.

Johnstud, R.O. 1960 A Decade of Nigerian Cotton, 1949-1958', *Nigerian Geographical Journal* 3: 2.

Jones, R.W. 1946 Orisa-Oko Yoruba Goddess of the Farm and Agriculture. *Nigeria* 23:18-21.

Keesing, R.M. 1935 *Kin Groups and Social Structure.* New York: Holt, Rinehart and Winston.

Kennedy, J.G. 1970 Circumcision and Excision in Egyptian Nubia. *Man* 5:175-191.

Kenyatta, J. 1953 *Facing Mount Kenya; The Tribal Life of the Gikuyu.* London: Secker and Warburg.

Krapf-Askari, E. 1966 Time and Classification. *ODU* 2: 3-18.

_____. 1969 *Yoruba Town and Cities: An Enquiry into the Nature of Urban Social Phenomena*, Oxford: Clarendon Press.

LaFlesche, F. 1912 Osage Marriage Customs. *Am. Anthr* 14:127-30.

La Fontaine, J. 1962 "Gisu Marriage and Affinal Relations." In ed. M. Fortes. *Marriage in Tribal Societies*. Cambridge: CUP.

La Fontaine, J. 1972 The Ritualization of Women's Life-Crises in Bugisu. In J. La Fontaine (ed.) *The Interpretation of Ritual: Essays in Honor of A. I. Richards*. London: Travistock.

Lambo, A.T. (ed.) 1961 *First Pan-African Psychiatric Conference*, Abeokuta; Nigeria.

Lane, E. W. 1944 *The Modern Egyptians*. London: Everyman's Library No. 315.

Lasebikan, E.L. 1952 The Yoruba in Brazil. *West Africa* (10 August), 843.

Law, R.C.C. 1973 Heritage of Oduduwa; Traditional History and Political Propaganda Among the Yoruba', *Journal of African History* 14: 207-222.

Laycock, H.T. 1950 Surgical Aspects of Female Circumcision in Somaliland. *East African Medical Journal*, 26: 445-50.

Leach, E.R. 1954 *Political Systems of Highland Burma*. London: G. Bell and Sons.

_____. 1967 *The Structural Study of Myth and Totemism*, Association of Social Anthropologists. Monograph 5 (1976 rep.). Fakenham: Cox and Wyman.

_____. 1969 *Genesis as Myth and Other Essays*. London: Jonathan Cape.

Leakey, L.S.B. 1931 The Kikuyu Problem of the Initiation of Girls. *Journal of the Royal Anthropological Institute* 277-85.

Levi-Strauss, C. 1966 "Introduction a l'oeuvre de Marcel Mass." In *Sociologie et Anthropologie*. Paris: Presse Universaire de France.

Lewis, H. 1995 Between Irua and Female Genital Mutilation: Feminist Human Rights Discourse and the Cultural Divide. *Harvard Human Rights Journal* 8: 1- 55.

Liell, O. Okedeji, G. Trout, and E. Vlachos. 1965 A Research Design for a Comparative Study of Urbanism and Fertility: A Progress Report, *NJESS* 63-9.

Lienhardt, G. 1961 *Divinity and Experience: The Religion of the Dinka*. Oxford: Clarendon.

Little, K. 1970 *West African Urbanization. A Study of Voluntary Associations in Social Change*. Cambridge: CUP.

Little, K. 1979 Women in African Literature *West Africa* 3241- 45.

Lloyd, B.B. Divorce Among the Yorubas. *Am. Anthr.* 70: 67-81.

_____.1960 Sacred Kingship and Government Among the Yoruba. *Africa* 3: 221-237.

_____.1966 Agnatic and Cognatic Descent Among the Yoruba *Man* 4:484-500.

Lloyd, P.C. 1953   Some Problems of Tenancy in Yoruba Land Tenure. *African Studies*, 12: 93-103.

_____. 1954   The Traditional Political System of the Yoruba *South-Western Journal of Anthropology*, 10:366-84.

_____. 1955   The Yoruba Lineage *Africa* 25: 235-51.

_____. 1955   Yoruba Myths-A Sociologist's Interpretation. *ODU* 2:20-28.

_____. 1959   Some Notes on Yoruba Rules of Succession and on Family Property. *Journal of African Law* 3:7-32.

_____. 1962   *Yoruba Land Law*, London: OUP.

_____. 1963   The Status of the Yoruba Wife. *Sudan Society* 2: 35-42.

Lombard, J. 1967   "The Kingdom of Dahomey." In. *West African Kingdoms in the Nineteenth Century*.D. Forde and P. Kaberry eds. London: OUP for IAI.

Longo, L. D. 1964   Sociocultural Practices relating to Obstetrics and Gynecology in a Community of West Africa. *American Journal of Obstetrics and Gynecology* 89: 472.

Mabogunje, A. 1958   The Yoruba Home. *ODU* 5: 28-35.

MacFie, J. W. S. 1913   A Yoruba Tattooer. *Man*13.

Mair, L. 1962   Indirect Rule in Iboland. *West Africa* 2335(3 July): 238.

Malinowski, B. 1953   Introduction *Facing Mount Kenya; The Tribal Life of the Gikuyu* by Jomo Kenyatta. London: Secker and Warburg.

Matherson, A. 1979 "Unkindest Cut of All." *The Observer* (16 September).

Mauss, M. 1954   *The Gifts, Forms and Functions of Exchange in Archaic Societies*, trans. by I. Cunninson. London: Cohen and West.

Mayer, P. 1950   Privileged Obstruction of Marriage Rites Among the Gusii, *Africa* 2: 113-125.

_____.1970   "The Witches." In M. *Witchcraft and Sorcery* M. Marwick ed. Harmondsworth: Penguin.

McLean, Efua and Graham S. 1985   Female Circumcision, Excision and Infibulation. *The Minority Report*. 47. Pergamon.

Mbiti, J.S. 1969   *African Religions and Philosophy*. London: Morrison and Gibb.

Mead, M. 1928   *Coming of Age in Samoa*. London: Cox and Wyman.

_____. 1963   *Sex and Temperament in Three Primitive Societies*. New York: William Morrow.

Mercier, P. 1965   "On the Meanings of 'Tribalism' in Black Africa." In *Social Problems of Change and Conflict*, P.L. van den Berge ed. San Francisco;

Meyerowitz, E. L. R. 1944   Ibeji Statuettes from Yoruba Nigeria *MAN*, 44:105-7.

_____. 1946 Notes on the King-God Shango and His Temple at Ibadan, Southern Nigeria. *Man* 46:25-31.

Malade, T. 1973 The Concept of Abiku. *African Arts* 7: 62-64.

_____. 1971 Ibeji Custom in Yorubaland. *African Arts* 4: 3, 14-15.

Morel, E.D. 1911 *Nigeria; Its Peoples and Its Problems*, London: Smith, Elder.

Morton-Williams, P. 1952 The Atinga Cult among the South-Western Yoruba; A Sociological Analysis of a Witch-finding Movement. *Waiser Conference Proc*, 43-49.

_____. 1956 The Atinga Cult among the South-Western Yoruba; A Sociological Analysis of a Witch-finding Movement. *Bulletin Ifan* 18: 3-4, 315-34.

_____.1960 The Yomba Ogboni Cult in Oyo. *Africa,* 30: 362-74.

_____.1960 The Yoruba Responses to the Fear of Death, *Africa* 30:34-40.

_____.1962 The Yoruba Kingdom of Oyo. In *West African Kingdoms in the Nineteenth Century* eds. London: OUP.

_____.1964 Outline of the Cosmology and Cult Organisation of the Oyo Yoruba. *Africa* 243-61.

Mudimbe, V. Y. 1988 *The invention of Africa; Gnosis, Philosophy and the Order of Knowledge.* Bloomington: Indiana University Press.

Murray, J. 1976 Church Missionary Society and the "Female Circumcision" Issue in Kenya, 1929-1972. *J. Rel. in Africa* 8:92-104.

Nadel, S. F. 1942 *A Black Byzantium.* London: OUP.

Needham, R. 1979 *Symbolic Classification.* California; Goodyear.

Neven-Spence, B. 1949 Female Circumcision in the Sudan. *The Lancet* 459.

Newbury, C. 1961 *The Western Slave Coast and Its Rulers.* London: OUP.

Niven, C.R. 1937 *A Short History of Nigeria.* London: Longman.

Nsugbe, P.O. 1974 *Ohaffia; A Matrilineal Ibo People.* Oxford: Clarendon Press.

Odugbesan, C. 1966 "Femininity in Yoruba Religious Art." In *Man in Africa*, M. Douglas and P. Kaberry eds. London: Tavistock Publications.

Ogunmodede, E. 1979 Social Customs: Female Circumcision. *African Currents* 14 (Spring edition): 30-31.

Ojo, G.J.A. 1963 The Changing Patterns of Traditioinal Group Farming in Ekiti, North-eastern Yoruba Country. *NGJ* 6:31-8.

_____.1966 *Yoruba Culture.* London: University of Ife and ULP.

Okedeji, O. 1970 Review of *Aladura; A Religious Movement among the Yoruba* by J.Y. D. Peel. *Am. Anthr.* 72: 649-51.

Okedeji, O.and F. Okedeji, 1966 Mental Stability and Social Structure in an African City. *NISER* 27: 151-63.

Okedeji, F. 1967 Some Social Psychological Aspects of Fertility Among Married Women in an African City. *NJESS*.

Okedeji, F. 1968 Some Social Psychological Aspects of Fertility Among Married Women in an African City. *Rejoinder*. 125-33.

Olumide, 1948 *Religion of the Yorubas*. Lagos: C.M.S. Bookshop.

Olusanya, P.O. 1967 The Educational Factor in Human Fertility. A Case Study of the Residents of a Suburban Area in Ibadan. *NJESS* 351-74.

_____. 1968 Some Social Psychological Aspects of Fertility among Married Women in an African City-Comments. *NJESS* 117-123.

_____.1970 A Note of Some Factors Affecting the Stability of Marriage among the Yoruba of Western Nigeria. *Journal of Marriage and Family* 32:150-55.

Ortner, S. B. 1996 *Making Gender: The Politics of Culture*. Boston: Beacon Press.

Osborne, O.H. 1968 "The Egbado of Egbaland." Ph.D.diss; Michigan State University.

Parkin, D.J. 1979 "The Categorization of Work: Cases from Coastal Kenya." Seminar paper Oxford University.

Parkinson, J. 1906 The Legend of Oro. *Man* 6:103-5.

Parrinder, E.G. 1947 Yoruba-Speaking Peoples in Dahomey. *Africa*, 17: 1.

Parrinder, E.G. 1956 *The Story of Kétu* . Ibadan: IUP.

Peel, J.D.Y. 1968 *Aladura. A Religious Movement Among the Yourba*, London: OUP/IAI.

_____. 1978 "The Christianization of African Society: Some Possible Model." In *Christianity in Independent Africa*, R. Gray *et al*. eds. 443-54. London: Rex Collings .

Perham, M. 1937 *Native Administration in Nigeria*. London: OUP.

Popper, K. R. 1965 *The Open Society and Its Enemies*. London: Routledge and Kegan Paul.

_____.1953 *Population Census of the Western Region of Nigeria 1952*. Bulletins 1-8 The Government Statisticians, Lagos.

Quinn, N. 1977 Anthropological Studies on Women's Status. *Annual Review of Anthropology* 181-225.

Radcliffe-Brown, A.R. 1965 *Structure and Function in Primitive Society*. New York: The Free Press.

Richards, A.I. 1956 *Chisungu, A Girls' Initiation Ceremony among the Bemba of Northern Rhodesia*. London: Faber and Faber.

Rogers, S.C. 1975 Female Forms of Power and the Myth of Male

Dominance. *Ame Ethno* 727-50.

Romany, C. 1993 Women as Aliens: A Feminist Critique of the Public/ Private Distinction in International Human Rights Law, *Harvard Human Rights Journal* 87.

Rosenthal, A. M. 1992 Female Genital Torture, *The New York Times* 29 December

_____. 1993 The Torture Continues, *The New York Times* 27 July.

_____. 1993 Female Genital Torture, *The New York Times* 12 November.

_____. 1993 Female Genital Mutilation, *The New York Times* December 24.

_____. 1994 A Victory in Cairo, *The New York Times* 6 September.

Sarpong, P.K.

_____. 1970 Traditional Beliefs *Insight* 5, 3.

_____. 1971 A Theology of Ancestors *Insight* 6, 2.

Schapera, I. 1940 *Married Life in an African Tribe.* London: Faber and Faber.

Schwab, W. B. 1955 Kinship and Lineage Among the Yoruba. *Africa* 28: 352-74.

_____. 1962 Continuity and Change in the Yoruba Lineage System. *Annals of the New York Academy of Sciences* 96: 590-605.

_____. 1958 The Terminology of Kinship and Marriage among the Yoruba. *Africa* 28: 301-13.

Schultz, T.

_____. 1975 Female Circumcision, Operation Orgasm. *Viva* (March).

Shorter, A. 1972 *Chiefship in Western Tanzania.* Oxford: Clarendon Press.

Simpson, M. 1937 "An Intelligence Report on the Oyo Division of Oyo Province" Mss. Afr. S. 526, Rhodes House.

Smith, R. 1969 *Kingdoms of the Yoruba.* Norwich: Methuen.

Smith, R. S. 1992 Female Circumcision: Bringing Women's Perspectives into the International Debate, 65 *S. Carlifornia Law Review* 2449, 2460.

Sperber, D. 1975 *Rethinking Symbolism.*Cambridge: CUP.

Sudarkasa, N. 1973 *Where Women Work: A Study of Yoruba Women in the Market Place and in the Home.* Ann Arbor: University of Michigan.

_____. 1977 Women and Migration in Contemporary West Africa, *Signs* 6:178-189.

_____. 1978 Female Employment and Family Organization in West Africa. In *New Research on Women and Sex Roles*, D. McGuigan ed. Ann Arbor: Center for the Continuing Education of Women, The University of Michigan.

_____. 1982 Sex Roles, Education, and Development in Africa. *Anthropology and Education Quarterly* 13: 279 - 289.

_____. 1987 "The 'Status of Women' in Indigenous Societies Indigenous African Societies. In *Women in Africa and in African Diaspora*, R. Terborg-Penn, S. Harley, and B. Rushing eds. Washington, D.C.: Howard University Press.

_____. 1996 *The Strength of Our Mothers African and African American Women and Families: Essays and Speeches*. Trenton: Africa World Press, Inc.

Talbot, P.A. 1927 *Some Nigerian Fertility Cults*. London: OUP.

Taylor, M.L. 1970 "Female Circumcision." Unpublished paper.

Thompson, R.F. 1970 The Sign of the Divine King: An Essay on Yoruba Bead-embroidered Crowns with Veil and Bird Decorations. *African Arts* 3:74-79.

_____. 1971 Sons of Thunder: Twin Images Among the Oyo and Other Yoruba Groups *African Arts*, 4: 8-13, 77-80.

Toubia, N. 1993 Female Genital Mutilation: A Call for Global Action (9).

Turner, J. G. S. 1932 *Medical Census of Southern Provinces. Census of Nigeria*. London: Crown Agents for the Colonies, 6.

Turner, V. 1962 "Three Symbols of Passage in Ndemba Circumcision Ritual: An Interpretation." In *Essays of the Ritual of Social Relations*, M. Gluckman ed.

_____. 1967 *The Forest of Symbols: Aspects of Ndemba Ritual*. Ithaca; Cornell University Press.

van Allen, J. 1972 Sitting on a Man: Colonialism and the Lost Political Positions of Igbo Women. *Canadian Journal of African Studies* 6.

van Gennep, A. 1960 *The Rites of Passage*. London: Routledge and Kegan Paul.

Verger, P. 1976 The Yoruba High God: A Review of Sources. *ODU* 2:19-400.

Warner-Lewis, M. 1996 *Trinidad Yoruba; From Mother Tongue to Memory*. Tuscaloosa; The University of Alabama Press.

Ward, E. 1938 *The Yoruba Husban-Wife Code*. Baltimore: Watkins.

Ward, I. C. 1952 *Introduction to the Yoruba Language*. London: Heffer.

Westcott, R.W. 1957 Did the Yoruba Come from Egypt? *ODU* 4:10-15.

Wood, J. T. 1996 *Communication, Gender and Culture* (2nd. Ed.). Belmont: Wadsworth.

Worsley, A. 1938   Infibulation and Female Circumcision, A Study on a Little-known Custom. *Journal of Obstetrics and Gynaecology* 686-91.

Zanotelli, A. 1971   Female Circumcision: A "Barbarous" and Immoral Rite. *Insight and Opinion.*

INDEX